PENGUIN BUSINESS

CORPORATE FRAUDS

Robin Banerjee is the chairman of Nucleon Research Pvt. Ltd, a global clinical research organization. He served as the managing director of Caprihans India Ltd between 2012 and 2022, and has held senior management positions at Hindustan Unilever, ArcelorMittal Germany, Thomas Cook, Essar Steel and Suzlon Energy.

Robin is a chartered accountant (FCA), cost and management accountant (FCMA), company secretary (FCS) and master of commerce (MCom). He is the recipient of two lifetime achievement awards from *CFO India* (Feb 2023) and Manufacturing Today (Oct 2023).

Robin holds board positions at several companies, chambers of commerce and business schools. He is a much-sought-after keynote speaker, a popular columnist, a business coach, a philanthropist and a gym enthusiast.

'I am an avid reader of Robin's books. He is an author of choice. Being a practising and successful manager himself, he never takes a moralistic stand; his books and comments are practical, real and never stripped of fair play. I would recommend this book to everyone: those who are in business, those who are not, those responsible to raise a voice and even those who remain silent but have something to care about—whether their wealth or their conscience! Like most books written by Robin, I am sure that this too will delight its readers. It will be a great reference in libraries, research institutions and academic archives.'

—**Ashok Barat, Ex-MD, Forbes & Co. Ltd; Past President, Bombay Chamber of Commerce and Industry**

'As a banker, investor or anyone with interest in the financial services, the first rule is to avoid the fraud trap. At the heart of all analysis lie numbers and sometimes numbers that lie. The quality of your analysis and understanding of the company is driven by the genuineness of those numbers. The trap is of corporate artists who have perfected the art of presenting numbers that tell a beautiful tale. Good bankers, investors and analysts are those who can smell these numbers and sift the truth from the tale. If you have read Robin's earlier books, then you would be familiar with what to expect. If not, then let him take you on a journey that gives you a detailed insight into the modus operandi of these elaborate corporate frauds. It is said that those who do not learn from history are condemned to repeat it. In his simple but straight-shooting style, Robin takes us through a crash course on the history of corporate frauds that will enable us to spot the next trap.'

—**Aseem Dhru, CEO and MD, SBFC Finance Pvt. Ltd**

'Robin's well-researched and deeply insightful new book focuses on a subject that is rarely discussed, though it impacts global economies everywhere. While books on individual scams abound, the larger issues involved in white-collar crime have rarely been examined, and it is this that makes Banerjee's work unique. Drawing on personal observations, anecdotes, intensive enquiry and his own visible concern over the issue, Robin takes an in-depth look at the growing deceit in the business arena, globally. He also delves into history and notes that companies down the ages have indulged in unethical behaviour. The author's objective, however, goes beyond identifying corporate crimes and the people behind them; he also explores the compulsions that fuel such traits. In an era where crime is taking on increasingly sophisticated dimensions and technology is a double-edged sword that both enables it and offers solutions, this book is long overdue. It also serves as an important reminder that criminal activity, however suave it might be, may offer short-term gains, but it is good governance that ensures a company's lasting value.'

**—B. Thiagarajan, CEO and MD, Blue Star Ltd;
Chairman, CII (Western India) 2021–2022**

'Robin Banerjee holds a mirror with a firm hand, again. As shareholders, professionals or even as consumers, we are impacted by wrongdoings of people and brands we trust—affected often in more ways than we may know. This book is an important service to keep our worldview open to the reality out there.'

—Damodar Mall, CEO, Reliance Fresh and Reliance Smart

'A cutting and incisive look at the corporate world and where the hidden secrets lie! Robin Banerjee has turned his magnifying glass towards the prevalent practice of 'fraud' in its many forms in the professional sphere. By understanding the real root causes behind unethical behaviour and classifying them in a way that is easy to understand and recall in our day-to-day activities, this book is an invaluable guide to avoiding the same mistakes that have led to many scandals in the corporate world. The book gives ample examples from the entire gamut of businesses of the way people and corporations are misled and shows us how to steer clear of these practices by being conscious of our actions.'

—Edward Menezes, Chairman, Rossari Biotech Ltd

'*Corporate Frauds*, the latest creation of Robin, narrates the spectrum of frauds and its aftermath that continue to haunt the economy. In fact, this book should be taken as a continuation of Robin's previous book, *Who Blunders and How?* Both together qualify to be an indispensable part of any employee induction programme across organizations, whether small, medium or large. Going forward, governance is one of the sustenance pillars for companies along with environment and social (part of the ESG) themes. I love this book on governance, which is written in Robin's inimitable style. I feel that every entrepreneur should live, imbibe and prosper through this book.'

—K. Nandakumar, Founder and Managing Director, Chemtrols Group; Member, CII MSME National Council

'Robin's book, *Corporate Frauds*, is a prescription for good corporate governance. I always believe you can learn either from your own mistakes or from somebody else's mistakes. But corporate governance mistakes are so costly that, in fact, they can cost you your life, freedom and reputation and so it is much better to learn from somebody else's mistakes. Therefore, I would definitely recommend this book as standard reading material for all professionals and students of management. I would also like to compliment the author for the fast-paced language, almost like an addictive web series. It is definitely a very engrossing and interesting read.'

—Piruz Khambatta, Chairman, Rasna Pvt. Ltd; Ex-Chairman, CII (Western Region)

'Once again, Robin has picked up a tricky subject, corporate frauds, to push our boundaries of knowledge. As humans push the boundaries of innovation using technology, it appears that fraudsters and cheats are the first to monetize the benefits of the new technology by combining it with plain old trust building. Fraud has moved from a one-off act by a misunderstood loner to a planned action by groups of otherwise honest individuals. Packed with contemporary and popular examples, this book is a fast read written in a direct style.'

—Ramesh Ganesan, CEO and MD, HDB Financial Services Ltd

'Amazing reading! Dark side of the corporate world at its worst. The book seems like fiction reading. A must-read for all.'

—Rishi Bagla, Chairman, Aurangabad Electricals Ltd

'Robin continues in his successful genre, with his third business non-fiction book. In this book on corporate frauds, he has dealt with different situations, as also the possible reasoning of the perpetrators. Robin's books are always easy to read and great for understanding.'

—Saurabh Nanavati, CEO, Invesco Asset Management (I) Ltd

'It is difficult to express this book in a few words. Every author brings all the glimpses and positive stories of the corporate world. It requires a third eye like "Shiva" to see the darker side of the world where we, the so-called corporates, live our day-to-day lives. Many of us do not even notice it; some may, but they choose to remain silent, and we have these so-called who are actually a part of the game. The book to me is gripping, a page-turner. The stories and facts shook me, took me to the darkest edge of certain dubious corporate conduct. Hopefully, this book will open the third eye wider and bring more discipline in corporate governance.'

—Sunil Pathare, Chairman and MD, VIP Clothing Ltd

'The book is just awesome. Every page is a learning experience. With every book of Robin, the narrative gets more gripping. It is a must-read for all: professionals, businessmen, students as well as housewives.'

—Sunil Chari, Managing Director, Rossari Biotech Ltd

'This is an amazing book which not only captures the past but also analyses the root cause which is responsible for bad corporate behaviour.'

—Nilesh Shah, MD,
Kotak Mahindra Asset Management Co. Ltd

'While greed and lust for money are the unstoppable evils that exist right through the human history, I feel there is still hope for minimizing pain and suffering of innocents in the world. Robin Banerjee's book on corporate frauds has a purpose to help people understand patterns of business crimes that cause them the pain and it carries warnings to be careful. No matter how strict the laws you make and develop technologies to stop fraud, the fraudsters find their ways to finally cheat innocent people. Robin's book is a pill or medicine to minimize people's ignorance. The narration of his huge research that he has done over global scams looks focused on creating awareness among people. The book is a must-read for every individual who keeps even a few coins in the pocket, because there could be someone around who is planning to snatch away the coins.'

—Sudhir Mutalik, MD and CEO,
Positive Metering Pumps (I) Pvt. Ltd

'Robin Banerjee has done a commendable job of comprehensively drawing up a compendium of all types of frauds occurring in the world today. In addition, he adds his insights on how to prevent and spot them based on detailed analysis of how they were perpetrated. It is a sad reflection of our times that such white-collar crimes are growing exponentially on a global basis and it calls for a clear need to inculcate ethical and moral behaviour in our society. It is a necessity for businesses to be run on the principles of trusteeship in a selfless manner as propounded by Mahatma Gandhi.'

—Uday Khanna, Ex-Chairman, Bata India Ltd;
Ex-MD and CEO, Lafarge India; Former President,
Bombay Chamber of Commerce and Industry

Frank, informative, interesting, gripping and mischievously thought-provoking. A financial thriller everyone must read.'

—**Vishal Vithal Kamat, Chairman, Kamat Hotels**

CORPORATE FRAUDS

Now Bigger, Broader and Bolder

ROBIN BANERJEE

PENGUIN
BUSINESS

An imprint of Penguin Random House

PENGUIN BUSINESS

USA | Canada | UK | Ireland | Australia
New Zealand | India | South Africa | China | Singapore

Penguin Business is an imprint of the Penguin Random House group of companies
whose addresses can be found at global.penguinrandomhouse.com

Published by Penguin Random House India Pvt. Ltd
4th Floor, Capital Tower 1, MG Road,
Gurugram 122 002, Haryana, India

First published by Sage Publications India Pvt. Ltd 2022
Published in Penguin Business by Penguin Random House India 2024

ISBN 9780143464587

Typeset in 11/14 pt Bembo by Fidus Design Pvt. Ltd, Chandigarh.
Printed at Repro India Limited

www.penguin.co.in

To the five most beautiful women in my life: my late mom, whose recent departure to the heavenly abode is the heaviest loss I have ever experienced; my better half Ananya, who cheerfully continues to tolerate my madness; our heart-throb and pride Roshnai; and the two cutest angels Arahana and Aheli, whose splendid smiles keep me going through all turbulences.

Contents

Acknowledgements

Writing a book on business crimes necessarily implies penning down the negative side of business practices. Most businesses conduct themselves appropriately, but there are some who cut corners for short-term gains. While writing this book, I learnt a whole lot of new ways, techniques and methods by which some entrepreneurs and managers could be giving short shrift to governance. Even though I appreciate that pressures for growth and profits sometimes overwhelm the necessity to be ethical, it is a conundrum and a fine balance which many need to master. While acknowledging my learnings from the episodes and experiences of corporate frauds, I apologize for my overindulgence in the area of this negative human trait. I could not help it, as unethical business practice is indeed the subject matter of this book.

My early learnings of good governance are from my alma mater employer—Hindustan Unilever. Numerous were my experiences where the organization would refuse to grease the palms of the powers that be, for gaining some early permissions (those days, the License Raj was in full swing). I got indoctrinated into the culture of doing business fairly, providing customers with goods and services of consistent quality at appropriate price!

As I moved on in my professional career, I saw many plusses and minuses of corporate behaviour. I am indebted to such highs and lows of managerial demeanour, the result of which is this book.

My sincerest gratitude to Ananya, my significantly better half, who has stood by me through thick and thin and keeps modifying my scribblings from time to time.

Abhishek, our son, has always been eager and keen to read my scrawls. He polished several places where the wordings were flat or were not making much sense. Roshnai, our daughter, trained in medicine, contributed with ideas to make the book easier to read and more lucid.

My writings would never have come into being without the encouragement of my journalist brother, Ruben, who used to tower over the Outlook group of magazines as its editor-in-chief. I wish I could write half as well as him!

Two of my gurus and mentors have always encouraged me in all my efforts. Debu Bhattacharya, Vice Chairman of Hindalco Industries and Uday Khanna, ex-President, Bombay Chambers and ex-Chairman Bata India Ltd, took great interest in going through my manuscript and suggest improvements. Both have shaped my approach to governance over the years, being my early bosses in my professional career. I would ever remain indebted to both these brilliant professional minds of the corporate world.

My good friend and neighbour, Ramesh Ganesan, CEO of HDB Financial Services Ltd, made brilliant suggestions while reviewing my manuscript. Being an avid reader, he keeps sharing great stories, especially from the financial world. He made sure that the 'Few Last Words', given at the end of every chapter of this book, provide key takeaways to the readers—a beautiful way of making a business book doubly useful to the readers.

Dolphy D'Souza, EY partner and an acclaimed author, being one of the most sought-after accounting experts in the country, closely read the chapter on 'Accounting Artifice'. He made superb suggestions to make the content more focused and relevant. I remember his hard-hitting comment on mergers and acquisitions (M&As) in India where some schemes display dubious accounting but eventually get court approval.

Ketan Bani, the Hong Kong-based finance wizard, shared his own disappointments with some top-notch corporates in their ethical practices. He did not miss to point out that even Maruti Suzuki India, the number one Indian car maker, is supposedly working hard to oppose air bags in cars on Indian roads, to keep their entry-level autos cheaper, without worrying about the safety of their customers. I am extremely grateful for Ketan's suggestions to improve the content of this book.

Santanu Syam, Director, Core Banking Transformation of KBZ Bank, Myanmar, while going through the whole manuscript, provided superb inputs. He very rightly pointed out that in spite of the hubris in the business world, there are still many good that prevail over the evil. There are pockets where shareholders are helping to set up good governance templates and whistle-blowers forcing to weed out unethical acts. Thankfully, there are several bright spots in the otherwise gloomy side of business practices.

Shankar Dey, Executive Director, APAC Financial Services, went through the manuscript almost with a toothcomb and suggested corrections like a professional editor. I sincerely acknowledge his deep interest in the book, including suggesting a lovely name for the chapter on technology-related frauds as "Technology Tall Tales"

Dr Ms Sangita Laha, Dean of National University of Study and Research in Law, Ranchi, helped me in shaping my chapter on cybercrimes. She suggested adding the new ways of cyberstalking—the unseen horror of the Internet age—and voyeurism—being the outcome of miniaturization of cameras.

I just cannot be grateful enough for the amazing quality of suggestions two close friends of mine made, while sifting through my manuscript. An acclaimed legal expert Swagata Bhattacharya, India Legal Head for Credit Suisse and finance guru Aseem Dhru, CEO for SBFC Finance, both going through with fine-combs to look for errors and omissions. Invaluable inputs they provided.

I had the opportunity to share my initial manuscript with two wonderful Outlook editors—Alam Srinivas and Anupam Bordoloi. My sincere thanks to the duo for their very useful feedback.

A book of this nature cannot be envisaged, worked upon and written unless family and friends lend their shoulders and extend their helping hands. Without their encouragement, nothing would have been remotely achievable. My deepest reverence to Ashok Chattopadhyay, Abhyuday Jindal, Achintan Bhattacharya, Adil Malya, Anuradha Bhatia, Ashutosh Mishra, Ankita Kariya, Anupam

Dasgupta, B. Thiagarajan, Damodar Mall, Debabrata Mukherjee, Edward Menezes, Firdose Vandrevala, Gopal Sehjpal, Harsh Chopra, K Nandakumar, Krishna Iyer, Kamal Mazumdar, Dr Lily Bhushan, Mohan Bhandari, Nafisa Yeasmin, Nandakumar K, Dr Niraj Gupta, Partho Rakshit, Padmini Patel, Piruz Khambatta, Ranjana Maitra, Dr Renu Shome, Rimjhim Banerjee, Rishi Bagla, Sanjay Kapoor, Saurabh Nanavati, Sundeep Sikka, Dr Shailashree Haridas, Somenath Mukherjee, Sriram Narayanan, Dr Swati Padoshi, Dr Sibichen Mathew, Sudipto Panda, Soumitro Panda, Dr Suresh Padhy, Sunil Mathur, Sushama Kanetkar, Sudhir Mutalik, Sunil Pathare, Dr Subhasis Ray, Kashmira Mewawala, Kapil Pathare, Uday Khanna, Vishal Kamath and Vikesh Valia.

The entire team of SAGE has always been exemplary. Manisha Mathews, my commissioning editor, has been super-supportive all through this arduous journey to research and spin stories on business frauds. My sincere thanks to Namarita Kathait and Neena Ganjoo, who were very proficient in handling the manuscript and converting it into a great finished product. My journey so far would not have been successful had I not been guided and supported by the two wonderful ladies from SAGE—Shafina Segon, AVP Marketing, and Savitha Kumar, AVP Editorial Production (at the time). My gratitude towards the fabulous SAGE team cannot be completed unless I mention my special appreciation to its leadership team, including Vivek Mehra, CEO, and Aarti David, Director Publishing.

I am obliged to Mini Narayanan, who took great pains in editing the manuscript initially, and all smilingly.

I sincerely apologize for my inadvertence in not acknowledging all my gurus, guides, buddies and confidants who have been instrumental in guiding, advising and educating me in all my endeavours.

My heartfelt bow, deference and salutation to all of you!

A few years ago, I invested in the shares of a company which was showing rapid growth in sales and profits. After about two years, the share price started crumbling. Around the same time, the company's chairperson was arrested allegedly for misusing bank funds. When the lenders started investigating the company's books of accounts, they realized that the accounting figures were fudged, with inventory and sales numbers grossly overstated. As an investor, I was cheated. The company played an elaborate hoax. Many of you may have been exposed to this sort of an experience that businesses unleash on the common man.

The world today hosts a rather strange mix of enterprises. Most of them are diligently serving our daily needs—from food to fuel, housing to hospitality, and entertainment to ecommerce. But many outfits are hoodwinking people, cutting corners and looking at short-term gains. And the bad news is that the latter version of businesses are getting bigger, broader and bolder. Surprisingly, the size and scale of deceitful activities within the business community are becoming murkier, messier and fuzzier, even as increasing regulatory strictures are getting pushed into service to contain it.

A similar experience of deceit is also rife in the sports arena. Remember that sports is also a thriving business. As the quantum of awards and sponsorships get larger, so does the lure for athletes and coaches to find new and creative ways to cheat. Athletics, gymnastics, skiing, cycling and weightlifting are all suffering from repeated scams. Even sports like cricket and football, which were once considered to be doping-free, are not devoid of scandals any more.

Over one-third of the athletes[1] preparing for big events are apparently taking banned substances. More distressing is that only about 10 per cent of them seem to be ever caught! Shocking, isn't it? The darker side of sports doping is getting dirtier. The number of performance enhancers currently estimated at 300 are on the rise, and it keeps ballooning as newer stimulants are discovered.

Just when you think that you have heard it all in doping, someone could spike your toothpaste, the coach could massage with a tainted ointment and the gym doctor could prescribe a banned painkiller.

Newer adulterators have taken over from anabolic steroids, which were earlier the mainstay of doping episodes. New 'designer' drugs are being introduced to make them undetectable in blood or urine samples.

One such latest development is blood doping. It involves transfusing blood or taking a drug which stimulates production of red blood cells to enhance stamina. In early 2018, 10,000 blood tests from 2,000 Winter Olympics athletes suggested that they had used red blood cell stimulants. Many had such thick blood that they should have been in hospitals.

Things are just getting crummier for professional sportspersons in their pursuit for excellence, glory and money.

The business world is no different from the world of sports, when it comes to making fool of others. Both the sporting and the business world keep elongating their con games to make more illicit bucks.

Greed is acting as the dope to inflict business crimes in many cases. Suboptimizing business practices, adulterating products, stealing money, bribing to extract illicit benefit, providing improper disclosures and doctoring financial results are becoming rather common and all-pervasive. An aphrodisiac for many, these are usually done to help a few and deliver short-term doles at the cost of long-term welfare.

In essence, business scandals are just getting weightier, wider and worse.

Look at the Indian corporate world. On the Valentine's Day of 2018—the day on which diamonds are gifted by the well-heeled to show their love—India's second-largest bank revealed that one of its prestigious clients, billionaire diamantaire Nirav Modi, fled the country after pulling off an elaborate heist of a whopping ₹11,000 crore ($1.6 billion).[2] He allegedly made a mockery of the bank's internal control system. His company acquired fraudulent letters of undertakings from one of the Mumbai branches of Punjab National Bank, for availing buyer's credit without any security, from overseas branches of Indian banks. Can you believe that the fraud was perpetrated for seven years, but no one got to know about it? The deceit not only by-passed the bank's internal control system but also skipped the apparent hawk eyes of multiple audit agencies.

Internationally, things have come to such a pass that even venerated banks like Goldman Sachs paid massive bribes and worked hand in glove with the political leadership, helping siphon off multibillion dollars from funds garnered for sovereign welfare funds.

In 2009, the Malaysian government entrusted Goldman to raise $6 billion (₹45,000 crore) in bonds.[3] It was a long-running welfare scheme called the 1Malaysia Development Berhad or 1MDB. Can you believe that Goldman, after generating a healthy $600 million (₹4,500 crore) in fees, is suspected to have conspired to misappropriate more than $2.7 billion (₹20,000 crore) from the bond proceeds it helped to garner?

In October 2020, the multinational investment bank agreed to pay at the group level a $3 billion (₹22,000 crore) global settlement with regulators, making this one of the biggest financial scandals in recent years. It is a sordid story of how one of the starred Wall Street banks played a role in looting the money arranged by them. Corporate dishonesty perhaps cannot get worse!

If we look for the most consistently scandal-plagued period in history, the 19th century takes the cake. The intensity of frauds fell for several decades till it showed signs of plateauing during the mid-20th century.[4] But then the escalations in reported financial frauds began. The number and quantum of business crimes have kept climbing ever since.

With business double-dealings mounting, lies and damn lies did not desert even the most prestigious corporates, like the much-acclaimed consultancy brand, McKinsey. What they did over 15 years is unfathomable.

The global consultancy firm took millions in fees to advise the American drug maker Purdue Pharma through slickly packaged product sales plans to market 'OxyContin', an opioid and highly addictive painkiller.[5] McKinsey helped structure the marketing campaigns, target those doctors they knew would overprescribe the opioid drug, and ways to circumvent restrictive retailers by offering mail-order deliveries to its keenest users. The result was an opioid epidemic, especially in the USA, which killed 400,000 globally and left millions addicted.

The consulting firm was aware that what they were doing was abetting and prescribing of a drug without a legitimate medical purpose. Ultimately, in February 2021, McKinsey agreed to pay $574 million (₹4,300 crore) to settle the opioid claims by the US states. And this is not the only felony by the famed management consultancy firm.

The motto of profit at all cost is driving many famed companies towards disregarding the higher societal purpose and shoving aside moral responsibilities. The lust for money seems to be getting gargantuan among many.

Just think. It is logic-defying as the more a person or an enterprise becomes prosperous, the higher gets the desire to hide wealth and avoid paying taxes which are legitimately due to the state.

Believe it or not, with global GDP at $80 trillion, the world's wealthiest have apparently stashed away a whopping $15 trillion in tax havens and shell companies across the world, masking them from the prying eyes of the taxmen.[6]

Further, out of $40 trillion of world's foreign direct investment (FDI), $15 trillion is wrongfully shown as investments routed through companies in tax haven countries to avoid taxes. It means that over one-third of global money transferred across borders between firms belong to the same parent company. This so-called 'phantom capital' is being touted as FDI, though this is money moving into shell companies which do not have any real business.

Let me give you an example of this malady. Luxembourg, a low-tax city-sized country with 0.6 million people, is stated to route over $4 trillion of FDIs.[7] The money flows from outside into Luxembourg-based shell companies and then flows out as investment to other countries, carrying very low tax accretion to dividends and capital gains which could accrue to the investments. Can you imagine that the FDI amount of Luxembourg is six times the country's GDP? Obviously, some trickery is going on. This is nothing but financial engineering to avoid paying tax on that monstrous mountain of money.

The matter is not only getting worse, but it is also making economies unable to understand the true impact of FDI on economic growth, as they do not know how much phantom capital is being moved around.

Would you believe that organized crime at the taxpayer's expense has dug holes in government coffers in a dozen European countries, amounting to a whopping sum of €55 billion ($65 billion)?[8] Tax trickery has gone bigger and broader! Germany, Denmark, Italy, France, Austria, Belgium and Switzerland have all fallen victim to this dubious financial ploy.

At the heart, these were tax dodges involving dividends in connection with trades known as 'cum-ex' (with and without dividends).

What are 'cum-ex' trades? Various nations impose a withholding tax on dividends paid to non-residents. This is because it is difficult to collect the tax from an overseas resident after the dividend is paid. If certain conditions are met, non-residents (say, companies or pension funds) can claim a refund of the tax withheld.

Who were involved? About a hundred different international financial institutions have been linked to the scam. These include big names such as Commerzbank, DZ Bank and Deutsche Bank.

How was the 'cum-ex' tax fraud accomplished? Typically, it involved three parties: the actual owner of the stock, a bank that borrowed the stock from the actual owner and sold it short, and a third party that bought the stock shortly before the dividend day. The bank would sell the shares with (cum) a dividend on or shortly before the dividend record date, and the shares would be delivered a few days after the dividend record date without (ex) dividend.

A design flaw in the tax codes of certain countries made it feasible to claim tax refund by both the original owner of the stock (who had received the dividend and paid tax on it) as well as the third party that bought it (who would typically receive the tax refund that the entity did not pay).

The three parties would then share the booty of the extra tax refund between them. And the amount could be as high as 25 per cent of dividend declared. The scamsters thus misled authorities to a massive heist of refunding tax which was never paid.

Is there a way to stop the ever-evolving nature of business scandals? Although not easy, some things seem possible with the help of technology. The rise of digital technology may produce new scandal-fighting tools; cyber records may potentially offer new levels of transparency; and artificial intelligence may be able to hunt down irregularities faster.

There are thus some possibilities of the 21st century presenting new tools to fight the dishonesties, though as of now, it does not seem that the scandalous world is ebbing in any way. The auditors, forensic accountants and market regulators are likely to continue having busy times.

Why Are Fraud Risks and Range Rising?

Aren't more regulations getting notified and more fraudsters getting caught? If so, then why are business crime risks increasing and scam sizes swelling?

The situation is similar to prisons. New jails are being built and more criminals are being imprisoned. But just because there are lock-ups, it does not deter the swindlers from looking for options of making a fast buck. Crooks continue to be on their prowl, prison or no prison.

Weird as it is, even with more deterrents, more deceits and deceptions are being witnessed in the business world. Business breaches are getting bulkier and more beastly.

Just note the size of the frauds which are taking place. Globally, financial crimes result in an annual loss of a whopping US$5.8 trillion.[9] Only four countries have GDP higher than that number—even India, UK and France's GDPs are lower. This takes a humungous toll—loss of jobs, erosion of savings, deceleration of growth and bankruptcies—leading to tremendous human sufferings.

To get an idea about the situation of corporate crimes, let us first look at the 'digital' side of business frauds.

A global information service company Experian conducted research among 5,500 consumers and 500 businesses across banks, financial institutions, cards and payment providers, online and mobile retailers in 11 countries including the USA, UK, China and India. In its *The 2018 Global Fraud and Identity Report*[10] pertaining to the 'digital world', the firm observed that almost three-quarters of businesses cited fraud as a growing concern. Further, nearly two-thirds reported higher levels of fraud losses in the recent past. Strange as it may sound, digital insecurity has led to lost businesses—with about one-fourth of consumers abandoning their transactions where they felt lack of visible security.

Why has digital deceit become so all-pervasive? And why are businesses struggling to cope up?

A key reason is that the modern world is getting increasingly wired. Just imagine that all our life savings are lying in so-called bank boxes (or is it black boxes?) accessible through the press of a computer button.

The paradox is that the defence against online fraud is also its susceptibility. The account set-up process requires consumers to provide wide ranging personal information, answers to secret questions and setting up of passwords. Things are just getting easier for the tech-savvy cheats to access confidential personal data.

Fraudsters are taking advantage of data breaches. Once pilfered, the information can be used to facilitate fraudulent activities. Unfortunately, this provides great value to personal information in the illegitimate markets of the dark web.

With the potential bonanza from digital fraud multiplying, so does the cybercriminal's incentive to stay ahead of the newest detection means, methods and machinations.

Even the worst disaster ever faced by the mankind—COVID-19 pandemic—did not escape the wicked eyes of the digital fraudsters. As people staying at home during 2020 and 2021 spent more time online with typically weaker digital security, Internet rackets increased. Offers of bogus drugs to avert or treat the virus, websites selling phony vaccines,[11] false promises of speedier receipt of government stimulus and quick clearance of bank funding—fraud got a brand new face.

Now let us look at the 'non-digitized' world of business crimes.

A *Global Fraud & Risk Report* by Kroll[12] says that the incidence of fraud continues to climb. Overall, 84 per cent of surveyed executives reported that their company fell victim to at least one instance of fraud in the past 12 months, up from 82 per cent in 2016. Incidentally, this figure was at 61 per cent in 2012. The wicked tentacles of the fraud octopus are entangling hitherto virgin territories.

For instance, the stock market which thrives on non-cyber mode is a sanctuary for swindlers. Time and again, stock prices of certain companies are maintained at distorted levels, which helps a few, either through doctored financial number disclosures or through insider trading. The world over, market regulators are becoming more active in bringing sanity into the stocks and shares trading—to deter the general public being taken for a ride by a few greedy souls. But the tricksters are not allowing things to get better.

Another array of dismal stories emanates from a few rich and famous choosing to mislead financial institutions. Many big boys of business are increasingly in no mood to return funds borrowed from banks, with some decamping to scenic tax havens to enjoy their sinful exploits. This is in spite of being financially capable of repaying the borrowed funds.

Wilful defaulters—as they are called—are proliferating by the day. Can you believe that there were over 1,900 wilful defaulters in mid-2020 who have not repaid a monstrous sum of ₹150,000 crore ($20 billion) to the Indian banking system (up from ₹55,000 crore or $9 billion in 2016), even though they were capable of doing so?[13] And the worse is that about 260 of them have wilfully defaulted over ₹100 crore ($13 million) each. Now look at the other end: If a commoner is in default of even one instalment to a bank, say against a car loan, the lender would hound the defaulter and make his life miserable. But the burly bad boys seem to be getting away scot-free.

Ponzi schemes are another malaise—hoax games taking advantage of people's innate desire to make quick and easy money! It is all about taking money from an investor with a promise of great return and attempting to pay back by taking money with similar false promises, from latter investors. This deception lasts till new investors can be misled. As you are reading this, there will be at least one new Ponzi scheme which is getting launched somewhere in the world, with no real business but selling make-believe stories to con people.

Things are obviously getting worse. Telling lies, hiding facts, doctoring numbers and hoodwinking people continue to show a rising graph in the world of business. An upgraded version of corporate fraud is in full swing, be it in the Internet world or otherwise. Con stars are all over, waiting to pounce on their innocent preys.

The simple reason for the enhanced mala fide act is greed. Short-term benefit over long-term good prevails in many human minds. This mindset creates the balance to tilt for some businesses towards taking shortcuts to extract immediate gains. It juxtaposes the ones practising good governance with a vision for long-term well-being.

Why Do Businesses Defraud?

I am a product of Hindustan Unilever, my alma mater for two decades. While working for perhaps one of the best employers in the world, the only other fantasy company for me was the American conglomerate, General Electric (GE). The legendary Jack Welch, who ran the company till 2001, was my dream CEO to work for.

But unbelievably, the industrial group of this stature has been accused by the US market regulator, the Securities and Exchange Commission (SEC),[14] to have 'misled investors' and 'violated antifraud, reporting and disclosure controls'. It essentially meant misleading investors about its financial condition.

What did GE do? It pulled forward future profits and cash flow and separately delayed reporting big losses in order to boost immediate results. Its power division was ostensibly the home of accounting mischief. This cost the conglomerate $22 billion investment write-off in 2017 and a $10 billion charge in 2018 relating to insurance liabilities underreported earlier[15]—in short, a massive $32 billion hole, which the company did not recognize earlier and covered up through accounting shenanigans.

Businesses have breached confidence reposed on them over the years. When promises made fall short or investors' expectations are not met, unethical behaviour sometimes ensues. When profits are not enough to declare management bonus or grant promotion, accounting juggleries could follow. When promises made to lenders or banking covenant fall short, doctored financial numbers might emanate.

Names involved in corporate guile often make the who's who listing and lead to disbelief when the recalcitrant list is made known.

It takes a colossal effort to become number one in any field, but the good work can get dented or ruined by governance concerns. An example of this phenomenon in India is the pharmaceutical giant, Sun Pharma, the largest drug maker. Its reputation has not been in sound health since the days it acquired another pharma major, Ranbaxy, in 2015. This acquisition was incidentally marred by an insider trading controversy and since then concerns on good governance. Entrepreneurs and managers need to give this matter some serious thought—is it worth slicing off the company's goodwill due to short-sightedness?

What did Sun Pharma and its well-known promoter and chairman, Dilip Shanghvi, do?[16] At the end of 2018, Australian brokerage firm Macquarie and an ex-employee whistle-blower alleged lots of 'murky waters'. The revelation raised questions on large guarantees given over two years to real estate firms owned by Shanghvi's brother-in-law Sudhir Valia; distribution of Sun Pharma's medicines through a related party company without prior disclosures; and providing sizable loans to undisclosed beneficiaries.

However, when Shanghvi was later asked about the governance complaints, he ducked by saying that those were old matters and explaining them then would put unreasonable burden on people. This seems to be an improper explanation from a person who was once the richest man in India.

Why should the illustrious GE attempt to doctor accounts to depict a picture better than the real one? Why should the unrivalled Sun Pharma's founder Shanghvi try to pinch odd gains into the pockets of his relatives? The key question therefore is: Why do businesses breach trust?

The asymmetrical approach to morality by some enterprises may be due to the unequal distribution of global wealth in spite of growth in the overall prosperity of economies. The skewed distribution of assets leads to sacrificing good moral behaviour and sound corporate governance at the altar of personal gains. Unless the matter of fair distribution of wealth is proactively addressed (and no clear method has emerged to achieve this), the world may continue to suffer unethical practices.

It is common knowledge that most companies' boards and senior management are usually hawk-eyed on revenue-fulfilment targets. With focus on profit and growth numbers, enforcement of strong ethics is not often on their agendas. In my opinion, the top management often overlooks the fact that unscrupulous behaviour crumples corporate cachet.

The longing to succeed, aspiration to meet promises made earlier, hunger for publicity, desire to gain short-term gratification, craving for bigger control and tendency towards acquisitiveness are often the reasons why some corporates boast and bluff.

The pressure of growing the business or to show profits could sometimes be overwhelming. This could entail many to adopt shortcuts, sacrificing long-term goals in the quest for immediate gratifications. Playing the game with a fine balance between the right and the wrong could help in optimizing business value.

Who Cheats?

A business outfit is not made of bricks and mortar. It's made of human beings who envision, plan and execute the business tasks. Ventures could be structured under different legal formats, most popularly as proprietorship, partnership or a company. However, when business frauds take place, normally the body corporate is penalized.

Remember that it is not the artificial legal entity—called the company or corporation—that cheats. It's the people owning or running it that call the shots. Hence, it is the psyche of the entrepreneur, the board or the top management which influences the behaviour of a business enterprise. Most importantly, it's the top boss who usually has the sizable sway.

In addition to the motley group of top honchos in an organization who could construct financial crimes, there could be others with their fingers in the pungent pie. These could include the employees, auditors, vendors, lenders or even the customers. Such financial infringements are normally termed as white-collar crimes and involve violation of delegated trust. The criminality basically involves the exploitation by a few, due to their position and power, for business or personal gain.

Corporate fraud is an intentional act, undoubtedly structured by humans linked with the concerned business organization. But as it is often difficult to pinpoint individual persons who would have had the criminal intent to have schemed the bluff, the people behind the fraud often go scot-free. This leaves the business firms—the artificial legal entity—being held responsible as and when frauds get entrapped.

That is why, time and again, you will find that colossal corporate frauds would have taken place, but no individual punished. For instance, in the massive LIBOR or sub-prime mortgage scams, running into billions of dollars, hardly any of the masterminds have been castigated, though necessarily hundreds of con artists would have played active roles in the deceit dramas.

However, of late, in some geographies including India, individuals have been taken to task and even jailed for dishonesty.[17] Examples include top executives of the Indian infrastructure finance group IL&FS for alleged financial irregularities; the promoters of the Mumbai headquartered housing finance company DHFL for purported fraud on its lenders; Yes Bank's co-founder and former CEO over accusations of money laundering[18]; and the German fintech group Wirecard's ex-chief executive accused of a $2 billion gaping hole in the balance sheet.[19]

Making the bluffing players responsible for their act is a sensible development. When certain parts of the business world are practising irresponsible governance, naming and shaming the deceivers is the only way the deadly deceit disease may get somewhat discharged. All corporates do not sidestep ethics, but many do. It is the sifting of the rotten eggs from a basket that gets very challenging.

Why This Book?

There is hardly any book or condensed literature available on common corporate cons practised across the globe. There are scam-specific writings, but none seems to have taken the business dishonesty's bull by the horns. None perhaps has addressed the entire gamut of business bluffs—from corporate corruption to cybercrime, from share market swindle to shell companies, from technology lies to insurance cons. No book has so far laid bare the underbelly of the vile games various businesses play.

A few years ago, I attempted to pen down the broad genre of business barratry through my book titled *Who Cheats and How?* However, over the last several years, the situation on business deceptions has gone from bad to worse.

This book is an attempt to unravel the shadier side of corporate thinking, behaviour and execution. I have tried to unravel the mysteries of the major routes businesses take to cheat you and me.

What are the major forms of trickeries that are being practised in the world of business? Which are the ones that are more serious and concerning? All of us have the right to know much more about what's going on inside the murky world of business duplicity and deception.

With the business crime size, nature and intensity rising, this book attempts to bring you a fresh insight into the subject of business scams.

Numerous stories, many anecdotes, several experiences and diverse dishonesties have been stitched together to provide you with a ring-side view of the corporate cheating circus which keeps getting enacted upon inside the business arena. The book provides you front row seats to the swindle spectacle.

Prevention is better than cure. The desire to control and fight business falsehood should significantly improve by knowing who plays such con games, how it is played and what one can do to avert it.

I believe that knowledge and expertise gained through this book should enable readers to fight the malady better—or is it to join the bandwagon? The choice is yours!

Go ahead and take a peep into the dark side of the business world. Savour the con corporates' cheat chronicles.

CHAPTER ONE

The Psyche: (Un) Ethical Manager

Many of you would have heard of Rajat Gupta, one of the most accomplished Indian corporate executives.[1] An IIT and Harvard Business School graduate, he retired as the chairperson of the revered consulting firm McKinsey and was a director of the acclaimed global investment bank Goldman Sachs. What he has been alleged to have committed is incomprehensible and least expected from a person of his stature.

Gupta was in a Board of Director's call of Goldman Sachs in July 2008. He dialled in for a conference call at around 3.15 PM. During the call, Gupta got to know that the market guru Warren Buffett's Berkshire Hathaway would be investing $5 billion in Goldman Sachs. This proposed investment was at a time when the bank was in dire need of capital owing to the onset of global financial crisis. The large fresh inward investment was obviously very good news for the company's stock price.

On hearing the news, Gupta made a call to his friend Raj Rajaratnam, his partner in Galleon Group hedge fund, between 3.54 PM and 3.55 PM. Rajaratnam purchased shares of Goldman Sachs a few minutes later, at 3.56 PM and 3.57 PM, yielding him a profit of over $1.2 million. It so happens that this transaction of Rajaratnam constituted about one-fifth of the Goldman Sachs shares purchased that day.

This is sheer wreckage of faith—an unethical act—helping a friend with inside boardroom information. Gupta was convicted of breaking trust which the corporate world reposes on board members. Incidentally, even after spending two years in jail, Gupta continues to plead 'not guilty'.

Let me cite another instance of ethical digression by a business manager with a different spin.

Vijay Sakpal was the human resource (HR) vice president of a large multinational FMCG company.[2] He had a sales and marketing background but became the HR boss showing promise of a good leader. A president's post aspirant, he knew his subject, understood the tricks of the trade and had good communication skills. Yet when it came to his next promotion, the Board repeatedly bypassed his eligibility. He was flummoxed as to why he was not getting his dream job.

What Vijay did not realize was that he was not honest in his behaviour when it came to his people who did not have a marketing-related academic qualification. He would always be biased against any other discipline, believing that only sales and marketing guys can be high achievers. This is an inappropriate mindset, especially from an HR head!

These could be the stories of many. We may believe that we are honest and yet knowingly or otherwise practise unprincipled actions. Our biases could lead to beliefs which may not be beneficial for the business. Very strangely, sometimes the quantum of potential gain may not be the criterion for being unethical.

Are We Really (Un) Ethical?

Most of us believe that we are ethical and impartial. We imagine that we can derive objective conclusions to any given situation and always work towards the best interest of our organizations.

A research report written by Mahzarin Banaji, Max Bazerman and Dolly Chugh published in *Harvard Business Review* (HBR)[3] under the title 'How (Un) Ethical Are You?' confirms that in reality, most of us fall miserably short of our magnified self-impression. We are in fact deceived by our own biases, with our unconscious preferences working contrary to our consciously held explicit beliefs.

We may believe with confidence and conviction that the hiring decision of a candidate would be completely unbiased without realizing that there would be counter-intentional and unconscious biases—whether race, religion, caste, family or even the school or college.

We may believe that during disputes, we will be unbiased; but in reality, the stance taken by us could be prejudiced towards ourselves, our friends or our family members. While this may look logical, from an ethical viewpoint, our posture is sometimes prejudiced and influenced.

The pervasiveness of biases means that the most well-meaning business managers unintentionally allow unconscious thoughts and feelings to influence seemingly objective decisions. These result in flawed judgements, moving the decision-making into probable unethical territory.

The HBR research report explores four related sources of un-intentional but unethical decision-making: implicit forms of prejudice, bias that favours one's own group, conflict of interest and a tendency to overclaim credit.

- *Tacit bias:* Most fair-minded people should normally strive to judge others according to their merits, but the research shows how people often judge according to unconscious stereotypes and attitudes, or based on 'implicit prejudice'.

  What makes implied predisposition so common and per-sistent is that it is rooted in the fundamental mechanics of thought. There coexist certain patterns. Say if there is thunder, rain is a likelihood; gray hair implies old age. This skill of asso-ciating things does serve well, but not always.

Our mental associations only reflect approximations of the truth; they are rarely applicable to every situation. Rain and thunder need not occur together, and a person may go gray early. In view of these associations which we would have noticed many a time in the past, we innately repose trust in arranging our thoughts and decisions according to our past familiarities.

Implicit prejudice arises from the usual and unconscious tendency to make associations. It is distinct from conscious forms of bias, such as religion, caste, nationality or sex. This distinction explains why people who are free from conscious prejudice may still harbour biases and act accordingly. With past experiences of associating black men with violence or a particular nationality with fraudsters or portraying women as sex objects, even the most consciously unbiased mind is likely to make biased links. These associations play out in the workplace and business situations, just as they do elsewhere.

- *In-group favouritism:* Can you think of a favour which you would have done sometime in the past? For example, the recommendation for taking a young person for a traineeship as the person stays in your building and helping out a friend from your college class in her sudden financial difficulties. Would you have supported these people if they did not belong to your group?

Not surprisingly, we tend to do more favours for those we know, and those who we tend to believe are similar to us: people who share our nationality, religion, race, employer, where we live, club or alma mater.

This preference for known groups leads to many problems. For instance, people in power or in majority may favour those like them or belonging to their community. Willy-nilly, it could exclude the minority and the underprivileged. Think of companies offering incentives to employees recommending their friends for a position in the organization—is it not favouring a group over the other? Does it not lead to selecting someone based on relationship with an existing employee, thus ignoring the best available talent?

You may be disturbed to know that some banks are more likely to deny a mortgage loan application from a black person than from a white person,[4] or someone belonging to certain religious communities,[5] even when the applicants are equally eligible. Experience says that these biased practices are prevalent in almost all regions where minorities could be disadvantaged while taking a funding decision.

The ethical cost of in-group favouritism could be high. Cost of bad debt for loans granted or unethical behaviour by the borrowers could entail losses, arising out of biased financial decisions. Organizations may suffer by hiring candidates who would not have been selected, had the recruiting manager not been biased by in-group favouritism.

- *Overclaiming credit:* Most studies show that the majority consider themselves above average on performance—from intelligence to delivering result. This self-overestimation bias leads to managers having an overblown sense of entitlement. This mental bias of treating one's own contribution greater than others, leads to judging co-workers in a lesser light.

Research has shown that when groups have been asked to rate their individual performance while working for a group project, it has been found that the totals for each study group averaged much in excess of 100 (the ideal percentage). Sadly, but not surprisingly, the more the sum of the total estimated group effort surpassed 100 per cent (in other words, the more credit each person claimed), the less the participants wanted to collaborate with each other in the future.

This excessive bias towards taking self-credit is unethical and adversely affects collaborations. People in a group become sceptical about whether the other person is doing their fair share. This leads to both tending to reduce the contribution of the other person to compensate for one's own excessive estimation. These developments adversely affect managerial performance.

- *Conflict of interest:* It is common knowledge that deriving personal benefit arising out of one's own position would normally lead to deliberate unethical behaviour. For example, doctors face conflicts of interest when they accept referral payments for prescribing clinical tests. While the prescription could presumably be for the best interest of the patient, whether all prescribed diagnostic tests were necessary will always remain in doubt.

  Similarly, lawyers often earn fees from clients based on the number of court hearings. However, out-of-court settlements are always cheaper for clients and a less-time-consuming option. But how can the lawyers be objective and unbiased in getting a quick settlement, when their fees are linked with prolonging the case and appearing before the court multiple times?

  Whenever there is a situation which has the potential to undermine the impartiality of a person because of the possibility of a clash between the person's self-interest and professional interest, it is logical to suspect unethical behaviour.

While we believe that we are ethical, most of us are unaware of our behavioural biases. Hence, we do not address the reasons behind bad decisions.

Awareness about ourselves being biased and to work consciously towards objectivity might just start making us more ethical.

Tailpiece

It is said that there are two types of people in this world, good and bad—the good sleep better, but the bad seem to enjoy the waking hours much more. That's what many managers do in real life. Imagining their actions are ethical and for organization's benefit, the subconscious mind often rationalizes and suboptimizes the thinking and actions. Such is the behavioural truth of life.

Why Do People Doing Well in Corporates Cheat?

Hard to believe, but a senior Citibank officer, Paras Shah,[6] earning an annual salary of £1 million (₹9 crore) was allegedly stealing food, yes food, from his London Canary Wharf canteen. The 31-year-old was one of the highest-profile traders in Europe's junk bond market but could not resist the temptation of shoplifting canteen food. He was suspended from his services in February 2020.

Let me cite another instance. Navdeep Arora worked as a senior partner at the consulting firm McKinsey & Co. in their Chicago-based office, earning decent bucks. But his greed overtook his intellectual integrity.[7] He submitted fraudulent invoices and expenses to his organization for over $890,000. After having committed the fraud, Navdeep left McKinsey and joined KPMG in London in 2014. However, he made the mistake of coming back to the USA without realizing that an arrest warrant was hanging over his head. In 2016, when he flew down to New York from London, as his current employer required him to do, he got arrested by the Federal Bureau of Investigation and jailed for two years. He just could not elude the long arm of the law.[8]

In another example, once respected Ramalinga Raju started Satyam Computers.[9] As he progressed distinctively well, he wanted to overtake his famed IT competitors by depicting his own company as the largest, with the fastest growth. To project false sense of comfort to his clients, he cooked up the books, falsified bank statements and ran one of the largest Indian scams of over a billion dollars.

Sometimes even the much acclaimed and decorated business leaders cheat.

One of the most honoured Indian woman executives—ICICI Bank chairperson, awarded with Padma Bhushan (third highest civilian award in India)—Chanda Kochhar bypassed good governance to dole out loans to entities apparently having business interests linked to her husband.[10]

Can you believe that billionaires sometimes cheat for a few thousand bucks? Do they believe in the old saying 'every drop makes an ocean'?

An American retail businesswoman and television personality, Martha Stewart, a Forbes billionaire, wanted to make a measly $51,000 on the sly through advance information obtained from an insider. She was fined and jailed for 'insider trading'.[11]

One of the best-known business executives of recent times, Nissan Motor chairman, Carlos Ghosn, earning over $8 million salary,[12] diverted his employer's money clandestinely to provide himself with luxury homes in Rio de Janeiro, Beirut, Paris and Amsterdam 'without any legitimate business reason'. Sheer idiocy!

Dishonesty by the rich and powerful takes many forms.

The list does not stop here. In fact, it is just the beginning of a long list of business tycoons committing hara-kiri to their career due to serious lack of judgement in their behaviour and motive.

That brings us back to the question: Why do people who are seemingly doing well in the corporate world cheat? Why do they risk their hard-earned reputation, either through momentary lapse or espousing lack of judgement? What drives some of them to illegal acts for trivial gains, when their wealth figures tell stories of abundance?

- *Greed* is the big cause. Love of money is the root of almost all evil!

But gluttony and avarice are not the only cause for the invincible to cheat.

- *Self-interest* for selfish behaviour is another trigger. For instance, determination to please one's client could lead to have an unethical side contract which turns sour.

- *Fear of failure* is another cause for fraudulent behaviour. Desire to perform and pressure to deliver past performance could add to the unethical conduct.

I am reminded of Bernard Ebbers, the former chief executive of the infamous telecom American giant WorldCom, who treated his company as his personal bank. He loaned himself a monstrous $400 million.[13] He did accounting frauds in projecting better-than-reality numbers. He was served with a jail sentence of 25 years, where he served 13 when released for ill health in 2019, only to die soon thereafter. He had apparently declared that he was consumed by the desire to prove himself as the greatest businessman.

Even when the rich and famous dupe others, and the apparent urge is to continue their reign of success, the underlying motive continues to be greed. The innate desire to ride the dream horse of fame and fortune is nothing else but selfishness and disproportionate desire.

Have you noticed that drivers in expensive cars are likely to drive faster, breaking speed limits or jumping signals more often, as opposed to drivers in smaller and cheaper cars? Ego and false sense of high self-esteem often lead to such irrational behaviour.

During the COVID-19 lockdown in India, inter-state migrant labourers were fleeing to their home states in search of food during April–May 2020. Many were stuck on the road due to transport shutdown. When city dwellers were requested to roll 'chapatis' (Indian bread) for these homeless and road-stuck workers, it's the poor who contributed immensely, with the rich agonizing over lack of domestic help in their homes. Strange are the ways of some rich and famous!

The psychology of being unethical by the well-to-dos is more complex. It does not end with the three primary causes of greed, self-interest and fear of failure syndromes.

Broadly, there are three other psychological dynamics which lead to crossing ethical lines. They are belief of omnipotence, cultural numbness and justified neglect. These emotional under-currents have been discussed in the article by Merete Wedell-Wedellsborg, titled 'The Psychology behind Unethical Behavior', published in HBR in April 2019.[14] Let me explain to you the cognitive undercurrents.

- *The belief of all-powerfulness* prevails over many. The people who are in power can become intoxicated by the influence and prestige which comes with their uplifted status. People eulogize them, and many run at their commands. This is when the omnipotent leader feels glorified and starts believing that rules of decent behaviour are not applicable to them. They tend to do whatever is felt appropriate by themselves, over-looking the consequences on others.

    A recent example of this belief of omnipotence was exhibited in the Indian banking sector. Rana Kapoor, founder and CEO of Yes Bank, was overseeing one of the largest private sector Indian banks.[15] He had the foolhardiness of sanctioning loans based on his own hunch. Apparently, even his senior colleagues were unable to rectify his sense of crooked judgements. Kapoor got ousted from his position, lost control over the bank and the government had to bail out the cash-strapped bank.

- *Cultural impassiveness* is another cause. When environmental influence leads to gradually accepting divergent behavioural norms, it often results in emotional numbness.

    For example, this can happen to a policeman or a lawyer dealing with top criminals. The cop or the advocate may begin to adapt the practice, language, food and dress of the offenders. Frequent interactions with the wrongdoers often lead to unknowingly mimicking the crook. A similar adversarial discernible trait often happens in organizations where adaption of existing poor corporate culture could lead to cultural indifference. Unethical behavioural patterns could seep in, and red flags of poor conduct fail to get noticed.

- Finally, it is about *justified neglect*. This is applicable when people do not point out ethical ruptures, as they believe in more immediate rewards such as staying in the good books of the influential.

Let us take an example of a company where sales are falling short of the guidance given to the market. The manager puts in some fake sales, justifying that it will be corrected in the next quarter. He further rationalizes by saying that small incursions do not matter. Next quarter, the sales continue to lag behind, leading to some more fake sales inclusion. The unethical rides the deceit tiger, creating a situation of hopelessness to get off.

The sense of power, increased resource accessibility and acceptability by others of possible immoral behavioural traits could make the well-to-do managers short-shrift ethics. Greed is often perceived as positive and beneficial by the well-heeled.

Right is right, and wrong is wrong, and managers should know the difference; but many times, they do not. The human mind is complex. And it is this intricacy which does not help us to identify precisely the reasons behind unscrupulous demeanour.

Tailpiece

It is said that power corrodes more than it corrupts, often as a result of clever justifications for ethical neglect. To follow good governance is a mindset—and minds are powerful tools which can be trained to behave conveniently. An unethical mentality can rationalize unprincipled moves, resulting in institutionalizing corroded behaviour.

The day the power of love overrules the love of power, the world will be a better place to live in.

Why Do Employees Cheat?

Employees sometimes play with company's laid-down systems to maximize either their own or the corporate's performance. Take the example of Volkswagen,[16] which admitted in 2015 to some of its employees creating a device which allowed the company's vehicles to cheat emission tests. In the following year, over 5,000 Wells Fargo bank's employees were involved in secretly opening millions of phony accounts in an attempt to achieve sales targets and receive bonuses.

There are so many instances of employees pushing the envelope of ethical practice to get ahead.

In 2017, Michael Baer, a professor in the W. P. Carey School of Business, completed a study (reported in phys.org)[17] on 1,000 employees in the USA about workplace cheating. It explores why employees cheat to enhance performance and what companies are doing to boost, perhaps unknowingly, unethical behaviour.

There are two major factors which could motivate employees to cheat, the paper said.

- One could be 'organization's pressure' on their employees to perform at a high level. The study found that as the pressure to raise performance levels increased, employees became focused on protecting themselves from getting into trouble. Accordingly, the employees ended up being untruthful by inflating their performance. In other words, they cheated.

  This is what happened in Volkswagen and Wells Fargo scandals. Investigations revealed that many of the employees felt threatened and ultimately decided that cheating was one way to meet the performance demands.

  A famous example of a disastrous outcome of excessive pressure due to tough goals dates back to the 1970s. It pertains to Ford Pinto, a subcompact car by Ford Motor Company.[18] The company's CEO Lee Iacocca pushed his team to build a car 'under 2,000 pounds weight and under $2,000 cost'. He was in a desperate hurry to get the car in showrooms for the 1971 model year. That meant one of the shortest production planning period: just 25 months, instead of the normal 40 months. The result was an unsafe car. An estimated 500 people died and hundreds got injured—linked to faulty design which made the gasoline tank explode after rear-end collisions. Due to the rush to complete the project, the Ford team overlooked safety testing while designing the car. The legendary Iacocca was fired in 1978.

- 'Personal gratification' is the other major reason for employees stealing or misappropriating corporate assets like cash or stocks, hoodwinking internal control systems or skirting trust bestowed by employers. This could be out of habit, compulsion or greed to corner some extra cookies. Making money on the sly is one of the most potent reasons for employees to cross the *Lakshman rekha* of ethics. Accepting something of value or money in return for a favourable decision (in short, bribery) is not uncommon among many managers.

  Just to cite an example, purchase managers of public sector enterprises are known to take kickbacks to source input items either at a higher price or of suboptimal quality. Bribery negates the nation's wealth creation by compromising quality and value.

There are other reasons for employees to embrace deceit and dupery.

- Many companies declare that they have an 'open door policy', but they 'discourage speaking up'. Creating a culture in which people can freely speak up is important to guarantee that the employees do not conspire or provoke misbehaviour.

  I know of an entrepreneur who could not take bad news. Once a customer rejected his supplies, leading to a huge loss on account of the goods sold being returned. But his manager fearing reprisal hid the fact by lying that all was well. The company could have easily taken action to rectify the production defects. Instead, the business went belly up shortly as customers lost confidence in the company's ability to supply goods of consistent quality. Discouraging plain speaking led to the fall of a dream enterprise.

- Another trigger for unethical acts is 'setting of conflicting goals' by the management. It creates motivational havoc among employees. A sense of injustice creeps in.

Let me cite an example. I once encountered a company in Delhi where the marketing head was told to double his sales, but the HR head was separately told to halve the number of salesmen as a cost-saving measure. The contradiction played havoc with the business. The incompatible goals led to dumping of goods to dealers by the diminished sales force, resulting in heavy return of goods sold in the following year. Organizations should have a common vision to achieve and not conflicting objectives to deal with.

- In any organization, people look up to the top for signals where 'leaders should not concede ethics'. It is the chieftains who show the way to others, how to think and behave. Communicating transparently, making products faithfully and behaving truthfully, all add up. If any compromise is attempted at the top, it provides signals down the line for compromising behaviour.

Many of us would have encountered departmental heads not apprising the true picture to the powers that be—with the intent to prove that the department is performing well—to get kudos and incentives. While the intent could be good, it may in reality lead to portraying a negative ethos across the business.

The bad news is that employee cheating is on the rise, with many research reports indicating the enhanced employee unscrupulous behavioural drift.

PwC's Global Economic Crime and Fraud Survey 2020[19] finds that 37 per cent of frauds were committed by internal actors, with another 20 per cent in collusion with employees and external actors. And the worst is that frauds committed by senior management were as high as 26 per cent being the most treacherous, as the top executives had the ability to hide frauds and bypass internal controls.

The EY *Global Integrity Report 2020*[20] (interviewing 3,000 employees in 33 countries) discloses some gory details of senior employee attitude towards ethics. The research finds that the more senior an employee, the more likely they would be to act unethically. High-ranking employees are more likely to justify unethical behaviour such as ignoring crooked conduct in their team, misleading external parties such as auditors or regulators, and being involved in bribery in order to boost their own career goals. This is disturbing, as leaders at the top set the tone and define standards of behaviour for any organization. And the worst is that 35 per cent of the respondents believed that unethical behaviour in their organization was often tolerated when the people involved were senior or high performers.

While maintaining integrity among the managers and employees is considered very important, it would be the business leaders who would need to focus on instilling employees to take individual responsibility for the integrity of their own actions. It is the tone at the top which swings things around—be it quality, attitude or ethics.

Tailpiece

Employee behaviour and integrity are largely driven by the corporate culture. If the top management does not espouse ethics, the employees are unlikely to exercise it.

Propensity to Cheat

As we go along with our daily chores, we sometimes cut corners just to hasten things—say jump an unpoliced signal, hoping there were no hidden traffic cameras. Or just to get work done quickly in your company, you allot an order to your relative, sidestepping the notion of conflict of interest, only to rationalize yourself that it was done in the best interest of the organization. Such small infractions look alright to begin with, but when they become a habit or get out of proportion, ethics takes a huge hit.

Many a time, infractions begin with baby steps. A little compromise here, and some bypassing of law there, seems innocuous and harmless. When nothing adverse happens, the matter of breaking laws and jumping rules becomes a habit. Bigger cheating, like siphoning off some portion of a corporate loan to buy one's own bungalow, becomes a trickery.

We have all been exposed to office behaviours involving stationeries being stolen, travel expenses being inflated or favouritism in recommending promotion. These acts normally start with trivialities but then start growing, vitiating the work atmosphere. It results in impacting trust, affecting company's performance and leading to a culture of unethical mindset.

How small transgressions can lead to greater infringements can be understood from a simple personal example. While driving, checking on a few WhatsApp messages looked blameless. But when nothing happened, reading emails while driving almost became a routine. That is an appalling behavioural aberration—only to be set right when a policeman one day caught me infringing and imposed a heavy penalty with a terse warning.

Think of some more examples of cutting some corners: doctors not giving full attention to patients and prescribing further medication based on cursory understanding of ailments and retail stores selling food products on the expiry date, knowing fully well that the customer is likely to consume post the last recommended date of consumption. Instances abound in our daily lives. These minor infractions, small cheating and little adjustments look alright, until these become big.

A big ethical impropriety will arise if a doctor suggests an operation, knowing fully well that it is not necessary to do so or if a retail shop habitually sells food products after the expiry date which could cause major health hazards to the consumer.

What is the way to avoid these cheatings?

The best way for a business is to lay down standard operating procedures, say a restaurant must ensure that the ingredients are checked by another person for being fresh and not out of date; a manufacturer of yoghurt to ensure that micro-biological tests are duly carried out; and a medicine manufacturer to ensure that complete records of all rejections are maintained. If strict written standard procedures are laid down, then bypassing controls become more difficult.

Normally, we would like to believe that we are good and honest people. But studies have shown that we are able to have this positive image of ourselves as long as we only cheat a bit and not much.

This human tendency to cheat small has been beautifully described through an experiment reported by Professor Dan Ariely in his book *The Honest Truth about Dishonesty*.[21]

In a study, the participants were given 20 simple math problems and asked to solve as many as they could in five minutes. They were then asked to put their solved papers in a shredder, before letting an experimenter know how many problems they solved. It was stated that the participants will receive $1 for every correct answer they would report.

What the participants did not know was that the shredder destroyed only the edges of the test papers, allowing the experimenter to compare how many problems they got right to how many they said that they solved. Almost 40,000 people participated in these experiments, with only 20 saying that they solved all the problems. This cost the researchers $400. The far larger impact, however, came from the 70 per cent of the participants—28,000 people—who cheated 'only a little bit' but ended up costing the researchers more than $50,000.

The initial casual slip-ups cascade into more serious ones, which then turn into habits. One knows that they are bad but it starts to feel excusable and even acceptable. It is hard to pinpoint the tipping point of transgression. It is easier to course-correct at the very beginning of the slimy slope than when one is sashaying full speed on the path of inappropriateness and impropriety.

It has been proven that when it comes to tolerating others committing frauds, the acceptability is more when it starts with small dishonesties and then grows to a bigger one, rather than a big fraud news popping up suddenly.

Tailpiece

Think of visible traffic cameras at signals—whether they work or not—their mere presence encourages good driver behaviour in not jumping traffic signals. Visible signs of good and ethical behaviour encourage others to practise it. Laying down guidelines of behaviour encourages acceptable conduct. It aids if there is someone who monitors bad behaviour. These steps may prevent even small transgressions.

But many a time, visibility has reverse implication—encouraging poor behaviour. If observed that others are practising bad behaviour, poor conduct gets encouraged, spoiling people's behavioural standards.

Cheats will be cheats—small or big, today or tomorrow—this, unfortunately is the human trait of many!

Tax Evaders' Psyche

News on tax dodging galore—every day in the media, there will be instances of swindlers somewhere trying to cheat their way out of some extra money.

The question is: Why are there so many instances of tax evasion? What is the psychology of tax evaders? Let us peek into the minds of these rogues to understand their psyche a bit more.

More wealth leads to more greed—a classical human psyche for some, to accumulate more, whatever be the implication. A worker may hardly be able to meet her ends through her earnings, but a high net-worth individual could happily park his funds offshore to evade the prying eyes of the taxmen.

Several tricks are employed to fool the tax system. 'Havala' (transferring money outside banking channel) transactions are not uncommon to remit ill-gotten wealth abroad and then routing it back at an appropriate time through round tripping. Over- and under-invoicing by businesses having international trade linkage are also often practised for stashing unaccounted money in tax havens or low-tax regimes. Many rich and famous love to play these games to evade tax, giving them intoxicating doses of satisfaction and achievement.

Audacity is the trait of many. By evaluating the risk and reward of tax deceits, some would venture into these murky trails. Consultants would sometimes advise clients of helping to structure deals which make taxation untouchable and untraceable. The fear factor is often the tipping point. Repeat offenders or appearance of low-risk threshold makes many jump into muddy puddles of tax avoidance. Honesty takes a back seat, and the thrill of cutting corners takes over.

High tax rates make many lie. Prior to the 1970s, Indian tax rates peaked at an eye-watering 98 per cent. With added burden of wealth tax, gift tax and estate duty, some were having negative income. The natural tendency in such a scenario will be to avoid tax. Currently, the tax rates in many geographies have come down, including in India. However, the old habits of generating black money and not paying the full tax liability are still holding sway. And some just enjoy not paying taxes irrespective of rates of taxes being fixed—savings arising from not paying money to the government provide innate joy to many.

You will be surprised to know that a 2018 study,[22] reported in *The Economist*, concluded that around 40 per cent of multinationals' overseas profits are artificially shifted to low-tax countries—from tax-less Caribbean paradises to tax-light hubs of Ireland and Cyprus. To undo this awful psyche of tax avoidance by the prosperous companies, the G7 rich countries and others are focusing on two main changes: reallocating taxing rights towards countries where economic activity takes place, rather than where firms choose to book profits, and setting a minimum global tax rate of 15 per cent. If this ever happens, it may ruin the carefully structured lucrative business models of the well-to-do corporations.

Corrupt tax-collecting system encourages a large number of moneyed players to play truant with the tax system. Strict implementation of law and presence of honest tax collectors can swing many to pay the taxes due. Presence of bribery and corruption among the bureaucracy help many to make merry.

Tailpiece

The psyche of tax avoiders is complex, influenced not just by economic motives but also by psychological factors. The ecstasy many derive by breaking the law and foxing the system is immense. It is almost like trying one's luck in a casino, knowing full well that the probability of winning is stacked against the player. But still, the joy of instant gratification keeps the gates of gambling dens busy. The mindsets of tax evaders are no different.

Tax planning is good, but tax avoidance is a crime. Tax evasion game is beset with risks, but as long as the dice keeps rolling favourably for evaders, the con game to beat the system will continue.

Why Do Some Turn Bad?

The other day I attended a corporate dinner. Wonderful people, professional approach and friendly to the hilt, and yet, later on I found that the group had been indicted for doctoring accounts of their company—showing non-existent sales. Why do these seemingly well-meaning folks get caught up in the hubris? How could some good people become bad?

Several theories exist about what provokes anyone to cheat, including some concepts elucidated in this chapter.

An old hypothesis which I learned way back in my college days is the famous 'fraud triangle'—a model created by the American criminologist Donald Cressey in the 1950s.[23] His theory is based on interviews with prison inmates. It talks about the need to have three elements for occupational fraud.

- *Pressure:* It is the motivation to commit fraud. It can be a deceit motivator, like heavy mortgage bank liability or pressing family needs.
- *Opportunity:* Given a chance, some would commit deception. Lack of business controls may lead to a swindle. If someone believes that it's easy to steal and an opportunity exists, a fraud could get committed.
- *Rationalization:* It is the mindset to justify that it is alright to commit a graft. An employee could feel that his employer is making a lot of money; hence, stealing from him is justified.

A mixture of the above three elements could cook up a deadly recipe of greed and result in bypassing controls for self-gain.

What is the tipping point for dishonesty? Apart from the basic tenets of pressure, opportunity and rationalization, there are a lot of other forces—both rational and irrational—which could influence a person becoming unscrupulous: fear of failure, conflict of interest, belief of all-powerfulness, creativity, witnessing others' dishonest acts, thrill of making money and so on—with human greed standing out as a sore thumb.

The human capacity to deceit is fairly high. Not everyone is crooked, but it is the bad apples—the outliers—which make the world of business a not-too-happy nesting ground for the honest. Unfortunately, the social sciences still do not intuitively understand how the psyche of dishonesty works on the humans. But the most important stuff is that we do not see it in ourselves!

Few Last Words

The emperor of business deception and duplicity was Enron,[24] which collapsed in 2001 when its massive fraud and hoodwinking got unearthed. And yet its ethics policy screamed: 'Agreements, whether contractual or verbal, will be honoured. No bribes, bonuses, kickbacks, lavish entertainment, or gifts will be given or received in exchange for special position, price or privilege.'

In India, the face which changed the perception of large-scale corporate malfeasance is Kingfisher Airlines. The once most preferred airlines company proclaimed 'Integrity' as the first item on its 'Values' statement. And what did the company do? It wilfully defaulted on debts drawn from banks and allegedly diverted the borrowings for non-declared purposes.[25]

The above virtuous statements could be familiar to many of you—for the organizations you may have dealt with—only to discover that poor governance is what several practise in reality.

Many companies have compliance policies which are usually signed by the employees while joining or taking a new assignment.

However, it is clear that it takes more than an ethics policy to make the workplace ethical.

Business managers often fall into the trap of unscrupulous demeanour when the environment tempts or psychological desire entices them to do so. Reasons could be many. Greed, immoral philosophy, exaggerated ego and weak corporate governance enable some to short-shrift the system.

A principled culture, tone at the top, appropriate internal control and value-based employee training would go a long way to develop ethical managers.

CHAPTER TWO

Corporate Con Artists

In India, there is an inherent dislike for mammoth business corporations—rooted in the bitter experience of one foreign company ruling the country for 200 years. **East India Company** remains history's most apocalyptic cautionary story about the abuse of corporate power—a stark instance of how the sinister interest of the shareholders can become that of the State.

East India Company, a corporate con artist, was a strange animal to begin with. It was a joint stock company established by a motley group of explorers and adventurers to trade in the world's riches. It gradually grew into an enterprise, is thankfully with respect to its viciousness and magnitude—a business house with its own army that conquered large tracts of India, grabbing jewels and wealth of the Mughal emperors.

The British company's plunder since the 18th century was so evil that the word 'loot' entered the English lexicon. This was one of the worst instances of an international business corporation transforming itself into a colonial power, accumulating unimaginable quantum of booties through belligerence.

While the company began as a traditional trading outfit when it was founded in 1599, it started showing the darker side quite early since 1602 when it captured a Portuguese vessel on its maiden voyage. But it was from the mid-1700s that the company ceased to resemble a conventional trading firm and turned itself into a looter.

In the infamous Battle of Plassey in 1757 under the leadership of Robert Clive, the company overcame Siraj-ud-Daulah's army of 50,000 near the mango groves of Lakash Bagh. The grateful East India Company appointed Clive as the governor of the Presidency of Bengal. Clive quickly began his advocacy for taking control of territories as well as trade in the region. But remember that he had the backing of the state, a sponsorship for extracting wealth from the underprivileged regions. The East India Company, emboldened by British state sponsorship, carried out flagrant acts with its private army, sustained through tax revenue and topped up handsomely with commercial profit. Then the rest became history.

Slowly but surely, the British took control of the Indian subcontinent under the mask of a business corporation. This episode of a company—state duo taking control over the wealth of a nation is the worst form of corporate ethical violation and violence of purpose in history.

Incidentally, this was not the only instance of business conning the system. There have been several other grisly instances of corporate loot and plunder. People voicing concern about the 18th-century-type corporate acquisition of state wealth for personal benefits do have reasons to doubt the inner intent of business establishments, at least sometimes.

Moving over to another blatant violation of corporate purpose, fortune hunter and land-grabbing settler, Cecil John Rhodes with his **British South Africa Company,** was the pioneer in the conquest of Zimbabwe.

At first, he bought from the local Zimbabwean king a written concession for exclusive mining rights and landed there with an army. Rhodes then declared war on the king. After successfully overthrowing the ruler, he named the country Rhodesia.

The British South Africa Company, a mercantile entity incorporated in 1889 by a British royal charter, was modelled on the East India Company and was expected to annex and develop settlements for the Europeans.

After years of exploitation, when they realized that they were losing ground support, the company handed over their authority to the British Colonial Office in 1924, completing another dark instance of corporate ethical desecration.

The stories of corporate exploitation of trust are too many. Instances of enterprises plundering state wealth had blurred the faith on business establishments.

Over 100 years ago, in the early years of the 20th century, William Knox D'Arcy, with encouragement from the British government, began looking for oil in Iran. He struck a concession agreement with the absolute Iranian monarchy, using the age-old method of bribery with the negotiators. Just after oil was struck, the British government bought the D'Arcy concession in 1909, and christened it the **Anglo-Persian Oil Company.**

The company then built the world's biggest refinery at the port of Abadan on the Persian Gulf. From the 1920s into the 1940s, Britain consumed the cheap Iranian oil and lived a gala life. This oil company was the most lucrative British enterprise anywhere on earth.

In order to protect their control over the oil wealth, the British with the help of Americans overthrew the passionate champion of Iranian oil nationalization, Prime Minister Mohammad Mosaddegh, and replaced him with Mohammad Reza Shah Pahlavi in 1953. But due to Shah of Iran's repressive ways and pro-Western stance, the political landscape in Iran changed. Democracy walked back after Shah fled in 1978 and Ayatollah Khomeini took over the reins.

Eventually, the oil company rebranded itself as British Petroleum, then to BP Amoco, and since 2000 as BP. The long era of corporate manipulation of a nation's wealth is a testimony to some harsh realities of exploitative business practices.[1]

Politicians and business corporations have ganged up together for centuries and across geographies. Fat contributions by businesses for electioneering and getting to choose candidates to occupy the seats of power have been known for long. It is an open secret that in democratic set-ups, corporate largesse often become the game changer.

In this game of corporate–politician nexus, perhaps the most infamous drama pertains to a coup planned under the aegis of the American manufacturing conglomerate **ITT**—International Telephone & Telegraph Corporation (renamed ITT Inc).

Way back in 1970, in Chile, the corporate hunger went berserk, with the company planning a coup d'état.

It is understood that the ultimate seat of power, the US White House, was offered by ITT that the company would be prepared to 'assist financially with sums up to seven figures' to block the impending appointment of Salvador Allende as Chile's president.[2] At the time, ITT owned 70 per cent of CTC (the Chilean Telephone Company, now Movistar Chile). ITT believed that Allende wanted to nationalize CTC, which was a telephone equipment-manufacturing concern. Declassified documents reveal that the company financially helped opponents of Allende's government prepare for a successful military coup. ITT apparently also funded El Mercurio, a Chilean right-wing newspaper. (As a revenge, in 1973, an ITT building in New York City was bombed for its alleged involvement in the Chilean coup.)

You may remember the *Strange Case of Dr. Jekyll and Mr. Hyde* by the Scottish writer Robert Louis Stevenson, written towards the end of the 19th century. The two alter egos of the main character have become synonymous with the exhibition of wildly contradictory behaviour, especially between private and public selves. The two opposite faces that some corporates portray have been no different. Many times, businesses show their gracious face to the society, only to keep topping up their coffers through their ominous acts.

Perhaps the most classical case of Dr Jekyll and Mr Hyde syndrome in the corporate arena was conjured up by **United Fruit**—the banana company desiring to create 'banana republics'. While the company sold the healthiest fruit, they practised conceivably the unhealthiest ethos.

The American multinational corporation United Fruit, believing in the spirit of liberal capitalism, dominated business and politics in Central America during the major part of the 20th century. Apart from harvesting the hearty fruit, the company wielded formidable influence over small nations, which were mostly corrupt and ruled by dictators.

By the 1920s, United Fruit's empire had spread across Central America. It included Jamaica, Cuba and the Dominican Republic. In South America, the company owned chunks of Colombia and Ecuador. With the world's largest private navy having 100 refrigerated ships, it dominated the European and US banana markets. Its ambition of complete supremacy made the company ruthless. The company gained a reputation of being cold-blooded when crossed and for working towards removing unfriendly governments.

United Fruit's first act of harsh stance included the invasion of Honduras in 1911.[3] Fearing power wielding by the corporation, the Honduras government blocked setting up United's production in the country. Undeterred, United Fruit financed an invasion for 'regime change' in the name of banana.

In 1954, the company manipulated in orchestrating a coup to get rid of the democratically elected Guatemalan government, as it had taken United Fruit's large tracts of unused land to distribute it to peasant farmers. The company bribed journalists and planted false stories of gunfire and bombs, blaming it on 'communist terror'.

After years of manipulation and aggressive marketing, it saw a declining fortune, mainly due to frequent banana plant diseases. In 1984, the company got transformed into the present-day Chiquita Brands International. The banana company—United Fruit—went bananas for the sake of its ambition to sell more bananas!

Have things changed of late? Can we say that the instances of corporates taking humanity for a ride only transpired many decades back? Unfortunately, that is not the case. The desire of corporates to show a good bottom line by influencing regulations to their advantage is still very much present. The propensity of the political class to source power through the fat reserves of businesses is still blooming. However, subjugation of states by corporations looks improbable. But corporate lobbying and scurrying for favours from the powers that be is more or less an accepted norm.

Just think that will Microsoft, Apple or Amazon, with over a trillion-dollar market capitalization each, be able to lord over any state today? No! In the modern world, it is unlikely that any state sponsorship will help a corporation build an empire. The public opinion being so deep-rooted through television, social media and smart phones, it will be hard for any business corporation to withstand public uproar. A loot of state wealth by a company aka East India Company is now a far cry. But exploiting people by lobbying, corruption, bribery or poor governance continues to be practised by some in the corporate world in various pockets across the globe.

While corporate con artists nowadays may not be able to cheat their way into looting the wealth of nations, the fact that they had indulged in booty cornering in the past is a moral setback on reposing trust onto their professed self-regulated governance principles. While most businesses practise sound business doctrines, a few of them still try to figure out ways and means to make that extra money for their own aggrandizement, achievement and advantage—which are in no way for the good of the people at large.

Lies and Damn Lies

None of us can say, 'I have never lied' or, for that matter, 'I do not lie.' All of us lie in some way or the other—small or big—depending upon the situation. Honesty is not always the best policy we have heard many a time. Human behaviour is peppered with lies and damn lies. Many of us make promises, knowing fully well that we cannot keep them; students often hide their misdemeanours through misrepresentation; children often play truant with truth whenever it suits them; parents tell holier than thou stories to their young ones; leaders often make false promises to the voters.

Corporate life is no different. How can our business lives be dissimilar to what we practise in our normal lives? We can talk about good corporate governance, announce awards for the best governed companies, but can we say that none of these companies cut corners in their daily business lives? The concept of truthfulness preached by gurus and evangelists is a mere fantasy in the business world.

Lies are sometimes damn lies! Think of some advertising campaigns. From time immemorial, we have watched ads showing certain variety of soaps making every woman look like a movie star, or using a particular shampoo or hair oil to have that perfect long and thick hair, or using a particular face cream to retain the youthfulness even in the sunset years.

Did the advertisers believe that their ad campaigns were wholly truthful? Of course not! A bit of stretching product functionalities is alright in this make believe world is what many would say. But what happens is that white lies are communicated with alacrity and disdain. The cosmetics, beauty, health, fitness and education industries are often built upon this duplicity.

Time and again, big names have misrepresented their wares by making superlative unsubstantiated product deliverable claims. **Gujarat Co-Operative Milk Marketing Federation,** the maker of the famous Amul milk, advertised to be 'fresh har pal' (fresh all the time).[4] It was a hoax. Amul milk was pasteurized milk. It has limited shelf life and claiming it to be fresh always is misleading.

Similarly, the much touted **Dr Batra's Positive Health Clinic's** (Geno Homeopathy) claim 'New STM which is an inventive hair growth treatment from France' was not substantiated with any details of the special treatment procedure based on French technology. It was considered to be misleading by exaggeration.

Time and again, the Advertising Standards Council of India has advised numerous corporates, including the famous ones, to desist from making exaggerated claims.

If we cannot repose confidence on the claims by big names of the corporate world, whom do we trust? And the list here is just a glimpse—you will be appalled when you see the catalogue of the recalcitrant.

One way to figure out the incidence of the problem in India is to track the Serious Fraud Investigation Office (SFIO). In 2019–2020, the agency probed into 361 companies believed to be involved in hanky-panky, against 132 companies probed in the previous year. Clearly, the number of corporate fraudsters is increasing manifold.[5]

In a recent instance, a Chinese tycoon, Wu Xiaohui, who rose to international prominence by buying the Waldorf Astoria hotel in Manhattan for $2 billion, was sentenced to 18 years in prison in May 2018 after having lied and defrauded investors.[6] What Wu did was use the company he founded, **Anbang Insurance** investment conglomerate with $316 billion in assets, to cheat investors out of $10 billion in one of China's biggest cases of financial crime. He devised a convoluted scheme in which he hid his control in Anbang through a web of companies, instructed employees to falsify financial statements, diverted insurance premiums for personal use and made false disclosures to regulators. In this way, he was able to skirt regulations and raise money from the public.

A big lie which has killed over 400,000 people in the two decades till 2019, in the USA, was modelled by a few pharmaceutical companies—the ones who are supposed to heal our pains. The medical fraternity argued that opioid drugs could be used to dull severe pain from cancer, arthritis, surgery or injury. They argued that addiction risks like that of opium or heroin could be reduced by special formulations and innovative prescribing practices.

Several pharma companies spent millions of dollars to falsely promote opioid as a cure-all without ill effects. **Purdue Pharma,** which sparked the boom in opioid prescriptions with high-profile marketing of OxyContin, was one such player, a large player.[7] **Johnson & Johnson** was also held accountable for intentionally playing down the dangers and overselling the benefits of opioids. Another wilful offender was **Insys Therapeutics,** which carried out intensive marketing plans of paying some doctors for sham educational talks and luring others with lap dances to sell its under-the-tongue fentanyl (a synthetic opioid) spray, Subsys. The list of opioid offenders is long—more than 1,000 US cities and counties, 22 opioid manufacturers, distributors and pharmacies.

The fundamental issue involved drug makers taking legitimate products—strong painkillers—and allegedly marketing them to loads of potential patients while understating the risks involved, leading to addiction so compelling that several 'patients' turned to the streets when their legal supply ran out. Many deaths involved addicts turning from proper prescription drugs to heroin and fentanyl, apparently being smuggled in from China and Mexico into the USA.[8] The tragedy is unlikely to end soon with tens of thousands more getting affected daily. One wonders how some pharma companies, who are supposed to be the ones curing you and me, get involved in wrecking the lives of so many humans!

Drug companies have carried out many sins over time: from cartelization to weakening competition; from price enhancing to price fixing; from hiding drug side effects to selling drugs for wrong application; from fiddling clinical trials to endorsing useless drugs; from bribing doctors to advocating skewed research papers; from promoting particular drugs to endorsing addictive opioids. The list of pharma transgressions is rather long.

A string of scandals involving pharma giants will make you understand the malady plaguing the industry. **Pfizer** settled several illegal marketing cases between 2002 and 2009; **Warner–Lambert** (Pfizer took it over) made a huge amount of money marketing the epilepsy drug Neurontin for uses that were not approved and not medically effective[9]; **Merck** unlawfully promoted its painkiller drug Vioxx for rheumatoid arthritis[10]; **Eli Lilly** misbranded its Zyprexa antipsychotic drug for the treatment of dementia in elderly patients; **Abbott** unlawfully promoted its prescription drug Depakote for dementia patients; **GlaxoSmithKline** (GSK) paid a whopping $3 billion in 2011 for unlawfully promoting certain prescription drugs like Paxil and failing to report its safety data; **Takeda** was found guilty in 2015 over its oral diabetes drug Actos for hiding the bladder cancer risks related to the drug.

Unfortunately, nothing much happens as the fines on corporations are inadequate compared to the harm they sometimes commit.[11] Plus, there are hardly any criminal charges against the ultimate decision-makers.

Tailpiece

Businesses are essentially meant to generate profits. But when corporate surpluses are garnered by conning others and painting rosy pictures on the canvas of deceit, problems arise. There is a common saying that cheating is fine till one gets caught.

Unfortunately, and shamefully, thoroughbred names have fallen foul of ethical business practice.

Why Do Corporates Con?

Businesses have cheated in plenty over the years. Names involved often make the who's who listing and lead to disbelief when announced.

There are plenty of reasons why businesses cheat.

Eagerness to maintain their reputation makes corporates engage in aberrant behaviours including acts of impropriety out of fear that they may not be able to meet expectations.

Peer pressure is another cause. The need to match or beat competing company's performance often leads to business crimes including doctoring of financial accounts.

The desire to get more funding is a cause enough for many corporates to lie. While borrowing, instances are plenty where the borrowers would have overstated their assets like inventory and receivables, only to be able to borrow more. Ask your banker friends for any number of such stories.

Moving on with the aspect of ethics transgression, examples of businesses fiddling information about the air quality, smoke emission and dirty water discharge are plenty.

Many a time, the desire to generate bottom-line (profits) leads to sacrificing quality or overcharging for non-existent services. Think of a situation that you are sleeping in a luxurious hotel room only to wake up in the middle of the night and find that the thermostat is not working. The hotel may have switched off the central air conditioner for some time during the night to save on cost! Imagine another scenario. You went to buy a small car. The dealer somehow sold you a car without airbags. Your safety was not the salesman's concern, his commission was!

Let me now cite one of the most bizarre cheating scandals to hit the lightly regulated Alternative Investment Market (AIM, a sub-market of London Stock Exchange for smaller companies). Inside the glass building close to London's Victoria station sits the main office of a small Nigerian oil producer, Lekoil.[12] The company plunged into crisis in January 2020 after a $184 million loan deal from Qatar's sovereign wealth fund to develop its main asset, an oil field off Nigeria's coast, turned out to be bogus.

The West Africa-focused company, listed on AIM in 2013, was hoodwinked through an exquisitely executed drama. Some people pretended to be the Qatar Investment Authority (QIA) and took Lekoil for a ride. Also involved in the middle was a Bahamas-based consultancy called **Seawave Invest,** to which Lekoil paid $600,000 to broker the funding deal with the QIA.[13]

Lekoil and those camouflaged as QIA representatives met regularly in the second half of 2019 in locations across West Africa, the Middle East and Europe. The fake QIA representatives went to considerable lengths to appear authentic, including producing sham business cards and letterheads. Lekan Akinyanmi, the Lekoil chief executive, himself led the negotiations for the company. He was advised by some of the best advisors. **Norton Rose Fulbright,** one of the largest law firms in the world, provided legal advice on the deal. **Control Risks,** a UK-headquartered global risk consultancy firm, prepared the due diligence report which apparently did not raise red flags. In fact, the loan's relatively low interest rate of 3.7 per cent should have raised suspicions.

If the massive, dramatized fraud had not been discovered, Lekoil would have had to pay $10 million fees just before the so-called first disbursement of the loan being negotiated. Since the deal announcement, Lekoil's languishing shares reached several peaks. But the euphoria suddenly ended when Lekoil disclosed that the so-called QIA was a completely false façade, and the funding deal was a big fraud.

The scandal has left Lekoil's future in tenterhooks, with the company blaming its advisers for failing to detect a phony loan deal.

With an experienced law firm and strategic risk advisors on the toe, how on earth could a fraud of this nature be fabricated? It was like a Hollywood movie portraying a con game.

To share another weird instance of cheating, you may find it hard to believe that even Warren Buffet can be bluffed! Buffet's financial services company Berkshire Hathaway was fooled into buying a seemingly solid German pipe maker which was actually going into bankruptcy.

Buffet's conglomerate is suing the USA-based international law firm **Jones Day,** which represented the owners of the pipe manufacturing company when it was sold to a Berkshire Hathaway subsidiary in 2017.[14] The lawsuit blames Jones Day for helping to trick Berkshire Hathaway into paying five times of what the German company was really worth.

The chances of recovering any money from the seller, Wilhelm Schulz GmbH, which fabricates the piping systems, stands bleak. The company has declared itself bankrupt and is facing a criminal investigation in Germany.

'The fraudulent transaction would never have occurred without the legal-firm Jones Day's substantial assistance,' accuses the lawsuit. It alleges the lawyers of withholding documents which would have exposed Wilhelm Schulz's disastrous financial position and called the legal firm a 'co-conspirator' in a 'massive fraud'.

It is alleged that the company owner, along with its managers, used false sales invoices and fake customers to make the pipe manufacturing company look more financially strong than it actually was and hoodwink Berkshire Hathaway to pay a very high price. The deal clearly shows that even the world's sharpest investor can be taken for a ride.

Clearly, this is a case where the legal firm was aware of information which would have revealed its client's dire financial condition but failed to disclose when it mattered.

Whom should we believe when even the big names in businesses are either parties to deceits or are negligent in unravelling deceptions? Lawyers and doctors are people we trust. But when they break the confidence reposed on them, then business structures could fall apart.

Frauds and scams crumple business image—whether the enterprises are involved in manufacturing or in services like legal, consultancy or medicine.

This absence of ethics is a recipe for poor corporate governance, leading to the risk of dents in a corporation's goodwill.

Tailpiece

Why do people and corporations who are seemingly doing well in the business world risk their reputation which they have built over the years with diligence and dedication? There is a conglomeration of reasons, but greed overwhelms them all.

Cheating to Hide Problems

Let me narrate a sordid story of how corporates cheat by hiding the truth.

Most of you would have heard the name **Ranbaxy Laboratories,** a pharma company which was once the biggest in India. A significant instance of corporate trickery was practised by this company. Once the poster child of Indian businesses Ranbaxy was shamed for practising devious acts. In 2015, Ranbaxy paid a $500 million penalty to US authorities as part of a settlement which included pleading guilty for two charges of violating drug safety and data manipulation.[15]

What did Ranbaxy do? They committed a massive fraud.

Dinesh Thakur, a chemical engineer educated in the USA, was hired as research executive by Ranbaxy way back in 2003. Almost since the day of joining, Thakur suspected something was amiss. He started looking for efficacy of Ranbaxy drugs—do they really work?

The events turned fast. While working for Ranbaxy, Thakur's three-year-old son developed a bad ear infection. He rushed to the local paediatrician. She prescribed the standard treatment—amoxicillin clavulanate, a strong antibiotic. Ranbaxy was making a generic version of this drug. Thakur knew about it and picked up the drug from his office on his way back from the doctor's chamber. He applied it on his little son, but unfortunately the generic version of the drug did not work and the child's fever persisted. Thakur rushed back to the paediatrician. She suggested not to depend on the generic version and recommended changing the drug maker to GSK. Upon using the GSK medicine, the child's fever came down within a day. Thakur's antenna of doubt on Ranbaxy's drug quality got alerted.

Thakur began deliberating: 'Do Ranbaxy drugs work as intended?' He found that the Ranbaxy's drug's 'bioequivalence' (generic drugs having the same effect as the branded drug) data was made up, fabricated or did not exist.

Thakur complained to the US Food and Drug Administration (FDA) in 2005. The agency's investigation found that Ranbaxy had a 'persistent pattern' of submitting 'untrue statements'. On at least 15 new generic drug applications, auditors found more than 1,600 data errors. This meant that their drugs were 'potentially unsafe and illegal to sell'. Ranbaxy was falsifying data to receive approval of its generic drugs and, based on it, selling the drugs all over the world.

Not practising ethics was perhaps in Ranbaxy's DNA. Between June and August 2007, the company again got caught in its own shenanigans. The company was aware that certain batches of Gabapentin (also known as Neurontin), a drug used for treating patients with epilepsy, had tested positive for 'unknown impurities' and had unreliable shelf life. But Ranbaxy still sold the medicine, keeping mum over the adverse findings.

'In essence, Ranbaxy used deceit as a competitive advantage to build and grow the business in the US,' quipped Ranbaxy's former vice president, Vince Fabiano.[16] (Ranbaxy was sold in 2008 to Japanese drug maker Daiichi Sankyo and then taken over in 2014 by Sun Pharmaceutical.)

Business corporations sometimes cheat to hide problems like poor quality. If customers get to know that the quality of the product is not upto the mark, they would reject it. Fearing loss of face or lack of business, corporates sometimes take the easy way out by lying. Compromising ethics is a giant mistake corporates often resort to. Should they get caught, damage inflicted on their goodwill is extremely serious.

To carry on with some more stories of corporate hiding syndrome, the US FDA, in a warning letter in December 2015 to **Cadila Healthcare,** one of India's largest drug makers, cited quality breaches and hiding own findings. Internal 'unofficial' records showed presence of bacteria in the water system, but official company records showed all was well.[17] Lab managers had the ability to delete data from software and, in fact, one file was deleted. Altering findings and masking troubles do entail transgressions on ethical standards harming any firm's brand image terribly.

Another pathetic instance of cheating to hide problems was by **Sri Krishna Pharmaceuticals,** an Indian company making drugs like acetaminophen (paracetamol) pain relievers, exporting to the USA.[18] They were found, by US FDA, destroying original batch records and then backdating replacement pages which were approved by quality and production managers.

In essence, the company failed to assure that manufactured drugs had the stated strength, quality and purity. These are serious misdemeanours, perpetrating long-term harm to Sri Krishna's brand, which is also a contract manufacturer for other drug companies.

Data falsification by businesses is a widespread malady.

The so-called quality-conscious Japanese manufacturers of **Kobe Steel,**[19] **Takata,**[20] **Mitsubishi Motors**[21] and **Toyo Rubber**[22] have all been involved in these unseemly acts. Similarly, **Tata Steel UK** is under investigation by UK's Serious Fraud Office on charges that Tata Steel's staff may have faked certificates on the composition of the products before its sale.[23]

Think of the ill will the countries get exposed to when corporate acts of chicanery take place—needless to mention the battering to the corporation's goodwill. In any case, poor-quality goods immensely harm the users and shatter their trust on products and services.

Short-termism is like one night stand—immediate gratification overshadows the big picture. Unethical acts are often committed for short-term optimization—biting into the corporate edifice which would have been built over the years. Squeezing a lemon too much and too quickly will only bring out its bitterness faster!

Few Last Words

Business crimes have assumed gigantic proportions. Worldwide, it is estimated that companies lose around 5 per cent of their revenue to fraud. The worse is that less than two-thirds of frauds are ever reported.

Judging from the news reports and surveys, corporate crime is all-pervasive.

The *PwC's Global Economic Crime and Fraud Survey 2020*[24] reconfirms this statement. The survey quizzed more than 5,000 respondents across 99 territories about their experience of fraud over the past 24 months. It found that nearly half had suffered at least one fraud—with an average of six per company. The most common types were customer fraud, cybercrime and asset misappropriation. And there was a roughly even split between frauds committed by internal and external perpetrators, at almost 40 per cent each—with the rest being mostly collusion between the two. The total cost of these crimes was an eye-popping $42 billion. That's a huge loss to bear.

What is the message from the survey? For every business, fraud threat is alive and kicking—a risk which cannot be ignored anymore. Unfortunately, many businesses are still looking the other way, hoping that they would escape the rogue's onslaught.

While more actions by governments are taking place to cleanse business practices, increasing episodes of corporates crossing the red line of good governance are being reported.

Business deception is now an intractable problem. The size and intensity is mounting. Increased numbers are jumping into the bandwagon of guile and graft.

The Bible rightly states: 'For the love of money is the root of all evil….' Proving the prophecy, business dishonesties and its concomitant breaches are clearly hurtling across the globe.

CHAPTER THREE

Corruption and Corporations

Let me begin with the story of **Grupo Odebrecht.** If you have not heard of the name, it means you are not from Latin America.[1] This is a Brazilian engineering big daddy behind the construction of the venues for 2016 Olympics and 2014 World Cup.

The company is a master of bribery. Odebrecht admitted to paying bribes in more than half of the Latin American countries, as well as in Angola and Mozambique in Africa. It was the largest-ever corruption case in Latin America's history.

In a bribery which involves inducing high-ranking officials, what could be the motive? Simple. The company sought to get massive government construction contracts. What is already known in one instance is that Odebrecht paid a massive $29 million to Peruvian officials in return for $12.5 billion in contracts.[2] (In June 2015, the group's CEO Marcelo Odebrecht, the grandson of its founder, was arrested. In December 2016, Odebrecht paid $2.6 billion in fines for its past mistakes—one of the largest sum of its kind in the world. The company filed for bankruptcy protection in June 2019.) Corrupt practices killed one of the largest Brazilian conglomerates.

From some recent instances of how multi-nation corruption is devouring portions of the global wealth, let me cite two legendary names in the business world—**Ericsson**[3] and **Airbus**[4]—both were involved in a lot of dishonesty and falsehood.

Most of us might have used the products of Ericsson, especially in the early days of mobile phones and recently the Bluetooth technology which the company invented. Now take a peek into the shady practices of this company in various parts of the world.

The Swedish telecommunications corporation realized their gross wrongdoing and could not dodge the regulators from the reality. It agreed to pay in December 2019 a whopping $1 billion to settle US criminal and civil investigations into foreign corruption involving high-level executives over a long period of time. The quantum of the settlement easily establishes the magnitude of the crimes committed.

The company admitted to a long-running scheme to use agents and consultants to bribe government officials in Djibouti, China, Vietnam, Indonesia and Kuwait.

What Ericsson did spanning over 17 years, between 2000 and 2016, is unthinkable of a company of such a stature. They not only paid cash bribes disguised as sham contracts but also practised in-kind bribes for government officials and provided off-the-books 'slush funds' (funds used for bribery) for making payments to potential customers who would ordinarily not pass its test of 'know-your-customer' (kyc) norms.

Expressing remorse, Börje Ekholm, Ericsson's chief executive, lamented that he was 'upset by these past failings', and the company had 'not always met standards in doing business the right way'. The words unfortunately do not seem to convey the extent of damage the two-decade-long illegitimate acts created!

And this is the problem with many corporations. If corruption is not seen as a grave act of illegitimacy, manipulating grossly the rules of fair business game, the deadly disease is unlikely to be cured through any dose of legal or punitive actions.

The misgovernance story of Airbus, which is similar to Ericsson, also involves multinational bribery. Finding themselves wrong footed, the world's largest plane maker agreed to pay a massive $4 billion in fines to settle a lengthy global corruption investigation. The settlement involved authorities in France, Britain and the USA.

What did Airbus do? It used intermediaries between 2004 and 2016 to bribe public officials in numerous countries to buy its planes. There existed an opaque system of hundreds of third-party Airbus agents who bribed officials in 16 countries, including Japan, Russia, China and Nepal, to buy the company's civilian jets and satellites.

The affair tarnished the company's goodwill and forced it to make sweeping changes in top management.

Just look at the big names which get involved in cockiness and chutzpah. If big daddies are playing with graft and hush money, how can we ever expect good conduct from the smaller bodies?

Corruption is a huge malaise infiltrating many parts of our planet. Between $1.5 and 3 trillion, equivalent to almost 5 per cent of the world's GDP, is usurped by corruption every year.[5]

Dishonesty and enticement are maladies most geographies have been afflicted with. Existence of weak state governance and asymmetrical wealth distribution is the breeding ground for this scum.

This virus is gorging our society in multiple ways.

It is sucking out money from bribe-giving economies, reducing consequently its tax revenue and curtailing its ability to invest in social welfare. It stunts economic growth and propels poverty. From the business angle, it encourages achieving results through the back door, rather than improved operations and better quality of offerings, resulting in enhanced transaction costs and lower efficiency.

When the finance manager of a business faces an overstated income tax demand or needs to hurry up a permission which his boss is looking for but is unable to proceed without oiling the palms of the concerned bureaucrat to make the files move, what does the manager do? This conundrum perhaps will never go away in a hurry—when growth in the developed world has stagnated leading most businessmen to focus on China, India or Brazil. Bribing is the cost of doing business in many countries. Although a colossal impropriety, it may not seem to be a big headache for all!

When it comes to bribery, the expenses are treated as cost of doing business. Business incurs various costs to generate surplus. However, if the bottom line can be enhanced by oiling the palms of the political class or the bureaucracy, then so be it. Corporate corruption involves a cost–benefit trade-off, together with potential risks. Whichever works better—business operations or bribery—is adopted to attain goals.

Government spends mainly on healthcare, education, IT, infrastructure and defence. These sectors are often the hot beds for lobbying and corruption. It is all about identifying where the government money is going, and how the business community can get a meaty chunk of the cake as its booty.

It is alarming that corporate corruption has come to be seen as a routine occurrence in most parts of the globe. It is interpreted after all as spending money to make more money!

World of Corruption

What happens when the most well-known competitive universities take bribes from the savvy parents of the top business echelons? What should be done when a teenage girl who did not play soccer magically becomes a star soccer recruit at Yale, costing her parents $1.2 million?[6] Or what happens when a student with no rowing experience wins a spot on the university crew team after a photograph of another person in a boat was submitted as evidence of her prowess with her parents wiring $200,000 into a special account?

What happens when parents working with famous employers such as the private equity king TPG Capital, bond giant PIMCO and the specialty finance bigwig Hercules Capital pay bribes to get college admission for their kids into top American universities? This was a huge college admission scandal in early 2019. Just think that if prominent business leaders foster such corrupt mindset, then what would be the state of governance at the companies they work in? Ironically, one of the parents at TPG Capital was in charge of setting up the 'responsible investing group' for the celebrated global private investment firm.

Numerous children across the globe dream to get into the best American universities. Unfortunately, the system is mired with corruption. The schools of scandal include names like **Yale, Stanford, Harvard** and other big temples of learning. These very top schools impart teachings on ethics and good governance but go on to short-shrift the values they profess to instil.

The middleman in the school admission scandal was apparently paid $25 million by the parents from 2011 until early 2019 to bribe coaches and university administrators to designate their children as recruited athletes, which effectively ensured their admission. The real victims were the hardworking students who got displaced in the admissions by far-less-qualified students—an unfortunate syndrome and fraud committed in an unequal society.

The questions that will perhaps remain unanswered for long is: How can the educational institutions teach ethics when many circumvent it? Are public ethics of several senior corporate executives as lax as their private scruples?

Most importantly, if such large-scale bribery takes place in the best global institutions, then what is to be expected elsewhere?

The morality of humans seems to be at the suboptimal level. Transparency International's *Corruption Perceptions Index*[7] ranks 180 countries and territories by their perceived levels of public sector corruption. It uses a scale of 0–100, where 0 is highly corrupt and 100 is very clean. The result of findings is worrying. More than two-thirds of the countries ranked scored below 50, with an average score of just 43!

The low Corruption Perceptions Index reveals the continued failure of most countries to significantly control the malady.

It undeniably points to the large-scale disappointing performance of the political leadership around the world. While there are exceptions, the data shows that despite some progress, most countries are failing to make serious inroads against corruption.

Some of the largest companies in the world operate in these countries fully knowing of the ground realities. The low Corruption Perceptions Index shows that there are investors who are willing to allocate capital to maximize their returns and turn a blind eye to the involvement of darker business practices.

Let me cite a few examples to provide you with the flavour of the corrupt world of business.

India's investigative agency CBI arrested **Bhushan Steel**'s vice chairman, Neeraj Singal[8] in 2014 for allegedly offering a bribe of ₹50 lakh ($77,000) to **Syndicate Bank** chairman, Sudhir Kumar Jain, for extending its credit limit.

South Korea's appeals court threw the world's biggest manufacturer of smartphones **Samsung**'s de facto head, Lee Jae-yong, back in jail in early 2021, for bribing former country president, Park Geun-hye, in an alleged attempt to secure control of Samsung; Park was impeached and sentenced to 20 years in prison.[9]

Engineering giant **Rolls-Royce** paid £670 million in penalties when found to have bribed 'middlemen'.[10] The pay-offs involved millions of pounds over 25 years to secure orders in seven countries—Indonesia, Thailand, India, Russia, Nigeria, China and Malaysia. Time and again, corporate big-wigs fall into the honey trap of corruption—either practising or propagating it.

Some more instances of the powerful getting sucked into serious graft include four of the past Peruvian presidents getting imprisoned for corruption, sadly etching a world record. US court convicted a Chinese billionaire, Ng Lap Seng, in July 2017 of bribing United Nations (UN) diplomats to help him gain backing for a conference centre in Macau, highlighting undue influence of cash at the exalted international body.[11]

The world is definitely losing its battle against bribery and corruption. The Kroll *Global Fraud & Risk Report* found that the incidence of bribery and corruption had increased from 15 per cent in 2016 to 21 per cent in 2017. This is an awful development.

In spite of levying hefty fines on businesses for bribery and corruption, clearly the practice is not going away. Governments across the world are continuing to introduce and enforce corporate criminal liability laws. EY's *The Global Fraud Survey* report says that despite over $11 billion fines having been levied globally under the US Foreign Corrupt Practices Act (FCPA) and the UK Bribery Act since 2012, almost 40 per cent of global executives still believe that corruption remains prevalent in business.

In EY's *Asia-Pacific Fraud Survey 2017* report, the worst fears were proven. The 1,700 respondents from 14 countries said that bribery and corruption being practised in their countries had gone up from 32 per cent in 2013 to 60 per cent in 2015 and then a high of 63 per cent in 2017. The survey also found considerable evidence of increasing fraud risk in the APAC region.

Perhaps one of the most arduous battles to win is a fight against graft. There are many recent instances of anti-corruption messiahs being taken to severe task. A UN-backed anti-corruption mission was expelled from Guatemala in January 2019 in what is seen as a bid to shield the country's ruling elite; the Ghanaian journalist who helped expose corruption in African football was murdered in early 2019. These amply prove how difficult it is to fight this demon.

Tailpiece

From bribery to the use of personal contacts, from vote buying to sextortion, corruption takes many forms. Persistent dishonesty is a big roadblock to spreading the benefits of economic growth to the masses. Malfeasance leads businesses to gain unfair advantage over those which believe in ethics and governance.

A corruption-free economy vastly aids in fairer distribution of wealth among the people, maximizing wealth generation from the finite means any economy would have. Till the time people realize the benefits of a corruption-free economy, this horrible business practice is here to stay!

Corrupt Corporate Campaigns

Even a child knows that climate change is the biggest risk facing mankind. But would you believe that top oil firms spend millions lobbying to block climate change policies? A report of March 2019 by InfluenceMap says that the largest five stock-market-listed oil and gas companies spend nearly $200 million every year lobbying to delay, control or block policies to tackle climate change.[12]

Chevron, BP, ExxonMobil, Shell and **Total** are involved in lobbying to push against a climate policy to tackle global warming.[13] Social media is increasingly used by them to push their agenda and to build a wrong public perception to weaken and oppose any meaningful legislation to tackle global warming.

After the Paris climate agreement in 2015, these massive integrated oil and gas majors said that they supported a price on carbon. But the report states that is a mere public stance; in reality, there are blatant gaps between their words and actions. You will be surprised to know that these oil giants show in their ad campaigns as if they support action against climate change but actually mislead people about the extent of their actions.

While publicly endorsing the need to act to reduce the carbon footprint, these companies are in fact increasing investment in large expansions of oil and gas extraction. The report castigates them saying that the companies spend on expansions will increase to $115 billion, with only 3 per cent of the amount being meant for low-carbon projects. Needless to mention that the oil firms rejected the report findings.

Some corporations often incur a lot to corrupt the minds of people by spinning stories which help them. The oil companies are perhaps doing that and ignoring the basic reality facing the earth and its inhabitants.

The world's most famous company, **Google,** also does it. The company lobbies hard. In 2017, Google outdid itself (and all other companies) in its efforts to influence Washington, spending more on lobbying than any other company that year, reports *USA*

Today.[14] Its wish list looks to include removal of restrictions on immigration, excessive taxation, antitrust suits and regulation of its advertising. Google says that it wants to be left alone to innovate and serve its customers.

Tailpiece

Businesses are supposed to practise good governance. But many don't; and that's a reality. Some profess bad behaviour to justify meeting of their own goals; several campaign and lobby to prove their wrong is right. Too many contradictions exist in the world of business.

A lot of business corporations seem to have lost their ethical compass they once had. Or is it that we are interpreting in a different way now that we are paying more attention to it than we did earlier?

Corruption and Indian Business

An American IT services corporation, **Cognizant Technology** wanted to set up three Indian campuses in Chennai and Pune. They needed to obtain planning permits and environmental clearances in a jiffy. So what did they do? They appointed the famous Indian engineering company **Larsen and Toubro (L&T)** to construct the campuses.[15] Then the Nasdaq-listed company decided to require L&T to make the facilitation payment of $3.6 million to the government officials in Maharashtra and Tamil Nadu for the quick permissions. The IT major reimbursed the illicit money paid by L&T, by disguising it as a compensation for cost overruns. The development shows the shady underbelly of cost of doing business in India. (In February 2019, Cognizant agreed to pay $25 million to settle the case with the US authorities.)[16]

It would be disheartening when you learn that a CNN survey in 2019[17] found that one in two Indians paid bribe at least once in the past year. It went on to say that corruption remains 'part and parcel of daily life in India'. The survey was large and gathered

190,000 responses across 20 of India's 28 states. The report went on to say that property registration and land issues were the biggest sectors of corruption, with the police force coming up next. The report found that people also paid bribes to the tax department, transport office, municipal corporations and other local authorities.

Unless you bribe, you cannot succeed has been an oft-repeated saying in India's corporate corridors. Many are heard saying that only if things were transparent, India would have done much better in the world of business.

Transparency International's *Corruption Perceptions Index 2020*[18] gave India a score of 40, lower than the so-called 50 as the acceptable index. The country ranked 86th among 180 nations studied—not an encouraging development at all.

Some more bad news! Seventy per cent of Indian chief experience officers (CXOs) are willing to bend rules to justify achieving financial targets against an average of 42 per cent globally. Shockingly, India's business leaders are more inclined to extend monthly reporting period, backdate a contract and book revenues earlier than they should be. These were from the findings of the *EY Global Fraud Survey 2016*.[19] This distressingly reflects some Indian corporate's mindset at the highest level.

An alarming number, 16 per cent, of chief financial officers (CFOs) and finance team members were observed to be willing to make cash payments to win or retain business—higher than 13 per cent for other than finance team members. This willingness of the finance folks to justify unscrupulous behaviour is deeply concerning, given their direct role to provide accurate financial information and control business assets. This is not a good development, especially when there is an enhanced focus of governments and societies on bribery and corruption.

Exasperated, the respected Indian industry veteran R. C. Bhargava, Chairman, Maruti Suzuki India Ltd, said in May 2020 when the COVID-19 pandemic was sweeping the country, 'The industry and the government have to change the way they interact. There was trust deficit due to corruption, tax evasion and other reasons, and that will have to change.'[20]

Tailpiece

Bribery and corruption continue to play havoc in most parts of the business world, including in India. This is in spite of political leadership's stance and promise to eradicate it. Long years of this dreadful affliction has made it impossible to destroy this malady in hurry.

It may take years before India can see cleanliness practised in its corporate corridors.

Anti-corruption Legislations

Businesses and governments are partners to economic well-being of any country. It is, however, well known that 'facilitation payments' are a part of the game which businesses often pay to hasten the process of permissions and licenses.

To discourage the business–politician–bureaucrat nexus, many governments across the globe have come out with anti-bribery legislations. Such regulations include the implementation of the US FCPA, the UK Bribery Act and the OECD Anti-Bribery Convention.[21]

The FCPA law in the USA bars businesses from giving any-thing of value to foreign government officials to win contracts. Donald Trump once told CNBC in 2012 and before he became the US President: 'It's a horrible law and it should be changed; every other country in the world is doing it and we're not allowed to. It puts us at a huge disadvantage….The world is laughing at us.' But the law remains. It brings in about $3 billion every year to the government by way of fines. The country does not go easy on companies using illicit favours to win business.

An example of the potency of the FCPA came to the fore when it indicted the daughter of the former president of Uzbekistan in March 2019 for receiving almost $1 billion in bribes from three publicly traded companies (Netherlands-based **VimpelCom**, Stockholm-based **Telia** and Russia's largest mobile operator **MTS**) seeking access to the country's telecommunications market. Ms Gulnara Karimova has been accused of soliciting and accepting bribes between 2001 and 2012.[22] Her father, Islam Karimov, ruled the country for 27 years until his death in 2016.

But intent may not always be the king. In the UK, where there is Bribery Act 2010, the lawmakers have been reviewing whether it is too onerous for small businesses. The relaxation agenda provides the possibility of watering down the anti-corruption provisions and providing level playing field with businesses located in geographies that are not overtly discouraging such mala fide practice.

However, it so happens that Britain's record in fighting economic crime over the past decade pales in comparison with the USA. The London-based anti-corruption NGO Corruption Watch examined cases and penalties between January 2008 and December 2018, comparing New York and London, being similarly sized financial centres. It observed that over the period, there were no successful criminal prosecutions of a bank in the UK, and just under £2.5 billion had been imposed in non-criminal fines. By contrast, the US authorities brought nearly 20 successful criminal actions against New York- and London-based banks and extracted over £25 billion in fines. The group blamed the legal framework in Britain, where it is not easy to prosecute companies and regulators impose 'only modest' penalties.

The good news is that several countries such as Brazil, the Netherlands and India have implemented anti-bribery legislations in recent years, allowing cooperation between the countries' investigators to coordinate.

India has moved a lot. The statute on corruption was earlier broadly governed by the Indian Penal Code, 1860. Then came in Prevention of Corruption Act (POCA), 1988, replacing the earlier 1947 POCA legislation, enacted to consolidate all laws relating to offences by public servants. However, the old POCA prosecuted only bribe taking and not bribe giving. The Prevention of

Corruption (Amendment) Act, 2018, added a lot more muscle to punish corrupt practices. This legislation allows the bribe giver, including a commercial organization, providing any undue advantage to a public servant to be prosecuted.

The Foreign Contribution (Regulation) Act, 2010, prohibits in India the acceptance of foreign contributions and foreign hospitality by persons such as judges, government servants, politicians and political parties. In addition, the Comptroller and Auditor General and the Central Vigilance Commission also play an important role in preventing corruption and loss to public exchequer in any contract involving the government including ventures of public–private partnerships.

India has a slew of other measures like the Right to Information Act, 2005; Lokpal and Lokayuktas Act, 2013; and Black Money Act, 2015.

Will things change in India? It took six long years after Lokpal laws were enacted to appoint the anti-corruption ombudsman for looking into corruption complaints at the national level. In March 2019, India's first chairman of the Lokpal got appointed. He will have his hands full, especially as the Transparency International's Corruption Perception score on India is sliding. The impropriety malady is deeply rooted, and it will take a long battle and political will to diminish the affliction.

Tailpiece

To fight the awful human trait of bribery to get work done, many businesses are fighting a grim battle to comply with the anti-bribery and corruption legislations, while several are continuing the toxic practice clandestinely.

Globally, more and more countries are promulgating new and more sophisticated anti-bribery and corruption laws, including aggressive implementations. Enforcement agencies of different countries are increasingly cooperating among themselves to fight the noxious habit.

The good news is that many parts of the world are announcing personal criminal liability for bribery. The new legislations are making individuals responsible, instead of the artificial legal entities, like the companies, paying for the lapses. This should aid in turning the leaf of the governance book for a better, corruption-free business world tomorrow. But will things improve? Unfortunately, the answer will only be known in the distant tomorrow!

Changing Face of Corporate Governance in India

The biggest accounting fraud in India, ironically, was found out neither by the auditors nor by any third party. It was the confession of Ramalinga Raju, the founder of **Satyam Computer Services,** which led to unearthing the scam. Raju, in January 2009, on his own volition, acknowledged the non-existent cash balance of ₹5,000 crore ($0.8 billion), though reported on its audited balance sheet. The scam was perpetrated during 2001–2008, a long enough period to grossly mislead customers and investors.[23]

Two of corporate India's best known names—Infosys and Tata— were rocked by allegations of questionable governance practices and that too by people who ought to know more. It is time to think about India's corporate governance inside the numerous board rooms.

Many Indian business families have for long treated their stock-market-listed companies as their personal properties, compromising corporate governance. Business magnates have relished jet-setting lifestyles at corporate expense and many a time have sucked out value through questionable related-party transactions between the holding and subsidiary companies. Minority shareholders were often unfairly treated. Some companies followed the practice of keeping the registered office at far-off factory locations, making it almost impossible for the minority shareholders to physically attend at a reasonable cost.

The Satyam fraud and poor governance by Indian entrepreneurs from time to time laid bare the inadequacies of the corporate governance framework in India. It led to the enactment of the Companies Act, 2013, laying down more stringent disclosure requirements by the directors, including independent board members and auditors.

For companies listed in the stock exchanges, the financial market regulator SEBI issued 'Listing Obligations and Disclosure Requirements' in September 2015. These stipulations are more stringent, especially for related party transactions, evaluation of board members' performance by the independent directors and conflict of interest with respect to board members and senior management personnel. It has also largely fixed the questionable practice of having registered offices at distant factory sites, requiring listed companies now to provide for electronic voting on stockholder resolutions, allowing minority stakeholders to give their say without making onerous journeys to far-flung locations.

The key question now is: Will all these steps improve Indian corporate governance?

'Good governance' in the Indian business world is many a time used as a euphemism for 'not being crooked'. India has a long way to traverse before an effective governance mechanism comes into existence. Even before the Satyam episode, the corporate regulations were not substantially different. Its implementation however remained questionable.

The fulcrum for good corporate governance is the presence of independent directors in a board, who are supposed to bring in balanced views and ethical behaviour. But unfortunately, most corporations are controlled by the promoters. Board members including the 'independent' ones are often handpicked by the powers that be and belong to the 'old boys club' being close to the promoters, chairperson or owing allegiance to the inner circle.

Forensic auditors are getting busier, unearthing possible misdemeanours. These are silver linings on the otherwise gloomy clouds of corporate governance, implying that some are perhaps trying to clean up their dirty stables.

While the new Companies Act and the Listing Agreement for stock-market-listed companies provide several corporate governance guidelines, just following the regulations does not guarantee good governance. It ultimately boils down to the ethics and principles of doing business.

'What is the best form of corporate governance?' is a debate as old as the corporate world itself. Good governance encompasses following proper accounting practice, qualified and experienced company boards (and not cronies of the owners), a good CEO with an oversight mechanism ideally through a non-executive chairperson, a transparent top-management reward mechanism and, above all, a consistent quality product or service sold at an appropriate price.

Tailpiece

In India, good governance is often regarded as 'not being shady'. In view of this rather lax benchmark, keep your eyes and ears open on the governance practices in the companies you are interested in. Any smoke could entail possible fire; any negative sound could be a potential red flag.

Corporate governance is like a car which has a driver with decent driving habits. A rogue driver can spoil the drive in the best car, but a good driver can make a journey even in a rickety car fairly comfortable.

Is the Corrupt World Getting Better?

Is the world of bribery and corruption getting saner? Are businesses behaving more responsibly? These are debatable questions. Both worlds exist. Some are making honest efforts to improve governance, while there are large sections seeking to extract some extra money on the sly.

Regulations are being brought into fold to prevent hush money use. Anti-bribery legislations are being implemented in many regions, including India, the UK, Europe and the USA. Some countries, like the UK, are creating a public register to try to end anonymous corporates, structured to make owners remain hidden. The USA, EU and India are planning to follow.

If you look around, chances are that you will spot that things are getting worse for corruption and bribery. Big names, great organizations and revered teams are being held accountable for splashing slush funds to get jobs done.

Just to cite a few instances: **Deutsche Bank** was found to have bribed between 2008[24] and 2017 by using a network of business development consultants to funnel kickbacks to woo clients across the world; **Alstom Network UK,** a subsidiary of the French rail and power company, was found bribing to secure a Tunisian tram contract and providing falsified evidence that its consultant was providing services in the country, when in reality it was a front for a company controlled by the brother-in-law of Tunisia's ex-president[25]; the Swiss government commenced investigating the world's biggest commodity trader **Glencore** over its failure to prevent alleged corruption in the Democratic Republic of Congo, where it mines copper and cobalt.[26] The malfeasance instances are abundant.

There is some good news too though. Whistle-blowers are getting more active, for instance, the gigantic 2,600 GB (gigabytes of data storage) Panama Papers leaks uncovering large-scale bribery or French authorities using whistle-blowers to sting the investment bank **UBS** with €4.5 billion penalty for advising wealthy clients in France and helping them evade taxes.[27] The matter of informants spilling the beans is an admirable development. On a lesser scale, initiatives such as ipaidabribe.com is helping to expose dishonesty in daily transactions.

In some parts of the world, examples of extreme harsh actions are being taken to show government's belief towards zero tolerance on corruption. In China, the former chairman of a Chinese state lender, **Huarong Asset Management,** was sentenced to death in early 2021 for bribery, corruption and bigamy. Lai Xiaomin, the ex-chief of the large lending company, was found guilty of receiving $277 million in bribes between 2008 and 2018.[28] This was a rare and sensational instance of Beijing's use of capital punishment for economic crimes. Whether such extreme actions will lead to cleaning the country of corruption or not, only time would say.

Some companies are doing a lot more to show that they are going beyond just ruling out corruption by building sustainable business models, sourcing from green sources and doing their bit to prevent global warming. For instance, Starbucks using Fair Trade Certified organic coffee; Nike producing its line of sustainable products by using environmentally preferred materials like recycled polyester; and Disney working to reduce indirect greenhouse gas emissions through the reduction of electrical consumption. Numerous are the ways being adopted by businesses nowadays to make things more sustainable and in-turn ethical, slowly though.

Anti-bribery and anti-corruption steps are subsets of the larger canvas of good corporate governance and responsible behaviour. It is true that these actions may lead to sacrificing some profits from shady geographies and practices, but that is a small price which businesses should pay for making our world a better place to live and do business in.

There are so much deliberations, regulations and literature on good governance, and yet there are equal number of crummy news of unethical behaviour perpetrated by some. More legislations are coming in, more good behaviour awards being doled out and more people being penalized for ill acts; yet higher are the instances where some are running away with ill-gotten wealth by hood-winking others. Strange is the way the world is behaving with contrary signals on how to do business.

Few Last Words

How bad is the situation?

Malfeasance, exploitation and nepotism are global problems costing both money and lives. While the incidence of pay-offs and shadiness is prevalent in both developing and developed nations, more noise is heard from the developing regions.

A precise measurement of bribery and corruption is not possible. Perpetrators justifiably employ every trick in the book to hide their dirty deeds.

The World Economic Forum estimates that corruption costs the 'world' economy 5 per cent of GDP each year. This would be a whopping $4 trillion. Further, in the forum's December 2019 report, it declared that corruption, bribery, theft, tax evasion and other illicit financial flows cost 'developing' countries annually a massive $1.3 trillion.[29] This would be enough money to lift 1.4 billion people above the poverty threshold (those earning below $1.25 per day).

In another estimate, it is reported that over $130 billion is lost to corruption every year throughout the European Union's member states, according to the EU Commissioner for Home Affairs.

Corruption is all-pervasive. Even in war-torn Afghanistan, of the $8 billion donated in recent years, over $1 billion has been lost to corruption. The needy have thus been sacrificed at the altar of the greedy.

The latest Indian numbers are unavailable. The last data I have seen, EY–FICCI's *Bribery and Corruption* report of 2012[30] provides a huge loss to the economy on account of corruption at ₹36,000 crore ($7 billion) between October 2011 and September 2012. This excludes some large scams such as 2G, Commonwealth Games and mining, which shook the country at that time.

What are the implications of these dirty games? Many disenchanted would have joined religious extremism, some terrorist outfits and several others just don't care for the country's law-enforcement agencies anymore!

It is difficult to conjecture why graft and malfeasance are rising and spreading, though there are pockets where things are getting better. A few plausible explanations could be income inequality, growing role of corporate money in political campaigns, increased political hold on economic decisions and innate incentives for business managers to twist rules to meet their ends.

What should be done? International cooperation, naming and shaming of bribe giver and taker, and political leadership's strong willpower can help defeat this long-entrenched virus in our societies. The good news is that the ever-growing awareness may someday help to minimize this demon of our human nature.

'It is not power that corrupts; it is the fear of losing power that corrupts' goes a popular saying, proving itself to be true over the ages.

CHAPTER FOUR

Technology Tall Tales

Do you recollect hearing about some super-duper technological developments which looked too good to be true? And you would have thanked the announcing organization for developing the breakthrough technology to help the mankind.

You would be surprised to know that many a time such hi-fi stories are maliciously strung by entrepreneurs when they are looking for money from potential investors or financial institutions. The high-tech mumbo jumbo sometimes become the Achilles heels for the financiers. Not to miss out an opportunity to invest in tomorrow's technology, some investors fall into the murky trap of the techy tales.

Let me give you an example. A 32-year-old Stanford University dropout beauty Elizabeth Holmes started **Theranos** in 2013, with tall promises of using revolutionary 'nanotainer' technology in the $75-billion laboratory testing business. She claimed the ability to produce accurate test results from just a few drops of blood deposited on a tiny glass vial, allowing patients to avoid painful needles and lengthy blood drawing sittings. The company was valued at $9 billion in early 2016.[1]

Holmes was a habitual liar. She carefully cultivated an image around her of a Silicon Valley whizz-kid, even wearing almost entirely black turtleneck sweaters which earned her the nickname as 'the next Steve Jobs'. In office parties, she used to tell her employees that the elementary blood-testing system 'is the most important thing humanity has ever built' and that anyone who disagrees may quit.

Then all hell broke loose. Medical studies raised doubts about the trustworthiness of the tests. US health regulators went even further. They warned that inaccurate test results put out by Theranos's California laboratory had placed patients' lives at great risk.

The company had to finally shut down in September 2018 and commence paying its creditors from whatever little money they had. The con artist Holmes and former Theranos's chief operating officer Ramesh Balwani were put on criminal trial for defrauding investors who ploughed hundreds of millions of dollars into Theranos. If convicted, they could face prison sentences which could keep them behind bars for the rest of their lives, unless they take the defence of being insane!

Entrepreneurs are sometimes prone to making aspirational statements about how technology can improve lives. There is often little or no reason, not to overstress or spin falsehoods to raise money if there are no serious negative consequences. This is what the Theranos duo did. But unfortunately, they played with human blood, resulting in a bloody bad game that turned against them.

Similar stories of technology fraud have been etched in the automotive industry.

Volkswagen admitted in 2015 to engineer its diesel vehicles to cheat emission tests. **Mitsubishi, General Motors, Daimler** and many other auto giants have acknowledged involvement in fuel economy or emission cheating.

Bosch, the world's largest auto-component company, has been fined for €90 million ($100 million) over its role in supplying components in the auto emissions deception scandal. Bosch was found to have delivered millions of control devices, which when fitted in cars, emitted more nitrogen oxides than allowed under regulations, helping therefore to fudge emission data.

Volkswagen has become the poster child of technology cheating. The much-hallowed VW letters got tarnished. The company continues to manufacture cars, but its colossal dishonesty may haunt their image forever.

Warren Buffet, one of the world's most successful investors, has often remarked that he does not invest in companies where he has difficulties in understanding the business nitty-gritties. He says that if you are determined to pick stocks, don't buy into a business you do not comprehend. He is fine with investing in Coca-Cola but not in Silicon Valley technology mumbo jumbo.

You need to be careful of companies which market themselves on technological platforms. There are likely to be many hovering around us to take advantage of our unguarded moments and possible lack of technological understanding. Do not make the mistake of jumping into the bandwagon of anything which does not give you the comfort of clarity.

Technology, Customer Convenience and Cheating

Technology has changed our world. We can now draw money without standing in bank queues, receive government permissions by clicking certain computer buttons, make friendships far and wide through numerous social media sites and even get married by exchanging vows over the Internet with the purohit, priest or maulvi stationed remotely. More so, with the onset of the COVID-19 pandemic, technology has taken over from boardrooms to bedrooms, classrooms to clearing houses, recruitment to record-keeping and geography has become history. The world has changed forever, and convenience has become the new normal.

The Internet and technology have started playing an increasing role in our daily lives and businesses, so has its attendant risks. Hackers can steal our money; enemies can generate negative social posts; and fraudsters can steal our personal data for illegitimate use.

Admittedly, technology has helped customers in transacting businesses; marketing wares and connecting with people. And yet technology-related frauds of phishing, man-in-the-middle, OTP scam, user credential duplicity and compromise of customers' mobile phone numbers, continue to play havoc. More of this is discussed in the next chapter.

New challenges are now confronting businesses. Just how well equipped are enterprises at accurately identifying customers online? To what extent are companies able to identify and manage fraud risk?

An Ireland-headquartered customer credit reporting company Experian, in its *2018 Global Fraud and Identity Report*, based on inputs from over 5,500 consumers and 500 businesses across 11 countries including India, China, USA and UK, evaluated what consumers think of security protocols today and gauged how confident businesses are in their ability to accurately identify their customers. The conclusion was that the digital marketplace has arrived.[2]

The Experian report says that almost all consumers own mobile devices (over 90%), followed closely by laptops (over 80%) and tablets (65%). Almost 90 per cent of consumers carry out online activities, reflecting significant and widespread hold of digital commerce for purchase and sale of goods and services, and conduct personal banking. As businesses undergo digital transformations in their front and back office operations, they recognize the importance of trust and the need for technology to enable it. In the same strain, fraud risks have swelled.

When it comes to online transactions, three-fourths of businesses are interested in more advanced security measures and authentication processes which usually have little impact on the customers. At the same time, businesses understand that their customers take comfort in the security measures they already have in place for digital transactions.

The survey revealed that over 80 per cent of businesses felt that the burden of fraud risk mitigation would be reduced if they were certain about the identity of a customer. While there are several obstacles to achieving this goal, it is now more business critical.

As businesses are moving online, a new business channel is a persistent and mounting risk. Managing fraud risk is a delicate balancing act between deceit discovery and the customer's digital experience. If a business can recognize its customers properly, there is a good chance of recognizing fraud. And this is what businesses will have to keep working on to stay ahead.

Tailpiece

Technology has enhanced customer experience, enabling them to enjoy the fruits of development simply by sitting at home or in office. The more customer friendly technology is getting, the more compromises are taking place with customer trust. But when customers pay, hackers sometimes take it away; make believe websites lure customers to pay for products or services which do not exist; customer credit or debit card embezzlement is becoming rather common.

The dark sides of technology are too many. However, it is this technology which can help fight the menace of technological lies.

Artificial Intelligence and Ethics

Imagine a world where Google is able to predict your next migraine attack based on your health history already with it. What a relief! The Google's artificial intelligence (AI) will get rid of your lifelong distressing problem where no precautions had so far worked. So far so good.

Now, what if Google is also employing its tools to find out all those who are suffering from migraine and badgering them with publicity materials on medications which will keep your headache subdued? It will be just one or two companies which could control your life.

Now think some more. Google calculates that you are likely to get a migraine attack, advises you to pop in pills, though in reality that attack was unlikely to take place. It was a miscalculation. Such mishits could however go horribly wrong when you substitute the 'migraine attack' info with 'heart attack'. Hell can break loose if the AI and its sensors take a wrong call with the data it has.

Think of this: Google has over a billion active users every month. With over seven billion searches every day, the company is sitting on a humungous load of user data. With all the data they have, Google hopes that one day it might be able to save your life. As the tech giant moves deeper into healthcare, it plans to create tools to be used by thousands of doctors and improve the accuracy of diagnosis with technologies like computer vision to read X-rays.

But just when Google was trying to access as much health data as it can and build new products, a scam broke out, alleging that Google engineers had access to medical records held by **Ascension,** USA's second-largest healthcare system.[3]

The challenge is already rife. How to persuade patients to trust Google with their sensitive data? The technological development has added to an imponderable risk.

If Google is going to fulfil its ambitious objectives in healthcare, it needs to convince health systems like Ascension to surrender their patient data and ease patients' concerns that the data will be used only for clinical purposes.

With the $9 trillion global healthcare business at its doorsteps, Google, Amazon and Apple are going full blast to unravel this golden goose of health-related business. All of them will be sucking out more and more health-related data, perhaps impinging upon our personal confidentiality. The bigger challenge will be combining data sources and learning from it.

Moving away from 'healthcare' to the world of 'high finance'—algorithmic trading—which has been prevalent in equities and debt trading for over two decades. Algo-trading has speeded up order execution, cut costs and enhanced volumes manifold. But it has come with risks of 'flash crash' and market manipulations. Ethics has not been its hallmark.

Now let us move to AI and machine learning. It is a technology involving learning from past experience and of course churning millions of data. It is supposed to do numerous tasks including trade without human interventions. In the mid of unimaginable possibilities and opportunities, there are substantial risks and hazards—ones that perhaps we are unable to even conjecture at this moment.

Imagine that the machine takes a massive trade position which goes awry, or declares someone a thief, though the person is not guilty, or prescribes wrong medical treatment!

How to crack the black box? The computer would have taken its action based on past human conduct and data, but once executed, it would be impossible to audit it and put around an appropriate risk-mechanism model to avoid future recurrence. Unless the machine tells you what it did, it will be impossible for you to know why it did something!

AI brings too many ifs and buts with it along with many questions around ethics and its ethical use.

Even the partners working with companies like Google fear the fate of their data and proper use of it. What will happen with it? Can ethical use of data for all times to come be assured? Questions galore!

Technology has started playing truant by compromising ethics. Text-generating AI technology can create havoc by sending out credible-looking emails and disinformation messages from any basement anywhere. AI tools have commenced spreading fake news in politics and business. Defaming rival's name and manipulating share prices with fake announcements are rampant. The 2016 US presidential election brought fake news into the public spotlight, when coordinated efforts were made by a Russian 'troll farm', the **Internet Research Agency**, to manipulate the election outcome through the use of AI.[4]

Tailpiece

Technology is not God. History shows that technology always did not work ethically. Electricity after invention has lighted our lives daily, but its misuse has killed many. The Internet is a boon, but misinformation blurted through it has doomed the future of many.

The companies working on AI need to recognize the necessity for a principled and regulated approach for developing and applying it.

Sundar Pichai, CEO of Alphabet and Google, said in early 2020, 'There is no question in my mind that artificial intelligence needs to be regulated. It is too important not to.'[5]

Not doing an ethical job through AI will be destructive to the future of mankind. The question is: Will we?

Digital Detectives

We brought home a small device—Amazon Alexa. It was kept on power-on mode for a few days. Then one day I was shocked out of my wits. When we asked Alexa to play some good songs, lo and behold, it played 'Bengali' songs. How on earth did it know that we are Bengalis? It seems that its AI picked up our home conversations and decided the type of music we could like. Now, could we lie to this little gadget saying that we are not from the eastern part of India?

Many of us lie. You cannot often make out if someone is saying the untruth. However, in this digital age, more and more evidence is created by storing data. Warehoused information will get used to prove points. Think of our Alexa. It knew we spoke the Bengali language at home.

Recently, a woman filed a complaint of being sexually assaulted. When her Fitbit was checked, the mini gadget revealed a different story. She was moving around at the time she claimed to be assaulted. It was a case of someone knowingly filing a false report.

Another instance is when a guy took a sick leave to go holidaying in Goa. His Facebook page gave him away, costing him his job.

Every debate can be ended with a Google search. Mobile messaging has unlimited capacity to store past conversations. Lying is just getting more difficult, with virtually all that we write and say, almost everything, getting stored somewhere somehow.

It is, however, difficult to predict how the networked and digitized world would shape up. Every indication denotes that the Internet of things (IoT) will make us more connected and auditable.

For every search you do online or for your every query, Google is ready with its analysis of your requirement in advance. It already knows your habit, the type of food you like, the destinations you cherish and the love life you aspire for. With every search, it just keeps learning a little more about you. There is hardly any secret and rarely an opportunity to lie.

All of us own smartphones which we carry around. It is so smart that it not only tracks every step of ours but also can let others track us and what we are up to.

Digital detectives have now arrived. Fraud-detecting software comb through terabytes of data, identifying patterns and spotting deceitful activity much faster and more accurately than human minds could ever do.

The Technology Quarterly in *The Economist* magazine had laid down some instances where these digital detectives got active.

For credit card frauds, detective software evaluates many parameters associated with each card transaction, including specific details of the items being purchased (derived from their bar codes), to evaluate the likelihood of foul play in the form of a numerical risk score. Any transaction that score above a certain predefined threshold is then denied or challenged.

For instance, the technology can track that someone is buying a diamond ring soon after buying petrol. This would be tracked as a high-risk transaction. Thieves often test a card's validity with a small purchase before buying something much bigger.

A small purchase at a shop that sells hard liquor is more likely to be fraudulent than a more expensive shopping spree at a wine shop, because expensive liquors are more likely to be better protected by a shopkeeper.

Buying two pairs of trainer shoes increases risk, as this may indicate plans to resell them. Shoes in teenage sizes push up the risk score further, since grown-ups are less likely to buy stolen shoes.

Sales in traditional black markets like London or New York bump up risk scores.

The fraud history of individual shops is also taken into account when technology tracks shopping habits and potential fraud risks.

Technology can track spurts and unnatural transactions when defrauders try their tricks. For example, the software can assign a customized scoring algorithm to each credit card, depending on its normal usage patterns. That algorithm is then updated with every ongoing transaction. If a card, belonging to a Mumbai-based person, is never used for buying an overseas flight ticket, it would normally block an attempt to book a flight to London leaving in a few hours. Plus, cards are often blocked when the volume of transactions for which they are used abruptly spikes.

Swindlers are no less clever. Instances exist where online fraudsters use their own tricks to beat the system. Sometime back, some American cheaters began buying CDs of classical music (when CDs were in vogue) with their purchases of expensive items, apparently in an effort to deceive anti-fraud systems (since classical-type music is generally assumed not to appeal to young, tech-savvy criminals). The detective software caught the trend. Soon thereafter, purchases that combine classical or opera CDs with expensive goods started receiving a higher risk score than purchases of high-cost items alone.

By reading a computer's Internet Protocol address, anti-fraud systems can 'geolocate' online buyers, raise or lower scores depending on where they are. Most systems penalize customers (say by reducing spend limits) in places such as Eastern Europe, China, Thailand and Vietnam. In a more dramatic step, many merchants block all e-commerce transactions from certain countries, say Nigeria, Congo and Liberia.

Digital detectives—technology to diagnose deceits—are trying to make it hard for the bad guys. Ultimately, it is the good ones who pick up the tab for the rotten citizens. Like in the detective novels, the algorithmic investigators arrive at their conclusion by combining small pieces of apparently irrelevant information.

The risk of technology being misused by the unscrupulous has become significant. Even the Vatican City—one of the most sacred places in Christendom—is worried. In early 2020, IBM and Microsoft signed a pledge called the 'Rome Call for AI Ethics', which is an 'ethical resolution' for Vatican to develop AI to protect the planet.[6] Even God is worried about tech fallouts.

Technology is making our lives easier. It is also trying its bit to catch the unscrupulous. But there is another side to technology—it could make us less happy. Whenever I see social media posts, the overbearing thought that comes to my mind is that everyone is so happy, so much better off than me! Almost every post shows success, togetherness and happiness. Isn't this hypocrisy? Perhaps most are lying when disclosing the truth to the world—and this is a growing side effect of some parts of new technology!

Few Last Words

The advent of technology is as much a boon as it is a concomitant bane.

Our lives have become so much easier; the world has gotten closer; entertainment choices wider. And yet our money lying in banks has become riskier; our private lives are more intrusive; modern facilities like electricity grids are more disruptable.

The contradictions of the tech world are manifold. The hi-tech world will need to meet with appropriate technology (automation and applied science) to maximize its benefits and minimize the attendant risks.

The biggest issue is whether technology can interpret the way humans could construe, take decisions and identify frauds. A good AI system learns continuously from data fed in and carries out tasks typically requiring human intelligence. As more data is getting fed, the algorithms are getting better in spotting frauds. AI is learning fast.

Today, we are surrounded by technology. We can hardly move an inch without using tech crutches. Yet most of us do not understand its nuances.

The problem is that the fraudsters are waiting to take advantage of our tech weaknesses to make a killing. Beware, every step of ours can be tracked—be it physical, financial or habitual.

Try not to dabble in businesses, investments or products which sound too technical and your understanding is doubtful.

It may be worth noting that technology is lunging to mitigate the techy menace.

In the world of technology, it is the humans who make the difference. A crooked but intelligent mind can unmake, through some techy moves, all that you have achieved so far. It's a scary tech world, unfortunately!

CHAPTER FIVE

Cybercrimes

We need doctors to cure our ailments; we cannot have quacks treating our maladies. The cyber world is facing a similar chaos—the world is desperately short of cybersecurity professionals. Studies show that we need millions more of cybersecurity experts to prevent fraudsters from emptying our bank accounts. Hackers have now become cyber physicians—and this is intolerable. We need ethical hackers equivalent to family doctors to make the cyber world safe.

I know of young kids encouraged by their parents attending hacker conferences and enjoying breaking into technologies. Eventually, they would perhaps be the security in-charge of my bank's ATM, preventing it from belching out cash for criminals or exposing vulnerabilities of the banking system.

Let me cite an example of a probable hacker mischief target. The Northrop Grumman B-2 Spirit stealth bomber can fly undetected for many thousands of miles to drop a thermonuclear bomb on pretty much any target on the planet, costing $2 billion to develop and deploy. But a terrorist hijacker or state-sponsored hacker can at a negligible cost cause havoc to any geography by either diverting or subverting the software-driven device.

Cybercrime has reached unprecedented levels. It costs the global economy $450 billion each year, making it more profitable than the global trade of marijuana, cocaine and heroin combined.[1]

When COVID-19 pandemic struck the world in early 2020, the cyber world became a wonderful productive target for hackers, with cyberspace remaining unsafe as always. The criminals knew that people were surfing more, looking for COVID-related search terms. They crafted targeted emails (called phishing) where clicking on the accompanying attachment would install malware on the user's system. Even the vaunted world body WHO was used as a smokescreen. Videoconferencing apps impersonated platforms like Microsoft Teams and Google Meet to attract potential victims—all these with ultra vires intent.

Phishing (disguised emails to trick recipients into certain intended actions) and malware attacks (malicious software executing unauthorized attacks on victim's system) were in abundance during the COVID-19 lockdown period. With many working from home, organizations were at a loss to rethink security strategy.

Taking advantage of the pandemic outbreak, consumers got targeted through fake listings, airline refund offers and travel deals, as criminals capitalized on the confusion around coronavirus travel restrictions.

Similarly, during the pandemic period, the number of scam emails purporting to be from medical authorities or hospitals climbed sharply, as criminals sought to exploit sentiments on timely vaccination.

The cyber scamsters are always on the lookout for opportunities to strike. The uncertain days of COVID times were no different.

Cybersecurity is now a daily struggle for businesses. Knowing no borders, cybercrime trends show a huge increase in hacked and breached data in workplace equipment such as computers, mobiles and other devices.

Ransomware is another huge malady. Here, the hackers through a malicious code encrypt data in a system, only willing to share decryption keys in exchange of ransom. Just to give an idea of the scale of operation, in India, there are almost 15 ransomware attacks every hour, and 1 in 3 fall prey to it.

The problem, however, is that most organizations have unprotected data and poor cybersecurity practices, making them vulnerable to data compromise. To protect themselves from malicious acts, companies must have cybersecurity awareness programmes for all employees. They need to make it a culture to prevent and institute security best-practices, as people are the weakest link in cyber defence.

Cyber risk is omnipresent. Yet organizations are struggling to make cybersecurity a proactive part of their business process and culture. The root cause is twofold. One, cybersecurity is treated as a back office job, plugged in as an afterthought without incorporating it as part of the process design. And two, most cyber leaders are either not senior enough or ill equipped to exert strategic influence within the organization. The very nature of cybersecurity's business importance, or the lack thereof, is letting the cybercriminals run amuck.

The world's computer systems, which normally hold all the data considered key intellectual property, are at an astonishingly high risk from cybercriminals and hackers. The governments, political leaderships and businesses have to do something about it. But the challenge is that no one yet knows the exact medication for this grave growing malaise.

Unfortunately, multiple surveys reveal that majority of boards and management teams are not yet trained in how to respond to cyberattacks. Successful cybercriminal assaults can represent an existential threat, enabling stealing and loss of data, or disabling equipment of any business, including critical national infrastructure (e.g., nuclear power plant). Yet most top managements look rather ignorant of the risk—a grave glitch!

Cyberattacks have another negative fallout. It can instil fear and disrupt everyday life, causing increased feelings of anxiety, stress and panic. Body's stress hormones are said to rise when experiencing network attacks on computers and mobile phones, leading to insecurity and enhanced threat perception.

Globally, cyberattacks have crippled businesses, infrastructure and public services—causing extreme disruption and panic, including financial losses—leading to irreversible or prolonged psychological distress.

While infrastructure disruptions may lead to possible loss of lives—for instance, electricity grid getting crippled or air traffic control systems afflicted—we also are living under the constant risk that our bank accounts may lie emptied before we wake up in the morning.

Make no mistake—every system can be hacked—and the more connected we are, the more vulnerable we become.

Cybercrime and Customers

Imagine losing money when you are supposed to receive some from a customer. And that too if the duped person—Harshita Kejriwal—is the daughter of the chief minister of India's capital city, Delhi.[2]

Harshita was trying to sell a second-hand sofa set on a portal. When she posted her interest, a fraudster approached her on the web portal. They finalized the deal. First, in order to gain confidence, the con star purchaser sent some amount to her account. Thereafter, he sent a QR code and asked her to scan it to receive the remaining money. When she scanned the code, ₹20,000 got subtracted from her account. Subsequently, she questioned the man about it. He told her that he, by mistake, sent her a wrong bar code. He then sent another code and asked her to follow the same procedure for receiving the money. When she scanned the code, she lost another ₹14,000. Harshita was duped. Just think that if the daughter of a chief minister can be duped so easily, what happens to minor souls like us!

Connectivity of varied and extensive data sources, networks and machine learning is enabling intimately interlinked service offerings. This is allowing people to pay bills, assimilate tons of information, access health services and do business even across the borders seamlessly. People's comfort has enhanced manifold through the seamless connectivity. Mankind is experiencing amazing benefits from digital services, yet the adversities are too many. The digital journey is continuously exposing us as a target for cyber fraudsters.

The seamless connectivity has enhanced manifold risks for potential attack entry points—such as application programming interfaces and third-party services—raising possible cyberattack threats, including placing personal data at great risk. This development of personal data explosion, access and storage is in turn magnifying the consequences of an attack.

Digital service sellers will need to evaluate the cost–benefit of consumer service vis-à-vis cybersecurity risk. Based on the evaluation, businesses will need to continuously upgrade cyber resilience for providing seamless digital service to customers.

An Accenture study points out some interesting experiences of retailers facing security breach.[3] Faced with the problem of cyber fraud, 12 per cent loyal customers of the affected retailers said that they had stopped shopping at those websites, and 36 per cent of the customers said that they would shop there less frequently.

Digital transformations brought new means to do business, but it has also enhanced risks. Customers need to trust companies with their data; companies need to honour the trust being reposed.

Online crime is growing rapidly. Various research reports are reconfirming that most businesses are facing enhanced fraud loss and cheating concerns. Fraud reports are stating that deceptions are moving between channels, such as web, call centres and mobile phones. New schemes, such as synthetic fraud, where criminals combine real and fake information to create entirely new identities, often labelled as identity theft, are evolving.

Then comes the bad news. The fraud surveys are showing that business executives are not very confident about their ability to protect their organization and their customers from fraud, especially the online variety. Traditional solutions relied on behavioural patterns that helped businesses detect fraud. New solutions mean new forms of online behaviour, and the old benchmarks used in detecting anomalous activities that might signal deceptions are no longer reliable. Consequently, as businesses innovate the digital experience, they feel increasingly vulnerable and not very confident in their ability to spot frauds.

Business managers are evaluating the cost and benefit while considering more advanced authentication methods. The ability to more accurately satisfy the customer needs vis-à-vis detecting the fraud will drive revenue. However, businesses are concerned that costs associated with more modern fraud detection may not offset gains from the incremental business.

Thus, a conscious choice mostly is to prioritize the customer experience. This sometimes explains why businesses stick with existing, and sometimes insufficient, solutions.

It is, therefore, critical that businesses figure out ways and means to identify fraud without compromising on customer experiences. It is easier said than done.

Time has come where this dichotomy of ease of doing business versus ability to identify fraudsters will need to be cracked. Whoever does it better will win this cat-and-mouse game with the cyber-criminals who are ever looking for means to make a fast buck.

There is one more aspect in the digital world, where clients are concerned. Customer trust must be considered a key feature for every offering, whether it is digital or physical product, especially containing some software. Loss of trust can lead users to abandon a product or company altogether. Hence, security and privacy concerns can no longer be taken for granted while designing a product strategy and architecture.

The game changer would be the means to identify your customer. This should enable you to detect frauds better and faster. Recognizing customers with multi layered easy-to-use systems, without compromising customer experience, will be the future of fraud prevention in the digital world—providing succour to the digital customers.

Tailpiece

Companies and consumers collectively face risks that are real and unavoidable in the digital world. Software systems are inherently vulnerable; the insights from data misuse are unpredictable.

We cannot push the risks arising from digital technologies under the carpet. Cybercriminals will continue to be on their prowl; data breaches and misuse will keep occurring. In essence, failures in the world of cybersecurity and privacy are inescapable at least in the short and medium terms.

To pretend that consumers are safe from tech onslaught is unreal. Unfortunately, the consumers in the new business world will need to stomach the tech risks, for now.

Impersonation Hoax

One day, my colleague in a remote office received an email purportedly from our common boss. At a quick glance, the email did look genuine. In fact, when looked closely later, one letter was found missing from his original email ID. Alternatively, the email could also have been from his hacked account, though in this case it was not so. The email stated that my colleague had been promoted and chosen for a very important global assignment, demanding confidentiality and promptness. The email requested my colleague to immediately transfer $5,000 to a Hong Kong account to make a payment for a permit. My colleague, believing the story and without much thought, transferred the fund forthwith.

What would have happened next is not very difficult to imagine. The money would have got quickly transferred to other multiple accounts, disappearing into a maze of money networks that often extend to China, Hong Kong and elsewhere. The rest is history, with very little audit trail remaining to catch the culprits.

Fraudsters have found a wonderful way to monetize trust. Impersonation and other hacking-related frauds also hinder recovery. Historical evidence shows that the general rate of recovery, even if companies act quickly to freeze funds, is less than 50 per cent.

The process of recovering money is lengthy and time-consuming. First, the lawyers will need to identify all the accounts receiving the money as it would have been split up and transferred and then apply for freezing of each account—if there is any money left in it. Lawyers would then need to get summary judgements to get the money returned, a process that can take years, if contested. The winners obviously are the con artists, as there is more probability for them to retain the hoaxed money.

This type of fraud is getting common for companies doing businesses around the globe. In the recent times, **Ferrari NV** (sports car maker) and **Arrow Electronics Inc.** (American electronics-company) have lost millions of dollars after employees were tricked into wiring funds to foreign accounts.[4] With global connections, remitting money across geographies especially Hong Kong gets easier, where the funds just disappear.

Identity theft is similar to the impersonation trick. This tactic involves stealing of someone's identity and using it to make transactions. 'Identity' can include an email address, phone number, IP address and, of course, credit card details. Cybercriminals can use these details to order items online under a fabricated name and then pay using the other person's credit card or account.

More dangerous is 'business identity' theft, where the business itself is impersonated. It involves misuse of key business credentials like its unique identification number, manipulation or falsification of business filings—all intended to derive illicit gain to the detriment of the victimized business. Just imagine that by appearing legitimate and opening a credit card in a company's name, cybercriminals can derive a bounty.

Tailpiece

The fertile minds of fraudsters are ever active to figure out new methods of making a fast buck. The stories of impersonation are plenty.

The way it works is not terribly difficult to understand. A popular trick is where the fraudster works his way through the organizational hierarchy until he is able to appear as the office chief, where the CEO's office mail ID gets stolen. The spoofed emails are sent to some carefully chosen vulnerable employees. The target receives the email and acts without reflection or questioning the source. The fallout could be quite damaging, including sharing of IP, designs, specifications and, of course, money.

Identity thieves are parasites of our modern society.

Cybercrime 'Push'

A Mumbai-based middle-aged television actor had some loans outstanding. He wanted to repay part of the loan. He rang the financing company several times on the phone number provided on its website, but got no response. Next day, he got a call from a person who identified himself as Rajgopal and claimed to be an employee of the lending company. He asked the actor if he wanted a loan.

On being told that he wanted to repay part of his outstanding, Rajgopal asked for the loan account ID. Within minutes, the actor received on his mobile details of the loan taken. The caller (Rajgopal) informed that the actor's outstanding was ₹2 lakh, which was in fact correct. Rajgopal then shared account number of a bank's branch besides other details for the repayment. The actor remitted ₹90,000 through his digital wallet.

The actor received no acknowledgement. Rajgopal did not answer his calls. The actor got suspicious. He could then somehow contact the finance company directly and asked if they had an employee named Rajgopal. There was no such employee in the financing company. The actor got 'pushed' to pay and the fraudster made merry.

The cyber fraudsters have figured out numerous ways to dupe the gullible.

'Push' is one such way, where you receive a call or email just out of the blue. This will be received either from a seemingly credible 'official' who claims to be from your bank or be your lawyer or from a business house you would have dealt with in the past.

The so-called 'official' would announce that your bank details have been compromised. He would then request you to immediately transfer your funds into a fresh account for safekeeping.

Alternatively, the 'official' would know about a big transaction you are about to carry out. Say, you may be buying a flat or a car.

Unfortunately, the innocuous 'official' would say that the account details that you were about to transfer the money to have changed. The fraudster may possibly say 'Would you please transfer the money to a new account? Can you please do it quickly?'

In the UK, loads of people are falling victim to bank transfer scams and the average loss is over £5,000 (₹50,000). In 2018, over 43,000 people reported an authorized push payment scam.[5] Customers instructed their banks to send an amazingly high sum of £236 million (₹2,400 crore) into rogue accounts.

This is modern-day bank robbery. Once you transfer money into the fraudster's account, you are unlikely to see the money again. This involves real-time payments, authorized in good faith. How will your bank know that you are transferring your lifetime savings to a rogue?

Tailpiece

While digital banking makes it easy for us to authorize large transactions, it is a different story when you realize that you have been pushed to be conned. Trying to recover the money pushed out which you have authorized yourself becomes an impossibility.

Capricious Crypto

A wallet containing C$180 million ($137 million) in crypto cash deposited by the customers of a coin exchange was suddenly found all empty! This horrible news was discovered after the crypto exchange QuadrigaCX's founder Gerald Cotten died in December 2018.[6] Cotten, who expired while travelling in India, had the sole responsibility for handling the funds and coins passing through the crypto site.

The master key to open the wallets was in Cotten's laptop, but he perished without revealing the password to access the encrypted data. Most of the digital cash that customers deposited with the exchange was supposed to be kept in 'cold wallet' to prevent it being hacked or stolen. The cash represented the virtual currency holdings of 115,000 customers.

Incidentally, Cotten's death forced the winding up of QuadrigaCX. The customers lost their crypto cash, as it got locked forever in Cotten's computer. While this example is not about any fraud, it brings to light that cryptocurrency is fraught with uncertainties. It is capricious and risky.

One learning is evident. The unregulated nature of cryptocurrency exchanges could expose customers to unpredictability, including losing their holding as it happened in Quadriga's case.

Bitcoin, a cryptocurrency, has been mired in with controversy ever since its launch in 2009. There are numerous rags-to-riches stories in Bitcoin, but equally plentiful have there been fraudsters earning millions from unwary buyers and investors.

'Blockchain' is the technology behind Bitcoin and other cryptocurrencies. The biggest challenge with the crypto industry across the globe is its lax regulation. Lucrative schemes keep getting advertised by the unscrupulous, and many fall into the booby trap of this unregulated currency.

Feigning Bitcoin-related stories, websites and outlets keep wreaking havoc on customer confidence. In 2020 alone, cybercriminals siphoned off about $24 billion (₹15,000 crore) from cryptocurrency users and exchanges, according to *Reuters*.[7]

The worst is that about 95 per cent of Bitcoin spot trading is faked by unregulated exchanges, reported an asset manager, Bitwise.[8] The analysis showed horrendous fraud numbers. Of all the volume reported in 70 out of the 80 exchanges, a substantial volume was 'wash trading'. It meant simultaneous selling and buying of the same stock—Bitcoin in this case—to create a sense of market activity. It means faking and lying. The result is that exchanges reported an aggregated $6 billion (₹45,000 crore) in average daily Bitcoin volume, though in reality the legitimate volume would have been only $270 million (₹2,000 crore), meaning that only 5 per cent was the true value of exchange transactions.

The success of Bitcoin led to mushrooming of several new cryptocurrencies across the globe. It is indeed difficult to keep an eye on the authenticity and performance of each one. These are known as 'altcoins', which incidentally can be cheaper. If Bitcoin is full of fraud bits, just think what could happen with altcoins—this alternate crypto may be even more dangerous.

New cryptocurrencies continue to emerge—there are over 2,000 of them. The massive valuation in 2017, its precipitous fall in 2018 and its rise from the ashes have led some—including tech scamsters—taking advantage of the volatility.

Tailpiece

The Financial Conduct Authority, a UK financial regulatory body, in its March 2019 report suggests that consumers purchasing crypto assets are often looking for ways to 'get rich quick'.[9] And the worse is that many consumers do not fully understand what they are purchasing.

Lack of transparency and regulation does make crypto a heaven for manipulators, speculators and fraudsters. 'Caveat emptor'—'let the buyer beware'—aptly applies to this new alternate currency.

Data Breach

Data equals information, equals understanding, equals supremacy.

The digital age and its success have given a new meaning to data—it has now become the primary form of currency.

Much of our daily lives is being captured, monitored and dependent upon the digital world. Thousands of private surveillance cameras are watching us as we move around; apps downloaded on our cell phones are monitoring our calorie burns; google maps are tracking our whereabouts; our text messages are getting captured; and our posts in social media are being followed.

Loads of data are getting into the hands of certain private enterprises who derive a wide latitude to use these for targeted marketing or selling it at a substantial price for onward research or marketing. Thoughts about its misuse are alarming.

This is where the problem of ethics begins. What if the data is misused, misinterpreted or mis-sold?

Personal data is a prime asset for the digital world, which creates a business dilemma. Companies are required to gather more data faster to maintain their competitive advantage and serve the customers better. On the other side, the data could be exploited, hacked, stolen, used or sold for profit.

Data breaches have now become fairly common, with data from millions of accounts being compromised.

The data could be breached in the business world essentially in two ways—either by the corporates holding the data for their own gain or it can be hacked into by criminals to access the information for onward sale or use.

Let's look at some instances among the 'social media' kingpins of using compromised data to augur its own cause.

In October 2019, **Twitter** admitted that it had 'inadvertently' used personal information such as phone numbers and email addresses provided by users for what they believed to be 'safety and security practices'.[10] Twitter however used the data to improve target advertising between 2013 and 2019, meaning that the 'inadvertence' may not have been an 'oversight' after all!

During 2020, **Google** had been accused of 'sharing' users' personal data between its services without acquiring specific consent to do so.[11] The Internet-related service company is apparently taking users' consent for certain uses of their personal data, say location tracking, but using it for a range of 'other services' that are completely invisible to the customers.

Let us look at some instances where the data from the corporate world have been compromised.

The **Marriott International** hotel group allegedly failed to protect the personal data of over 300 million guests in one of the largest data breaches in corporate history.[12] The hackers had apparently gained unauthorized access to guest records worldwide in a security breach of the guest reservation database between July 2014 and September 2018. The data included guests' names, home and email addresses, telephone numbers, as well as passport and credit card details. The hotel group was fined £18 million by the UK data security watchdog in October 2019. The saga did not end here. There was a further data breach in early 2020 of 5 million guests.

If you are a frequent **Domino's** customer in India, you may find your personal data in the dark web. The popular pizza seller suffered a huge data leak sometime in mid-2021.[13] Data of 18 crore orders got breached. Hackers have leaked information pertaining to phone numbers, email addresses, and payment and credit card details of the users.

As we go through our increased online lives, personal data is getting more and more critical, though as customers we do not often realize the risks we are exposed to when our data is compromised by no fault of ours.

Tailpiece

Information is power and data access provides that supremacy. Data breach leads to ethical lapse. As data is the new currency of the digital world, more and more instances of data's ethical breach are likely to come out in the open.

Keeping data secured and being conscious about the growing data-related risks may help in mitigating some of the data perils.

Digital Frauds Abound

Senior vice president of an international bank based in Mumbai, Sanjay Kapoor,[14] was walking along the Palm Beach Road one balmy morning, when he got a message on his mobile that ₹10,000 ($130) were deducted from his debit card, supposedly used in Worli, another part of the city which is several miles away. Before he could realize what was happening and institute a no-payment advice, 14 more transactions took place within a couple of minutes, depleting his balance by ₹1.5 lakh ($2,000). This is not an uncommon incident, as many of us have been a victim ourselves or have heard of a near and dear one being conned.

This was a case of debit or credit card being cloned and misused by skimming your data while you go to your ATM to withdraw cash. This is like an identity theft for debit or credit cards.

Scammers use hidden electronic devices to steal the personal information stored on your card and record your PIN number to access your hard-earned cash. Skimming involves two steps. The first part is the skimmer itself, a card reader placed over the ATM's real card slot. When you slide your card into the ATM, you are unintentionally sliding it through the counterfeit reader, which scans and stores all the information on the magnetic strip.

The second step is to gain full access to your PIN number, without breaking a sweat. That's where cameras come in, hidden on or near the ATMs—tiny spy cameras to get a clear view of your PIN number punching. Just remember that the mini cameras could be hidden on nearby brochure racks. Having a fake key board is another trick which is employed sometime.

Sanjay Kapoor's card fraud would have occurred in one such ATM where a skimming device may have been fitted.

With increasing levels of online business and enhanced dependency on IT, every organization and each one of us individually must harness the safety belts to deal with growing sophisticated ways of cyber frauds.

The active developments in IoT, proliferation of the web and more sophisticated everyday use of electronic items such as mobile phones, have added a new dimension to the nature of corporate fraud. With over 90 per cent of all business records now being created and stored electronically in most parts of the world, we need to develop new technologies to retort to the ever-growing and evolving nature of digital threats.

Let us now look at some of the more common digital frauds which we may get affected with:

- *E-ad menace:* You must have seen many advertisements announcing quick-get-rich schemes or free air tickets, without realizing many of them are fakes—bogus digital ads. As an example, in mid-2019, Indigo Airlines cautioned job hunters of fraudulent job offers in the airline's name.[15] On the canvas of digital frauds, e-advertisement scams definitely form a significant part.

'Ad frauds' in the digital world have become a huge business. With the global digital advertisement market size at around $240 billion, the component of cyber ad fraud is almost one-tenth at $19 billion, with India's share in 2018 at $1.6 billion. India is thus involved in 1 in 10 of all reported cyber ad deceits.

Thieves rob banks; the cybercriminals have found new banks in digital advertising to pilfer from.

Barring bogus ads, there are many other menaces to bother about. There are agencies who fake the 'engagement and retention' of customers on a site. On nascent sites like entertainment and financing, clients are tricked into believing that they have acquired more customers than actual. To make money, the scamsters make it look as if there are more people looking at the ads than there really are. 'Click farms' exist where large number of human workers, on payment of compensation, click on ads on behalf of third parties, creating illegitimate clicks. Many use 'sourced traffic' where sites show more visitors through third parties, generating artificial inorganic traffic. 'Ad injection' is another malady, where inappropriate ads are placed without the knowledge of the website or the owner.

- *Man in the middle:* Communication between companies and their customers is vital. However, a simple email conversation can become the target of a 'person in the middle attack'. This type of fraud aims to get hold of sensitive data by intercepting digital exchanges like emails and log-in credentials. This can be done using malware, eaves-dropping techniques, unsecured public Wi-Fi networks or even badly protected company networks.

  Crucial or classified details obtained from these conversation interceptions can then be used to facilitate business identity theft or account theft.

- *Chargeback con:* It is a friendly fraud. In this instance, the swindlers order a product or service using a credit or debit card and then instantly claim that card has been stolen. The company reimburses thinking that the person is an innocent victim of a card theft. However, the cybercriminal keeps the product or service and the business loses twice. There could be an honest mistake too—but sometimes it is difficult to distinguish between a fraudulent transaction and a genuine error.

The above list is just a peek into the cyber vulnerability all of us are up against. The diversity of digital deception could be boundless.

Tailpiece

Since the beginning of e-commerce in the 1990s, businesses have been facing digital fraud. Its threat and adverse implications are increasing with each passing year. The cyber crooks are ever evolving new ways to con businesses. With every step businesses take, the fraudsters take two steps. This Tom and Jerry game is getting tougher by the day.

Tech is the weapon to kill the technological menace; the antidote for cyber virus is the cyber tech itself.

Strangulating Steps to Sabotage Cybercriminals

British Airways, which once boasted to be 'the world's favourite airlines', invited its customers' ire, when personal data of 400,000 people got stolen by hackers in the summer of 2018 including their credit card details.[16] The airlines was imposed a heavy fine of £20 million ($25 million) for the data breach. But what really peeved the customers was the reaction of the management which refused to take unconditional responsibility for the problem. This unacceptable attitude impacted the reputation of British Airways's brand.

Every company management is expected to ensure cybersecurity. Unfortunately, some top managements do not take this responsibility seriously, and many boards are underprepared for this role. Unfortunately, small and medium-sized companies are most at risk as they often fail to anticipate and instil appropriate cybersecurity.

In the modern world, the ability of companies to manage cyber risk has far-reaching implications for corporate goodwill, stock prices and professional reputations of the board members and managers themselves.

A PwC UK report on *Digital Fraud*[17] outlines some precautions that companies should consider:

- *Proactive health check:* Businesses must attempt to carry out proactive rather than reactive digital health checks. The top management must be aware of the risks and responsibilities. A heightened awareness of both personal and collective liabilities of the management helps a lot.
- *Make fraud security inclusive:* Companies should work to make fraud security a 'business as usual' process by training staff and implementing a clear security policy. Businesses should also aim to entrench all-round, good digital security-awareness culture.
- *Cost–benefit analysis be the driver:* Companies should use risk assessment strategies to ensure that their investment is targeted towards those security controls that offer the greatest benefit.
- *Adopt the best practice:* Enterprises have several choices for controlling and preventing digital frauds. Some have outlived their utility. Hence, organizations should aim to implement internationally recognized standards of best practice.
- *Put in a back-up plan:* Companies should put in place contingency or disaster recovery plans to ensure that should an untoward incident occur, it is in a position to respond swiftly and efficiently to minimize any disruption to the business.
- *Traditional and sophisticated controls to be used:* Enterprises should ensure that their security defences are integrated and adequately up to date to respond to the ever-changing and increasingly sophisticated technologies being utilized in cybercrime. These technologies might include identifying spyware, instant messaging and voice-over Internet protocol. However, companies should also bear in mind that hi-tech solutions should sit alongside

traditional techniques and processes for tackling the crime.

- *Global digital identity tool:* This is another set of methods used by the banking community to detect frauds, as stated by UK Finance's *Fraud the Facts 2019* report. It says that the special software analyses billions of real-time transactions across geographies, coupled with additional data on device, behavioural and threat intelligence inputs. By combining these with historical data, banks are able to build a picture of identifying potentially dishonest activity.

  Tools like behavioural biometrics are being used by banks to identify potential frauds. Some banks have adopted software which monitor the way a consumer could type and swipe on their devices. It also identifies the environmental noise from where the customer is calling. Any unusual background sounds are picked up for analysis. Changes in behaviours are picked up by the software for flagging possible suspicious activity and could prompt a call from the bank.

- *Cyber insurance policy:* Cybercrime risks are insurable. Such policies have become more comprehensive and cover more than they did earlier. Negotiate one before the ghost strikes, and not in the mid of the episode. It should normally cover most costs associated with a data breach like counsels to guide you, forensic firm to unravel mischiefs and even a ransom that the company could pay to get its data unencrypted.

'Take Five' is a campaign being run by a financial trade association UK Finance and the UK government to popularize simple steps to avoid cyber frauds. Drawing inspiration from it, I give below my 'adopt sixer' steps, which are all common sense. Regrettably, it is uncommon to have common sense which lends many of us to be scammed.

1. Beware that a genuine bank or organization will never contact you out of the blue to ask for your PIN, full password or to move money to another account.
2. Use a strong password which is not easy to guess and do not

use the same password for all accounts. Use a hard-to-guess but easy-to-remember password. You may use password manager to remember passwords.

3. Never transfer money to any unknown account.
4. Do not be tricked into giving a trickster access to your personal or financial details.
5. Always question uninvited approaches and contact the company or vendor directly.
6. Never answer or act upon any email or phone calls, announcing too-good-to-be-true offers and then give your personal information, howsoever sketchy it could be to start with.

The best way perhaps for organizations to reduce the risk from cybercriminals and prevent external hacking is to understand a hacker's mindset. Corporates need to think like a hacker to comprehend their actions, anticipate and confront them. Hackers are usually skilled, intelligent and risk takers, waiting to exploit a vulnerability in the system to break in. They are mostly great actors and communicators, capable of manipulating people's psychology to part with crucial data and perform desired actions. You need a hacker's mentality to hack the hacker's habits!

Tailpiece

Cybercriminals are notorious for their ability to strike when the iron is hot—when system usage enhances as it happened during the pandemic period of 2020 and 2021.

For businesses, it is a race to stay ahead of the cyber scamsters. Staying ahead of the cybercriminal games, keeping the workforce trained and taking an insurance policy will help reduce the risk for your company.

Cyberstalking, Voyeurism

Six former eBay executives in the USA were caught cyberstalking after harassing a couple who wrote critical blogs about the company and annoyed its management.[18] You will be surprised to know that the executives sent a 'box of live cockroaches, a funeral wreath and a bloody pig mask' to the co-owners of the EcommerceBytes news site publishing the blogs—a horrible behaviour to say the least.

'Cyberstalking' is getting common, with over one-third of adults experiencing some sort of harassment online, with the majority of targets being women.

The meaning of cyberstalking involves a person, abuser or stalker embarrassing another person by misusing the Internet or electronic media. A stalker may contact a person by an email, social media, messaging apps or other online media. To intimidate a person, a stalker may post messages, pictures or information online about the person, or just track someone's location or online activities, or send parcels or letters containing uncomfortable content.

'Voyeurism' is another scum of the new tech age. Over half of women seem to have encountered this, including in their work lives. With cameras getting smaller, it's a field day for voyeurs to spy on women at private places.

Recently, stories reported in the press of Airbnb guests finding cameras hidden in lightbulbs and routers, with a family finding in Ireland a hidden camera inside a smoke alarm, apparently livestreaming everything it recorded. [19]

The tales of voyeurism will scare anyone who stays in an Airbnb—and there are many of us who do or used to do before the pandemic! The company lists more than 6 million rooms, flats and houses to rent in over 80,000 cities. These are often cheaper and more conveniently located. The practice of voyeurism is an awful fraud on customers' trust committed through a company of such size and reach.

One instance of voyeurism that caught a lot of eyeballs was in India when Ms Smriti Irani, the Indian Central government minister, went shopping in Goa in April 2015. While visiting a leading ethnic apparel outlet—Fabindia—she raised an alarm when she spotted a CCTV camera pointing towards the change room. Several store staffers perhaps were behind the episode.[20]

A voyeur usually means a person who derives sexual gratification from the covert observation of others as they undress or engage in sexual activities.

Things get worse when the private pictures or videos get uploaded, unknown to the victim, in the social media, to take revenge, extract compensation or just for the sheer pleasure to disrepute someone.

Cyberstalking and voyeurism are both punishable offences. The Indian Penal Code and the Information Technology Act, 2008, addresses the criminal acts in India. World across, similar provisions exist, as no civilized society tolerates such vices.

Cyberstalking is the concealed terror of the Internet age, with voyeurism being the outcome of miniaturization in high-tech gadgets especially cameras.

Few Last Words

Can you believe that in Finland, a hacker robbed tens of thousands of patient records from a psychotherapy centre and started black-mailing victims to keep the data private?

The cyberattacks, which started in 2018, came to light in end 2020. Apparently, the crooks accessed records of 40,000 patients with mental illness or emotional difficulties from a centre run by Vastaamo, a private company running psychotherapy clinics across Finland.[21]

The hackers approached patients directly with demands for €200 in Bitcoin—increasing to €500 after 24 hours—in exchange for their records being deleted. About 300 notes from therapist sessions were leaked on to the dark web.

This is unprecedented human behaviour—goons targeting the most vulnerable sections of any society and trying to make money by disclosing the innermost secrets of some of us.

This incident is a wake-up call on cybercrime and its collateral cybersecurity.

Cybercrime incidence is galloping. According to *Cybercrime Magazine* November 2020, cybercrime inflicted a global loss of $3 trillion in 2015, with this number doubling to $6 trillion in

2021, and a massive possible loss of $10.5 trillion annually by 2025.[22] This would entail the largest transfer of economic wealth ever. Cybercrime costs include devastation of data, productivity loss, intellectual property theft, personal and financial data heist, embezzlement, fraud, post-attack disruption to business, forensic audit, restoration of hacked data and reclamation of reputational ravage.

These horrible developments and the possible catastrophic losses lead to the key question: Why are we not able to fight the murky menace with the formidable and daunting military capabilities the world possesses? Most countries would easily deter and scare off any would-be attackers. But why does the same logic not work in the cyber realm?

There are four broad reasons for our incapability so far to fight the peril. First, fighting cybercrime is significantly more daunting than the conventional ones with most parts of the world already widely wired. Second, while cyberattacks are relatively cheap, cyber defence is costly and strenuous. Third, each country's laws to deal with cybercriminals are different. Finally, and more importantly, it is very difficult to attribute a cybercrime. Whom do we fight? Hackers and their hacks are hidden behind layers of veils without any clear address.

Things may, however, be getting better. The currently used poorly written and outdated codes could be replaced by more secure alternatives. Even passwords could be replaced by safer facial recognition software. Use of two layers of authentication, that is, the usual password and a one-time additional password from say your mobile could prove useful. Deep fakes could be identified by constant verification of eye and face movements to ensure that the person behind the keyboard is not faking.

It is hoped that policymakers and designers work to ensure that the digital world remains safe and our privacies intact. We deserve a safer world from the goons of the cyberspace.

CHAPTER SIX

Banking Deceits

We keep our hard-earned savings in banks. What if I now tell you that your money after all may not be fully safe! Just look at some key findings in India. Bank frauds worth more than ₹1,40,000 crore ($19 billion) were reported in the year ended March 2021.[1] This was nearly double of ₹71,000 crore ($10 billion) in the previous financial year, and up 6 times as compared with ₹19,000 crore ($3 billion) in 2015–2016 full year. If this trend is to be believed, we need to really worry, as our money lying with the banks is becoming unsafe with the each passing day!

Let me give you another bad news. In India, many from the lower strata keep their life-time savings in the cooperative banking sector. And that has now become a virtual looting mechanism by their ownership, or so it seems. The central bank has been issuing notices of closure with persistent regularity to various cooperative banks. I understand that over 150 cooperative banks have been shut down in the state of Maharashtra alone in the last three decades.[2]

With monotonous consistency, small cooperative banks in India fail without any prior notice—sinking the savings of the common man—with fraud and mismanagement being the main cause.

One instance of corporate malfeasance and banking woes which left a deep impact on the Indian banking system involves the once high-flying businessman Vijay Mallya—the 'king of good times' and ex-CEO of Kingfisher Airlines. The fugitive is disliked in India, as his faltering company failed to pay banks, creditors, pilots and cabin crews, despite his own lavish lifestyle. He is under pressure from India's public sector banks to repay ₹9,000 crore ($1.3 billion)[3] in debts following the airline's demise.

Vijay Mallya's fraud on the banks opened new chapters for tougher Indian banking norms, like prohibition on ever-greening (lending new money to pay back old money) of irrecoverable loans and proper disclosure by banks of bad loans.

A serious issue which the Indian banking sector is grappling with is non-performing assets (NPAs) or bank loans in default. The quantum of bad loans have already touched the dizzying number of ₹10 lakh crore ($130 billion) in 2020–2021 (total banking advance in India is around ₹100 lakh crore [$1.3 trillion]).[4] The horrifying irrecoverable loan syndrome data has been shared by none other than the governor of India's central bank himself. It means borrowers are not paying back loans taken; and if this happens increasingly, our money in banks will become more and more insecure.

You may not be too surprised to know that a 2017 EY survey felt that the 'rise in NPA and stressed asset numbers is due to diversion of funds to unrelated business or fraud'. It boils down to corporate misdemeanours and poor governance.

More bad news is when banks play truant while doing their own business. A classic recent example is **Wells Fargo,** one of the world's largest banks, which tried to squeeze out profits by signing new accounts without customer consent. Since 2011, for over five years, Wells's employees, trying to meet aggressive sales targets, opened millions of fraudulent bank accounts.[5] The shrouded sham accounts scandal was monumental to say the least.

Trust is the base on which the banking system stands. When customer confidence gets compromised through bank frauds, whether from within or from outside, it is unnerving. Banking system must set up strong control systems to avoid banking deceits at any cost. This is required to protect banking image, goodwill and customer faith—or else the wheels of trade and commerce will screech to a halt one day!

Banking deceits work both ways. It's like the two-headed snake: one, when banks are cheated; and two, when banks cheat on us. Strange, but that's how the unethical side of money business works!

Crook Banks

It can be exceptionally alarming when we trust our money with a bank only to realize that the money managers were scoundrels.

Let me tell you a story which took place in the 1970s and 1980s. Needless to mention, versions of this con game keep appearing from time to time, ruining the life savings of millions of trusting common folks.

This story belongs to the very unscrupulous **Bank of Credit and Commerce International (BCCI),** which took money from more than a million depositors from across the globe, to become a personal money bank for its Arab owners and Pakistani managers.[6] In addition, to its favoured customers, millions of dollars were lent without asking for proper documentations and in violation of bank's lending thresholds. Fake front customers were placed to mask the real borrowers.

The hoodwinking continued in several areas. Teeming and lading schemes were widely followed. Deposits from fresh customers were adjusted against unpaid interest and principal repayments from the defaulting customers. When loss mounted, the bank lent money to its existing shareholders so that they could buy more stocks of the bank. The proceeds from the share sale would help bump up its equity (faking enhanced quality of bank's balance sheet), which would have got battered due to losses. This would mean that the bank was round tripping its own money.

From the early days, bankers and regulators were uneasy about this bank. It was something of a big black hole—a 'stateless' bank that operated in the USA and about 70 other countries including one branch in India, registered in Luxembourg, run by Pakistanis, largest owner being the Abu Dhabi government, headquartered in Britain and serviced by outposts in the tax haven, Cayman Islands.

Police had nicknamed BCCI the 'Bank of Crooks and Criminals' for its fondness for customers who dealt in arms, drugs and hot money.

The bank practised a shady mix of deceptive banking. Phony loans, unrecorded deposits, secret files and illicit share-buying schemes, all channelled through a network of shell companies, friendly financial institutions and rich Arab front men to mask the fraud.

The bank tricked the outside world by shrouding it with an aura of credibility by making charitable donations and paying consulting fees to the high and mighty of the society. Among the prominent people who had an account with BCCI included former US President Jimmy Carter and former British Prime Minster James Callaghan.

Juxtaposing the connections with the well-heeled, the bank maintained secret accounts for hordes of notorious people and institutions, including the Iraqi President Saddam Hussein, Panamanian ruler Manuel Noriega, drug dealers and arms traders. It was once stated that 'BCCI was the bank of convenience for people with money to hide.'

When the lid came off the scandal in 1991 with the collapse of the bank, people and regulators were aghast as to how a banking fraud of this form and nature—the largest thus far—could have taken place?

The multi-billion-dollar scam, leaving over 6,500 customers gasping to get their money back, was tied to drug money laundering, illicit arms trade, influence buying and even financing of an unreleased Brooke Shields movie. The shrewd perpetrators managed to evade regulation for two decades by scattering its main operations among multiple geographies having different legal frameworks.

It seems that from its very inception, the bank was envisioned and structured to cheat. If this be so, unless the regulators are very careful, such things can happen again. The unfortunate part is that hubris by banks keep cropping up.

Let us take an example of a recent fraud by one of the largest cooperative banks in India—the **Punjab and Maharashtra Co-operative (PMC) Bank,** a four-decade old institution, with 137 branches spread across half a dozen Indian states.[7]

The modus operandi, though not unique, was rather shrewd. The bank gave loans to its major shareholder, a realty firm **Housing Development and Infrastructure Limited (HDIL),** even when they defaulted in making repayments.

For over a decade, the bank structured and schemed loans to inappropriate borrowers. The bank used over 21,000 dummy accounts to hide non-repayment of the loans getting disbursed. Some of these accounts were also password protected. The idea perhaps was to show small loan amounts so that any default is not taken as a red flag. Loans given to these accounts were ultimately passed on to HDIL or its promoters, the Wadhawan family.

What PMC Bank did was utter lack of banking sense. It extended loans of over ₹4,000 crore for years to just one group HDIL, up to 73 per cent of the bank's total assets (limit is 20%), and that too without adequate collaterals.

The banking system works on spreading its risks when loans are granted. The mere fact that three-fourths of the loans were made to one group automatically made it a business crime.

The lender and the borrower were hand in glove with each other, with the chairman of PMC Bank, Waryam Singh, being also a director in one of the HDIL group companies. Not to end here, Singh in fact chaired the bank's meetings where the loans to HDIL were approved—a clear case of conflict of interest.

Now the question is: How did the bank escape its audits?

When the country central bank, RBI, came for inspections, apparently the PMC management submitted fraudulently manipulated data for conducting sample checks. The bank fiddled with management information systems and NPAs identification process. The bank is understood to have given special access codes on its core banking software (CBS) for HDIL accounts with restricted visibility to only a few of its 1,800 employees.

While running the script for system identification of the NPAs, it deliberately excluded the HDIL accounts. The bank's own MIS software called 'Opine' had a script for generating lists of newly sanctioned or disbursed accounts, but the undisclosed loan accounts were excluded from this list.

The sample of accounts thus picked for inspection did not contain undisclosed accounts of HDIL group. Thus, the fraud of giving loans to accounts where loans are not serviced remained outside the knowledge of the inspecting teams. The bank therefore carefully carried out the scam by structuring its operating and control mechanisms such that the lacunas remained outside the ambit of the regulators.

It is ultimately the commoners and their life savings that get stuck in these con games. Even in PMC Bank, hundreds of customers are still struggling to recover their own money, deposited trusting the banking system. Unless the regulators regulate the banking system properly, God save the unsuspecting common folks from the crooks and cheats who keep lurking around for unguarded opportunities.

Tailpiece

Time and again, swindling and phony banks have cropped up. Even banks that were started with the right vision and mission went astray down the line. Access to someone else's funds is the reason for greedy actions to corner some easy money.

Fraudsters do take advantage of lax banking system when the lenders are incapable to appraise loan proposals. Data submitted and stories spun around by potential borrowers, when not adequately challenged or properly vetted by the lenders, do lead to loans turning bad.

Sadly, our most trustworthy partners, the banks, could turn untrustworthy!

Rogue Credit Culture

'A diamond is forever' is the tag line of De Beers, the world's household name for diamonds. Nirav Modi diamonds, which aspired to be the Indian De Beers brand equivalent, however failed to get its name etched as a diamond jeweller forever.

The unassuming Nirav Modi, owner of the once famed eponymous brand, grew up in Belgium, got admitted to Wharton School but failed to continue. He moved back to India in 1990 when he was 19. He trained for the diamond jewellery business under the sharp eyes of his uncle Mehul Choksi, promoter of another scam hit, stock-market-listed company, **Gitanjali Gems.**

In 1999, Nirav Modi branched out on his own, under the banner of **Firestar Diamonds,** starting his own diamond jewellery-making facility in India. Meanwhile, the diamond industry was undergoing two major shifts.[8] First, brands loomed large on the landscape that was once ruled by mom-and-pop boutiques and family jewellers. Clients began moving to branded jewellery—assurance of ethics was needed to repose trust. Second, design started taking precedence—shifting to 'wearable' creativity instead of just traditional diamonds and stones.

Nirav Modi took full advantage of these shifts in consumer preference. He realized that the luxury jewellery market was red hot, pushing into the ultra-luxe retail jewellery market in 2010. With the tagline 'Haut Diamantaire', he launched his jewellery business branded **Nirav Modi** with eight boutiques worldwide, including high-street luxury stores in London, New York and Hong Kong.

Nirav Modi was just flying higher and higher in the $275 billion global jewellery market. Firestar group turnover grew to a whopping ₹14,700 crore ($2 billion) by 2016–2017, and he expressed his vision of having 100 stores by 2025. His name became the stamp of corporate India's growing global status.

His diamonds sparkled on Hollywood red carpets, adorning the necks and earlobes of celebrities like Kate Winslet. Back home in India, the Nirav Modi brand was splashed on hoardings across Delhi and Mumbai, bearing the image of its global brand ambassador, actor and former Miss World, Priyanka Chopra.

Then came out the fraud—the mega heist structured by the borrower, aided by the lender. Nirav Modi used the classical method of relying on bank insiders, greasing palms and dodging technology more than using it.

His lender, **Punjab National Bank (PNB),** stunned markets when it declared in February 2018 that its Mumbai branch in Fort area had lost over ₹11,000 crore ($1.5 billion). Nirav Modi, three of his relatives (his wife, brother and uncle Mehul Choksi) and three firms (**Diamonds R US, Solar Exports** and **Stellar Diamonds**) in which Modi and Choksi were partners got embroiled in one of the largest scams in the Indian financial market.

How was the fraud committed? It began with the diamond firms approaching PNB for financing import of rough diamonds. The much popular letter of credit (LC) facilities were opened by the bank in favour of Nirav Modi's firms, which allowed credit for a certain period. Nirav Modi bribed his way to obtain the LCs without any security, which is the primary requirement for any such facility. What these LCs allowed were imports for which payment can be made by the importer to the bank later, that is, after the agreed credit period.

Based on the strength of the LCs, Nirav Modi firms got PNB to open letters of undertakings (LoUs) apparently for one year (though legally, it could not exceed three months) on foreign branches of certain Indian banks. (LoU is a bank guarantee which allows bank's customer to raise money from another Indian bank's foreign branch in the form of short-term credit.) When these LoUs were shown at the foreign branches, these banks remitted funds to PNB's nostro accounts (accounts PNB had with the overseas banks). The available funds were then drawn and utilized by Nirav Modi's team.

It was expected that Nirav Modi's firms would settle their obligations with PNB on the expiry of the LoU period. This last leg did not happen; and this was the problem and obviously the swindle!

About 150 LoUs were fake—issued by a few PNB employees. Based on these unauthorized LoUs, PNB employees misused

SWIFT network to transmit messages to foreign banks communicating details of sanctioned LoUs by wilfully not recording these SWIFT messages in the bank's core system. These omissions made the transactions bypass the main PNB banking control system.

When the news of the fraud got flashed all over—ironically on a Valentine's Day—Nirav Modi's abrupt upsurge to eminence came crashing down.

Why did he cheat? A logical reason could be his need for continuous funding. The pace of growth of his business was so fast and furious that it was perhaps difficult for him to fund his enormous marketing cost, supermodel remunerations, new luxury stores and investing in working capital.

Nirav Modi tagline 'Say Yes, Forever' was literally followed by the lax Indian bank by continuing to heed his request for incessant loan guarantees, fraudulently or otherwise.

Nirav Modi's troubles mirror those of another Indian tycoon, Vijay Mallya. (Both Nirav Modi and Vijay Mallya are holed up in the UK with the Indian government desperately trying to lock them up in Indian jails.)

When corporate tycoons run away with the money they have borrowed from banks, what credit culture are we talking about? It is sheer corporate crime of the highest order.

Instances abound on entrepreneurs running away after loan defaults, especially when they have the ability to pay but do not do so. These instances raise doubts on the prevalent credit culture among the Indian corporates. It is true that all businesses cannot be painted with the same brush. But thousands including big names like **Winsome Diamonds,**[9] **Zoom Developers,**[10] **Varun Industries,**[11] **S. Kumars**[12] and **DSQ Software**[13] have taken the banking system to the cleaners.

Exasperated over the behaviour of certain borrowers, India's largest banker lamented in 2017 that they no longer trusted 'steel companies'. It was a sad day. Arundhati Bhattacharya, ex-State Bank of India chief, slammed steel firms for being non-transparent in their data presentation to the banks—disappointed over the way the industry misrepresented by twisting facts while seeking loans. It was a bank chief's way of expressing annoyance over corporate India's attitude towards credit culture.

Many woes of non-payment in the Indian economy are due to past instances of political gridlocks, delayed permissions and economic slowdowns. But it does not provide the license to any borrower, not to repay its liabilities willingly. Poor business conditions leading to banking defaults are excusable, but not when the borrower wilfully defaults. Sadly, numerous borrowers default in paying bank debts even when situations improve. This is poor corporate culture.

Tailpiece

Credit is oxygen to business. Its adequate flow is a necessity for any business to function effectively. The loans disbursed need to be supervised and recovered by the lenders in accordance with the lending terms. But what if the borrower does not, purposefully? This is a significant issue of banking fraud. Money borrowed if properly utilized for intended purposes are generally duly paid back. But if the borrowed sums are siphoned off, money laundered or used for unapproved projects, it becomes a huge hoax.

Not returning money borrowed is a deception which renders short-term gains to the borrowers but obliterates their long-term well-being.

Long and Short of Borrowers

In India, if you wanted to go on a foreign holiday, **Cox & Kings**, one of the oldest travel companies, would have been among the preferred choices. A company of great vintage, heritage and prestige became bankrupt in 2019. The company not only let down its customers and vendors but most importantly its employees and lenders.

One of the reasons for this company's demise was very poor financial practice. It is understood that the company borrowed short-term loans on the strength of its standalone business balance sheet and would invest in overseas subsidiaries as equity.[14]

This is a clear case of borrowing short to lend or invest long. The financial mismatch is a massive misstep. If a company borrows short, it implies that the money needs to be repaid at short notice. How can such money be lent or invested with a long-term horizon? It defies common logic.

In addition to the awful financial management, Cox & Kings has been accused of misusing bank borrowings by siphoning it off through creation of multiple layers of onshore and offshore subsidiaries across the globe. The oldest travel outfit practised lengthy hocus-pocus all the way.[15]

A similar problem played out for India's hitherto largest non-banking financial company (NBFC), **Infrastructure Leasing & Financial Services (IL&FS)**.[16] The company failed in 2018 after having notched up growth for decades.

What went wrong? IL&FS piled up too much debt, mostly to be paid back in the short-term, while cash flows from its lending assets were skewed towards the longer term. The business model of IL&FS was to lend for building infrastructure such as roads and bridges. It necessarily assumes a long gestation period for repayment. However, the company went on borrowing for short-term periods of six months to one year, with the presumption that the lenders will roll over the loans.

And what happened? Many lenders, feeling uncertain about IL&FS's future, decided not to give fresh loans (rollover the old loans) when the earlier loans matured. Hell broke loose, and the company went belly up to be rescued by sacking the board and replacing it.

Many companies follow poor financial practice of borrowing short and using it for long-term purposes, therefore staging a fraud on the short-term money market lenders.

To cite a normal practice, for a home purchase, you will not take a bank overdraft or personal loan for one year and hope to roll it over every year. You would rather take a housing loan repayable over say 20 years. A typical short- versus long-tenured loan decision.

It is common sense that when lenders lend, they need to match the length of time for borrowings from depositors or other sources. If a bank is lending for a project with repayment period of five years, how on earth can it borrow correspondingly for just six months? The primary reason for such mismatch is that short-term borrowings are cheaper, with long-term lending rates being steeper. The banks then keep hoping that the sources from which they borrowed would keep rolling over the facilities. What if they do not? That's when things explode.

Tailpiece

The inherent promise of borrowers is that they would be repaying the borrowed money on time with interest. However, if the money borrowed is lent for a longer duration where repayment can only happen after sufficient length of time, the trust reposed by the lender is then seriously compromised.

Hoodwinking Banks

While many common borrowers face serious difficulties in meeting the equated monthly instalments (EMIs) of their loans and face harassment if any EMI is missed, several big fat defaulters seem to 'live life king size' without much of a worry. Many of these defaulters have the ability to pay but do not pay the lenders— tagged as 'wilful defaulters'. They are scums of our society, as they lie to the banking system to borrow.

The size of such muck in India is huge. For instance, in March 2021, there were around 2,500 (up from 2,200 in previous year)[17] borrowers who did not deliberately repay banking loans, though they had the ability to do so. In fact, the so-called 'wilful defaulters' owed about ₹150,000 crore[18] ($20 billion) to the banking system. The worst part is that over 20 such wilful defaulters had an outstanding of over ₹1000 crore ($135 million) each. Just imagine the quantum and quality of trickery these borrowers would have perfected over time to suck out so much money from the lenders with the ultimate intent of not repaying!

Another facet of conning banks is fraudsters looting banks. Over the last decade, more than 53,000 cases of frauds were reported by the banks in India involving a massive amount of over ₹200,000 crore ($26 billion).[19] The sheer number of banking frauds are galloping—rising 30 per cent (from 6,800 cases in 2018–2019 to 8,700 in 2019–2020). The worst part is that there is concentration of large-value frauds, with the top-50 credit-related frauds usually constituting 75 per cent of the value of the frauds.

The modus operandi of misleading banks into committing large-value frauds could include opening of current accounts with banks outside the lending consortium without a no-objection certificate from the existing lenders; diverting funds by borrowers through various means, including routing through associated and shell companies; using credit sanctioned for purposes not intended by the lenders; and taking unwarranted risks by speculating with bank's money.

In the UK alone, over £1 billion was stolen by the fraudsters in 2019.[20] This is nothing else but modern-day bank robbery.

The borrower frauds have gone overboard in India. Forensic audit of over 200 companies facing corporate insolvency resolution action under the Insolvency and Bankruptcy Code has revealed irregularities of more than ₹1 lakh crore ($13 billion), including diversion of funds. Such is the menace of cheating concerning borrowed money!

All types of irregularities have been noticed. Misdeeds include diversion or siphoning of funds; unauthorized creation of assets; undervalued transactions through related or other entities; circular transactions; preferential transactions with a group of creditors and customers; gold plating of projects; and transactions defrauding creditors.

Let me tell you some stories how certain businesses have cheated banks

The famed real estate conglomerate and owner of Taj Expressway, **Jaypee Group**[21] had large tracts of unencumbered land bank of about 850 acres, worth over ₹5,000 crore ($670 million). By misrepresenting to its existing lenders which had loan liabilities overdue, the large land tract was mortgaged to borrow further money from another set of lenders. This fraudulent behaviour was being executed when the group had already sold 30,000 flats in its much-hyped Noida township, Wish Town, launched in 2007 but had only delivered 9,500 apartments. This left home buyers high and dry. The infrastructure conglomerate could have easily used the available land to secure loans or sell them to raise funds to complete its promised housing project which remained incomplete where customers had already paid their hard-earned money. But with fraudulent intent, it did not.

Another instance of a big banking deceit: **Bhushan Power & Steel**[22] is being probed by the Enforcement Directorate for a fraud of ₹47,000 crore ($6 billion)—loans from 33 lenders between 2007 and 2014. Borrowings by the promoters were apparently diverted for procurement of personal assets by the former chairman, Sanjay Singal. The company declared that these funds were used for purchase of goods, which never took place.

The rogues follow numerous ways to fool the banking system. In fact, between 2015 and 2019, 38 defrauding borrowers fled India.

The deceit instances cited will enable you to understand how the trust of the banking system is often misused by the con artists.

Tailpiece

Banks are defrauded in various ways. No rocket science techniques are needed—forged documentation, flawed certification, multiple funding, project cost, overvaluation or non-existence of sufficient collaterals and siphoning off funds. If not anything else, many well-heeled borrowers just decide not to repay.

There is another aspect—a social side—when loans are obtained by fraud or siphoned off. This means that the money which should have been used for productive purposes like setting up a real factory will not happen, hence no new jobs, no additional supply and no fresh taxes. It is an instance of victimless crime at a colossal community cost.

Numerous are the ways to amass wealth by the unscrupulous. One way is to treat bank 'debts' as 'gifts'!

Peer-to-peer Deception

Would it not be wonderful if money could be lent or borrowed within our friend circles, bypassing the intermediates like banks? Familiarity and trust are the fillips. The Internet has boosted this ability to approach a broad spectrum of people for lending purposes. A peer-to-peer (P2P) lending platform is a virtual marketplace where actual lenders could meet genuine borrowers. But it goes on well until trust is compromised.

P2P lending is a form of crowdfunding. It connects borrowers with lenders without the intervention of any intermediary like a financial institution. Its popularity has grown over the last decade as it provides the possibility of receiving high returns on investments. However, P2P lending poses unprecedented risks of default and duplicity , as risk evaluation possibilities are scant or can be misrepresented by the borrowers.

This neo-borrowing, however, went awry in China. Police cracked down in 2018 on P2P lenders, freezing Rmb10 billion ($1.5 billion) across 380 companies. They fanned out across Asia in pursuit of financial runaways. The operation is aptly named 'Fox Hunt'. This chase commenced when hundreds of investors took to the streets in China to demand repayment of money lent through the P2P platforms.

The so-called P2P lending, a $200 billion business which connects private lenders with borrowers online, was once a thriving industry in China. Some say that the size of the market could be over $400 billion. The government had little oversight over thousands of businesses which rapidly opened shop.[23]

It was touted as the way to promote innovation and the future of banking.

But in recent times, what appeared to be a harmless way of lending and borrowing has turned itself into a huge scandal, involving billions of dollars. It appears that the P2P platform was a guise for some to bait high returns to collect large sums of money.

The so-called 'shadow banking' sector has got infiltrated with wealth management products and trusts. This unregulated sector, of late, is under government crackdown in China. It is feared that by mid-2020, the crackdown resulted in a mammoth $115 billion in losses for the average Chinese investors.[24]

Bloomberg reports that China's multi-year clampdown on its P2P lending industry has shaved off the number to just about 30 platforms by mid-2020, down from about 6,000 at its peak, with fugitives fleeing the country failing to return money to the investors.

In India, P2P lending has been in vogue since 2014 but was largely unregulated till 2017. The country's central bank (RBI) has since notified that these lenders will need to be registered as NBFCs.

Although there are several websites claiming to be offering P2P lending services in India, RBI publishes a list of companies which have been registered as P2P lending NBFCs. The size of the Indian P2P lending market is estimated at ₹200 crore ($26 million).

The good news is that in India, the defaults do not seem to be as large as in China. That is probably due to RBI's intervention in putting across regulations, with borrowing limits set at ₹10 lakh ($13,000).[25]

But what people should be aware of is that Ponzi-like schemes could squeeze through the P2P model, fooling many.

In China, in one such incident in 2016, a company had collected Rmb50 billion ($8 billion) from 900,000 investors under P2P funding story, but was found to be 'a complete Ponzi scheme'. Police used two excavators to uncover some 1,200 account books that had been buried deep below the ground. Established in 2014, **Ezubao** was one of China's highest-profile P2P lending sites, promising investors annual returns of up to 15 per cent. Ding Ning, its 34-year-old founder, allegedly diverted money into his own real estate projects and used it to pay off existing investors. Ding has been since arrested.

Investors need to be wary of schemes which seem too ambitious in promises and returns.

A typical P2P lending scam normally comes into the open when the lending platform, after a period of mysterious activities, blocks investors from withdrawing their money and then eventually shuts down. The question that always remains unanswered is whether the P2P platform was created with the intent to deceive people or did it close down due to bad business calls.

Few Last Words

Banking deceits are too many, ranging from disguising as genuine businesses who take out loans only to file for bankruptcy; from gold plating projects to fabricating future project cash flows; and from criminals trying to game the system to circular financing.

The genesis of banking deception arises from either of the two fundamental failings: one, the banks' inability to monitor utilization of loans granted; and two, the borrower conning lenders for inappropriate usage either in collusion or due to banker's poor appraisal skills.

When a loan is taken, say for buying a car, the bank can easily monitor fund deployment by paying directly to the auto dealer. But as the loan amount becomes bigger, the lenders lose the ability to monitor appropriate use of funds. Similarly, if the borrower lies by producing false documents or maliciously enhances project cost or just siphons off amount lent, lenders can do very little but to run to the police or to the judiciary.

There is another possibility to funding swindle. It is when the lender and the borrower join hands to wreak havoc—creating perhaps the nastiest instance of corporate cheating.

Banking is the business of money. Countless prying eyes are normally trying to con the system. With many intelligent minds ogling at the booty, combating banking fraud menace would continue to be a challenge for all times to come.

The steep bank losses and nasty frauds have shaken the banking system substantially. Several steps including enhanced audit quality, training of managers, an improved fund monitoring system and an implementable penalty mechanism should go a long way to improve sanitization of the lending industry.

Financial system is like the vein through which blood flows to make the businesses run. If the blood vessels get contaminated, clogged or collapse, health of any body, business or economy would quiver.

CHAPTER SEVEN

The Art of Hiding Shady Wealth

The lure of money and the art of hiding ill-earned dark money is rather lucrative for many of the so-called respected souls in our society.

In South America, journalists used to consult a respected teacher—Professor Bruce Bagley—as an expert while reporting on drug trafficking, money laundering and corruption. For instance, in 2016, Professor Bagley was consulted over two nephews of the Venezuelan president who had been charged with drug trafficking. The professor who taught international studies at the University of Miami told news agencies, 'the nephews are just the tip of the iceberg, and corruption is rampant in power circles in Venezuela.'[1]

Such is the lure of ill-gotten money that a mere three years later in 2019, the federal prosecutor found out that Professor Bagley was more than an academic expert on the criminal world. He was in fact a money launderer himself, being arrested for his involvement in a scheme to hide the origins of over $2 million in proceeds from bribery in Venezuela, apparently keeping aside about 10 per cent of the money for himself as a commission. So even an esteemed professor could not escape the enticement of dirty money.

Money laundering is a method to hide shady wealth. It is a process by which criminals attempt to conceal the illicit origin and ownership of the proceeds of their unlawful activities. It helps to cleanse ill-gotten money by transforming the proceeds from wrongdoings into funds of seemingly legal sources. Typically, it involves multiple transactions and usually routing the money through banking channels to prove authenticity. If successful, the money laundering process provides legitimacy to the proceeds over which the criminals would maintain control. In short, the process disguises criminal origin of funds so that they can be freely used.

It is essentially an art of converting illicit money into legitimate money. In other words, converting black money into white is an act to hide bad money under a good cover. It involves a series of actions such as concealing, disguising, converting, transferring or removing the illicit money.

As you are aware, money which remains outside the accounting books is nothing else but black money—something on which no duties or taxes are paid.

It is not only an offence to launder ill-gotten gains, but one can also be prosecuted for knowingly helping manage another person's illicit money. You may note that an offence gets committed while helping another person in laundering money only when it can be identified that the cash handled was from proceeds of a crime, such as corruption, bribery, theft, drug dealing and even tax evasion.

Let me tell you a typical story of money laundering.

This is a laundering case involving over $400 million.[2] The gang involved got convicted recently, though the swindle was going on for over five years.

The incidence starts from the drug money off the streets of London. Thousands of pound sterling get collected in cash by the bosses of a drug ring. They are however unable to bank the dirty money. Hence, they need some conduit to make use of the illegitimate wealth.

Then enters a Moroccan crook, Hamza, with connections in Europe. He connects with Ali, an airport cleaner in London. Ali picks up the money and flies to Dusseldorf.

He then hands over the booty to Salma, a lady ambulance driver. Being a woman, it is easier for Salma to drive the short distance to Belgium. She then contacts a gold dealer, Zakaria.

For a gold dealer, it is simpler to convert cash into gold. Plus, it is more convenient to transport gold than cash. Zakaria even arranges fake receipts so that the gold looks legitimate.

Zakaria then hands over the gold to Kumar who flies with the treasure to Dubai, where the gold gets sold in the gold-souk. The sales proceeds received in cash in Dubai, known as a tax haven, are then transferred through the banking channels to various parts of the world.

The original trace of drug money by then gets completely obliterated.

The police somehow got a wind of this international play. Almost all the players got arrested except the Moroccan, who was the kingpin. He must be ensconced in a lovely beach, away from the prying eyes of the law enforcement agencies, perhaps changing his identity and waiting to carry out his next con game of laundering some more dirty money.

The above is a typical instance of how dirty money amassed gets converted into legitimate use through the use of various agencies including the banking channel.

Money laundering involves hiding from the tax net illegally acquired money and then being able to use it by providing a mask of legitimacy.

A typical route for money laundering would obviously first involve the collection of dirty money, say by sale of drugs or armaments. This illegitimate money is then deposited in a bank. The dirty money thus gets mingled with good money in the financial system, losing its trail of the original source.

Let me take another example.

Say a helpful bank typically transfers ill-gotten funds received to the bank accounts of company AB. This money could get transferred through a wire transfer to an offshore bank account. The offshore bank would then lend to company XY. This company XY pays the money to company AB who would raise false invoices on company XY.

This would imply that the money goes back to company AB, who initiated the layering of the money received. This helps the money to go back to the so-called originator company AB. This flow seemingly legitimizes the deposit into company AB account, as the money travels through banking channels.

Alternatively, the company XY could choose not to return the money to company AB. It could procure expensive properties from the large loan received from the offshore helpful bank. These assets could include luxury condominiums, investments in financial products or commercial properties. While carrying out laundering, money is invested in such a way that even the investigating agencies would be unable to trace the main source of wealth.

Money laundering is as old as the tax system itself. Human ingenuity has long been playing with the system to avoid paying tax on income. Money made through extortion, gambling and others is often the hot bed of avoiding tax, and then to launder it so that it can be used for legitimate purposes.

Banks, Businesses and Laundering

Over $20 billion dirty money was moved between 2010 and 2014 into Europe, the USA and other countries, by over 500 people, of whom many were Russians. The massive larceny was tracked down in March 2017. The law enforcement agencies of Moldova and Latvia believe that the actual money involved may even be a colossal $80 billion.

'Laundromat' was the code name given by the network of investigative journalists—Organized Crime and Corruption Reporting Project—who exposed this gargantuan money laundering scheme.[3] The 'Laundromat' scheme was creatively structured to wash dirty money. It involved fictitious London-registered companies in many cases.

Typically, company A would 'loan' a large sum of money to company B. Company B, being a fictitious company, obviously had no intent to pay the debt. Other businesses in Russia—fronted by Moldovans—would then guarantee these 'loans' on behalf of company B, promising performance in favour of company A. Company B would fail to repay the debt. Moldovan judges, mostly under the influence of bribes, would authenticate the 'loan', allowing Russian companies to honour the so-called fake guarantees and transfer real money to a bank in Moldova. From here, the cash would go to a bank in Latvia, inside the EU.

At least 19 Russian banks were involved. One of them was the **Russian Land Bank (RZB)**, laundering $10 billion. From Russian accounts, money was sent to other accounts at **Moldindconbank** in Moldova. From there, it was transferred to **Trasta Komercbanka** in Latvia's capital, Riga. (In Moldova, 15 judges, together with senior bank managers, central bank officials and bailiffs, are awaiting trial.)

The colossal sum of money laundered went via the global financial system to 96 countries. That included bigger nations such as the USA, the UK, Germany, France and China.

The ill-gotten wealth was used for purchase of diamonds, designer chandeliers, home cinema equipment and expensive wallpapers. Some of the money flowed into London real estate, including a pub in Bloomsbury and a townhouse in Kensington. Money flowing to the USA were used on aesthetic dentistry, luxury diving watches and other items.

It is common sense that when banks involve themselves in money laundering, things can't get worse.

Let me cite an instance where even basic banking norms were not followed by a global bank. **Deutsche Bank's** internal probe revealed in 2019 that it processed at least €175 million of dirty money for the Russian criminals.[4]

Deutsche's procedures on anti-money laundering provides that corporate cheques for cross-border payments must be verified by 'two' different employees independent of each other. However, the bank's internal audit found that some payments were processed after just 'one' verification.

It is hard to even imagine that if global banks do not follow basic process controls, then what may many smaller entities be doing.

Deutsche Bank is bracing itself for potential fines and prosecution of individual managers.

The problem of money laundering is leap frogging. And banks are getting increasingly involved and sometimes in monstrous proportions.

The UK's monetary watchdog, Financial Conduct Authority, has fired warning shots to its banks by threatening to use its criminal powers in cases where London firms launder dirty money. It lamented that the city is acting as a global laundromat, washing hundreds of billions of pounds of dirty money from around the world.

Another huge shameful money laundering act led **Danske Bank,**[5] Denmark's largest lender, to fall from grace. The bank has gone from being one of Europe's most respected financial institutions to getting caught red-handed in one of the world's biggest scandals.

An internal report by Danske revealed in September 2018 that the bank had failed for years to prevent suspected money laundering involving thousands of customers at its tiny branch in Tallinn, Estonia, between 2007 and 2015. The report prompted Danske's chief executive and chairman to step down. In December, the police in Estonia arrested 10 former Danske employees on charges that they had been involved in a network of money launderers.

And the likely amount involved? An unbelievable figure of €200 billion ($227 billion)! The scandal involved non-resident customers mainly from Russia and other ex-Soviet states. The scam also embroiled **Deutsche Bank, Bank of America** and **JPMorgan Chase,** with money possibly passing through these banks.

The bank management overlooked a simple test: too much profits in a sector where margins are wafer thin. The Estonian branch apparently made a 400 per cent return on capital in an industry where even double figures are difficult to reach.

There must have been a good reason why a small group of customers were willing to pay any bank so much. It involved some 15,000 Danske customers, mostly non-residents. Obtaining entry to the EU banking system via Estonia was priceless to these customers.

The Swedish bank **Swedbank,** the largest lender in the Baltics, also got itself engulfed in this money laundering episode.[6] US regulators are probing the bank after internal documents revealed by Swedish public television broadcaster SVT showing about €135 billion in high-risk non-resident money—mostly from Russia—flowed through its Estonian operations for over a decade. Broadly, it's an issue of Swedbank dealing with large number of risk-prone foreigners who should never have been onboarded.

Both these Nordic banks were making a lot of money in a small foreign branch in Estonia, far away from their homeland. The magic formula turned out to be alleged money laundering for Russian crooks and czars, who were using the banks to shift suspicious cash oversees. Money flowed in and out, often linked to trade and foreign exchange transactions—originally considered as 'low-risk trade finance'—and the banks took a cut along the way. But in reality, a significant slice of this 'trade finance' was illusory. Money was allegedly passing out of Russia to offshore shell companies, with fictitious trade transactions being concocted as the cover.

The banks should have known. But their anti-money laundering controls were either lax or not put into place. The question is: did the banks purposely ignore the red flags? At least in Danske Bank's case, there was little insight into what was going on locally at the Estonian branch using a different computer system, with most documents being in Estonian or Russian language. Swedbank's involvement in this mess, however, is less clear, though they too handled a significant amount of money transfers. The Russian criminals were obviously getting an extremely good deal on their fake business, with the two banks, who either were foolish to have control weaknesses or were complicit in the dirty money scandal.

The saga of other banks' involvement in money laundering continues unabated.

Australia's financial crime-combatting agency has accused **Westpac bank** of the biggest breach of money laundering laws in the nation's history.[7] The regulator alleged that the country's oldest and the second-biggest bank by market capitalization did not adequately monitor and report A$11 billion ($7.5 billion) in suspicious transactions which included transfers related to crimes as heinous as potential child exploitation—that too for a period as long as 2013–2019 on an unbelievable quantum of 23 million suspicious transactions!

Apart from banks playing foul, some corporates are no holy cows. Let me cite an instance of how a 'business' laundered wealth generated.

REI Agro, an Indian company claiming to be the world's largest basmati rice player and marketing 'Raindrops' branded rice, has been charged by the Enforcement Directorate with serious money laundering allegations.[8]

It has been alleged that REI Agro has laundered bank loans of over ₹3,800 crore ($500 million) by diverting funds fraudulently for the purpose other than for which the same was sanctioned. The company promoter-directors Sandip and Sanjay Jhunjhunwala allegedly committed all sorts of mischiefs and were both arrested.

The duo arranged fake purchase and sales invoices of rice and paddy through brokers and dealers of Delhi. The fake stocks were shown for drawing working capital loans from banks. They then diverted these funds for acquiring assets, instead of using the money for procuring paddy. They have also been alleged to have illegitimately diverted ₹600 crore ($80 million) through Kolkata-based shell companies to the accounts of associate companies. The company had also arranged fake bills of steel for ₹25 crore ($3 million) and shown it as capital expenditure but received back the amount in cash.

The lure of laundering has attracted loads of illustrious people.

The famous steel magnate Lakshmi Mittal's younger brother Pramod Mittal could not avoid the bait. The younger industrialist was arrested in mid-2019 in Bosnia over allegations of fraud and money laundering of €11 million through **Global Ispat Charcoal Industry Lukavac,**[9] of which Mittal was the supervisory board chairman. This company is Bosnia's biggest metallurgical coke producer. If found guilty, Mittal could get jailed for 45 years! (How fortunes swing! Pramod Mittal, once one of Britain's wealthiest men who spent £50 million on his daughter's wedding in 2013, had reportedly been declared bankrupt in June 2020 with debts running to more than £130 million.)

The central banks of various countries have been taking to task the banking system for their laxity towards following money laundering norms. But still the deception is all around.

In its efforts to punish the recalcitrant bankers, in early 2019, the Indian central bank imposed fines totalling ₹11 crore ($1 million) on 7 banks for their failure to report frauds, exchange of information with other banks and not following anti-money laundering standards. The list included the who's who of the Indian banking system—**HDFC Bank, Kotak Mahindra Bank, Allahabad Bank, Andhra Bank** and **Indian Overseas Bank.**[10]

What did the banks fail to do? The lenders botched in maintaining records on the origin of some of the fund transfers, failed to provide information to other banks on the source of funds in the chain of transactions and did not carry out proper verifications on distrustful transactions, including payments to suspected child exploitation facilitators in Southeast Asia.

Anti-money laundering for banks would essentially mean that they may not process some transactions or may even refuse to have someone as a customer. If the rules of the games are properly followed, especially by the financial institutions, it would then be tough for the scamsters to keep skimming the society of taxable wealth.

Money laundering is a scum of the society. It involves ill-gotten wealth, be it terrorist, drug or criminal money, all avoiding tax nets. Bad money is routed through the banking system, which often chooses to close its eyes on 'know your customer' (KYC as it is popularly known as) processes and substantiation on money sources. Bankers need to set up systems to identify risky customers and transactions.

It is a never-ending game to counter the movement of money acquired through illegal means. The criminals are always seeking new ways to transfer the proceeds of crime. The effort is all about keeping pace with the ever-shifting techniques used by the crooks to move illicit wealth. The truth, however, is that even after banks pouring in millions of dollars into anti-money laundering compliance programmes, the size and intensity of laundromat are not showing signs of cleanliness.

Tailpiece

'Catch me if you can' is the buzz word among launderers, who keep shifting their pace and practice to launder illicit treasure. Unknowingly or knowingly, many banks get caught up in this whirlpool.

Laundering has been in vogue since times immemorial. Consider the ill-famed case of tarnished BCCI's scam of the late 1980s—which saw the world's seventh largest private bank hoodwinking regulators to practise illegal dealings. It involved infamous names like Iraq's President Saddam Hussein and Panama ruler Manuel Noriega.

Moving on to the present, the recent €200-billion Danske Bank scandal caught in 2018 makes it appear that the laundering game continues unabated, with banks still unable to catch up with the tricks and trade of the tricksters.[11]

On a lighter note, when the COVID-19 pandemic was blowing through the world fast and furious in mid-2020, a South Korean in Seoul put a considerable number of banknotes for laundry in a washing machine—to remove possible traces of the coronavirus! The loss was sizeable.[12]

The bad news is that the size and scale is just getting larger—the emergence of business and banking breaches in a bigger, broader and bottomless proportion is indisputable now.

Money Laundering Recipe

Drug traffickers, swindlers, corrupt politicians, public officials, gangsters, extremists and con artists are the ones who are usually on the lookout for ways and means to launder their illicit wealth. Most of these swindlers are in serious need of a good laundering system, as they deal almost exclusively in cash, causing grave logistical problems of hiding, moving, accessing and using it. Usually, the cash available is large and typically stalked by law enforcement officials.

Just imagine that a drug trafficker dealing with just 30 kg (70 pounds) of cocaine may garner about ₹200 crore ($30 million) in Delhi streets. The criminal would obviously need the bounty to be hidden and moved out immediately so that it does not get confiscated.

Even if the launderer spends his cash on houses, cars, luxury holidays and restaurants, how much can he use in these modes? Soon he will run out of means to spend his large catch. That is where the money laundering or hiding the untaxed and ill-gotten cash comes into play.

In practice, laundering usually involves injecting cash gained through illicit means into the legitimate financial system in a way to disguise its origins, so that the money appears to come from a clean source.

There are numerous techniques to launder money, few known and many unknown, as fraudsters have several smart alecks to advise them.

Money laundering normally involves three basic steps.

Let us take a look at these three popular steps used by the launderers.

1. *Placement:* The launderer first tries to 'place' the dirty money into a legitimate financial institution. This is often in the form of cash deposits in banks. This is the riskiest process, as large amounts of cash are to be deposited, making it pretty conspicuous.

    If deposited in banks, then there is an additional problem of banks requiring to report high-value transactions.

The cash could also be placed into circulation through channels other than banks, like the money markets, casinos, retail trade, foreign exchange bureaus and also through normal businesses.

The 'placement' process could include the following:

- *Smuggling of currency:* It involves physical and illegal movement of currency and monetary instruments out of a country. 'Hawala' (informal money transfer through a network of brokers) could be a method used.
- *Collusion with banks:* This is when financial institutions connive with illegal groups like arms or drug dealers. This would involve taking deposits of forbidden money without depositor's due diligence and tracking the source of funds.
- *Currency exchanges:* Forex bureaus which are involved in the business of exchanging foreign currencies for local money could be used as a cohort to money laundering. It can convert illegally acquired foreign exchanges into official local currency.
- *Security brokers:* Stock brokers can help depositors to purchase shares and stocks by camouflaging the original source of the funds.
- *Blending with other cash:* The way to hide cloudy cash is by mixing it with good cash. Financial institutions are often used for this method.
- *Set up front companies:* It is using money from illicit activities to set up fake companies. This enables the funds from illegitimate sources to be masked in legal transactions, where the front companies will be treated as legal entities.
- *Purchase of assets:* Property purchase is a popular way to launder wealth. This helps in converting bulk cash into valuable but saleable assets like a prized condominium.

2. *Layering:* Steps to layer are taken to make it difficult to track the origin of dirty money. Complex steps are taken in sending

money through 'layers' of financial transactions to change its original source and form.

This is the most intricate step in any laundering scheme, and it is all about making the original dirty money as hard to trace as possible by the law enforcement agencies.

Some popular methods of 'layering' are as follows:

- *Banking roulette:* The cash deposited in the banking system could be played with by making several bank-to-bank transfers, or wire transfer between different accounts in different names in different countries, or make multiple deposits and withdrawals to continually vary the amount of money in the account.
- *Convert cash to another monetary form:* When the illegal money is placed within the financial system like a bank, the proceeds can then be converted into a monetary instrument like banker's drafts or change the currency itself.
- *Buying high-value assets to sell them later:* Assets such as boats, houses, cars and diamonds, bought through illicit funds, when resold locally or abroad, get difficult to trace the funding source. This is done to change the form of the money.

3. *Integration:* This stage involves making the black money re-enter the mainstream economy to 'integrate' into legitimate-looking form. It gives the shape to money as if it's coming from legal transactions. At this point, the criminal will have a bright chance of using the money without getting caught. It is very difficult to catch a launderer during the integration stage if there is no documentation during the previous stages.

Some 'integration' methods used are as follows:

- *Property dealing:* It is the use of shell companies to buy property from illegal funds. This will make detection of property ownership difficult. Plus, sales proceeds of the property could be treated as legal.
- *Front companies and fabricated loans:* Front companies are sometimes set up in countries with corporate secrecy laws

like Switzerland and Dubai. Bad money is then lent from these front companies to the launderers so that it looks as though it is legitimate.

- *Fictitious import–export bills:* False import–export invoicing is often used by unethical organizations. This helps easy integration of illicit money into the formal financial system. False export invoices or overvalued exports involve depositing of funds into the domestic banking system. Over-invoicing of imports will enable transfer of funds outside the country through a formal banking channel. The illicit money received through over-invoiced exports can also be sent out to any other country through over-invoiced imports.

- *Bank's blind eye:* Banking guidelines globally provide that banks should take all reasonable steps to ensure that they do not knowingly or involuntarily assist in hiding or moving the proceeds of corruption. It means screening customers to determine whether they are people with a shady back-ground. If so, the banks are supposed to file a 'suspicious activity report' when such customers transfer unusually large amounts of money. The willing assistance of banks makes money laundering detection difficult.

- *Mix money in legitimate companies:* Genuine businesses could be apt for investing dirty money. It helps to get bad money mix happily with good money. Examples would include restaurants, nightclubs, casinos or even parlours and spas. Revenues from crime would be injected alongside genuine income from these businesses, including salons painting nails or dressing hair. Money is then banked, taxed and legitimized. Everything becomes hunky-dory.

Since the 1980s, the amount of money laundering has just ballooned. An estimate by the United Nations Office on Drugs and Crime reported in *The Guardian* puts the annual sum between 2 and 5 per cent of global GDP.[13] If this estimate is correct, it would be between

$1.5 trillion and \$4 trillion. The matter obviously is dreadfully enormous. The newspaper then goes on to state, 'Of late the flow of money to the tax havens are likely to exceed 10 per cent of global GDP, and is just growing. If this is so, then corporate deceits are spreading its tentacles!'

Tailpiece

Modes of money laundering involve an illegal process of obscuring the origin of money obtained illicitly by passing it through a complex chain of banking transfers or commercial transactions.

The schemes are structured such that the money does not suffer taxes, can be used for illicit purposes or returned back to the launderer. In essence, skilful recipes are concocted to produce white money from black bucks.

Money laundering helps providing oxygen to organized crime!

Illegal Foreign Currency Usage

A famous money laundering trick identified was through the black market peso exchange, perhaps one of the most insidious black currency usage system in the Western Hemisphere.

Way back in the 1990s, the Colombian officials were flummoxed by the way US goods were being imported into the country. They huddled together with the US Treasury Department to figure out the method of the illegal imports. When they considered the use of drug money and illegal foreign trade, the officials discovered that the methodology being used was achieving twin purposes— converting dirty money into legitimate currency and importing goods without customs duty payment.

The black market peso exchange is a trade-based money laundering technique commonly used by narcotics traffickers based in Colombia and Mexico.

This complex set-up relies on the fact that there are businesspeople in Colombia—typically importers of international goods—who need US dollars in order to conduct business.

To avoid payment of import duty into Colombia and save on Colombian government's taxes on the money exchange from pesos to dollars, some businessmen would go to black market 'peso brokers' who charge a lower fee to conduct the transaction outside of government intervention. That's the illegal importing side of the scheme.[14]

The contraband activity goes like this:

The drug kingpins, usually Colombian or Mexican, would have sold the illicit drugs in the USA for US dollars. These dollars will need to be ultimately converted into local currency of Mexico or Colombia. The drug dealers will typically approach the peso brokers who will convert the US dollars at a commission. Genuine importer-traders in Colombia would buy the electronic goods in the USA by using the pesos from the peso exchange. Once the imports take place, the import proceeds will be settled by paying pesos usually in Colombia.

Everyone gets satisfied. The importer in Colombia could buy American goods and sell it in his home country, albeit at a lower commission of converting the foreign exchange. The narcotics dealers who sold their illegal wares in the USA gets US dollar converted into pesos ultimately. The peso exchange dealers make money through foreign currency conversion commission.

Let me tell you a story as to how it usually works.

Abraham is a money intermediary, but he is different from others in the world of money-broking business. He buys dollars in the USA, which come from street drug sales. Abraham's way of working is such that he shifts the risks of getting caught from the drug traffickers to himself. Once he picks up the dollar drug money, it is his duty to get the pesos back to the drug traders in Colombia. If the money gets seized or something goes wrong, Abraham will be responsible. He may have to pay with his life if the money is not paid off.

It will normally work this way. Abraham will get a call from a Colombian trafficker or their US colleagues. They will negotiate an exchange rate of Colombian pesos for US dollars, normally 40 per cent below the official exchange rate. Once the rate is agreed, the drug trafficker will arrange to get his black dollars delivered to Abraham's office or at a secretive location.

The money can be delivered in various ways including a car stashed with cash, with the car key. The drug trafficker's deal is now done. He now waits for the pesos to be delivered in his home country bank account, a few weeks later at the most.

Abraham's side of the work begins. He has a contingent of runners. They would deposit every time less than $10,000 in cash into hundreds of American bank accounts—the 'smurfing' method will be practised. Once the money is banked, it takes the form of legitimate money and can be moved around.

Abraham's colleagues in Colombia meanwhile will make currency deals with legitimate Colombian businessmen who have pesos but want to buy cheap US dollars to purchase goods such as cigarettes, liquor or white goods in the USA. The exchange rate could be about 20 per cent below the official exchange rate. They pay the pesos in Colombia to Abraham's office. In turn, Abraham will use the US dollars being held by him in the USA to settle the liabilities of Colombian legitimate importers in the USA.

The matter became so widespread that it is suspected that even large legitimate companies like General Electric, Whirlpool, Phillip Morris and Intel may have all been involved in this system in the past.

The likes of Abraham are the conduit for legitimate international economic transactions, but by using drug money.

The dollar Abraham gets from the traffickers goes to the legitimate businessmen in the USA (like cigarettes, liquor or white goods sellers), and the pesos he gets go to the drug traffickers in Colombia. He gets commissions and the difference in exchange rate, making it a wonderful business but with bountiful risks.

Some launderers do get caught. A court in Laredo, Texas (at the USA–Mexico border), found in 2019 six individuals—four men and two women—guilty in connection with a two-year multimillion-dollar money laundering scheme.[15]

It happens essentially because legitimate businesses in Central and South American countries suffer from a lack of US dollars to conduct international business. To avoid financial regulations, these businesses rely on 'peso brokers' to organize an exchange of legitimate local currency for dirty US dollars.

This method ensures that the dirty drug money does not cross international borders. It instead is used to purchase legitimate goods from unsuspecting businesses on behalf of legitimate South American businesses, whose genuine imports are used to find pesos for the illegitimate drug dealers.

This system of black market peso exchange involves several key advantages for the trafficker: It helps to avoid the risk of having large quantities of cash detected at international borders, to avoid reporting of large money deposit requirements for financial institutions in many geographies and to achieve quick access to local currency like pesos.

Tailpiece

The peso exchange syndrome is not unique. Variants of it are operational in many parts of the world. When it gets detected and busted, it vanishes only to reappear in another avatar somewhere else.

One new variant is the entry of Chinese money brokers. Virtually unheard of a decade ago, these Chinese players are moving large sums quickly and quietly. What are they doing? Essentially, routing cartel drug profits from the USA to China then on to Mexico with a few clicks of burner phones (mobile phones meant for temporary use) and Chinese banking apps—and without the bulky cash ever crossing borders. The launderers pay small Chinese-owned businesses in the USA and Mexico to help them move the funds. Most contact with the banking system happens in China, a real black hole for the USA and Mexican authorities.

Ingenious are the ways warped minds function, and definitely the world has not seen the last of this black market peso exchange modus operandi.

Shell Companies' Shelter

On the 74th floor of the Time Warner Center in Manhattan, USA, condominium number 74B was purchased in 2010 for $16 million by a mysterious entity called '25CC ST74B L.L.C'. It was traced to the family of Vitaly Malkin, a former Russian senator and banker who was barred from entering Canada due to suspected connections to organized crime.

A few floors below, three condos were owned by another shell company, Columbus Skyline L.L.C., which purportedly belongs to a Chinese contractor Wang Wenliang. His construction company was found housing workers in New Jersey in hazardous, unsanitary conditions.

Behind the dark glass towers offering a sheen of both snootiness and secrecy at the iconic Time Warner Center overlooking the Central Park, most of the owners have managed to keep their identities concealed. They registered the condos against shell companies, which in turn are in the names of trusts, limited liability companies (LLCs) or other entities which hide the owners' names.

The New York Times pierced the veil of secrecy of more than 200 shell companies and documented in 2015 a decade of ownership in Manhattan's real estate market.[16]

The secretive landlords represent the high and mighty of the society, like wealthy foreigners, tech entrepreneurs, chief executives, doctors, lawyers and stock traders. The foreign owners included government officials and close associates of officials from Russia, Colombia, Malaysia, China, Kazakhstan and Mexico. Some of these owners were also subjected to governmental enquiries including financial frauds.

These multimillion-dollar purchases were possible without questions raised as the US laws tolerate movement of untraceable money through shell companies.

Enormous amount of wealth keeps flowing unchecked around the world. The reasons could be many, including sleaze, corruption or tax avoidance. These dreadful acts get encouraged by an ever-more-borderless economy and a proliferation of ways to move and hide assets.

The flood of flight money has created colonies of foreign super-rich in the global financial centres such as London, Singapore and Dubai. The phenomenon of the sky-penetrating dwelling—Time Warner Centre in New York—is just an example of the global trait of unaccounted and untaxed foreign money making inroads into high-end real estates through the ever-growing route of using shell companies.

The New York Times report had pointed out that about $8 billion is spent each year on New York City residences which cost more than $5 million each. This is more than triple the amount a decade ago, citing a report in the website PropertyShark. And the worse was that in 2014, over half of those sales were to shell companies, masking the name of the real owners.

Some of the Time Warner Center owners are the billionaires on *Forbes* magazine's annual list of the world's richest people. It has been home to numerous celebrities, including the Indian mining magnate and chairman of Vedanta group, Anil Agarwal, 'King of Latin Pop' Ricky Martin and the American actress and talk show host Kelly Ripa.

The high-end real estate economy obviously does not mind not knowing where the money is coming from, as long it keeps pouring in. It's an opaque economy for some of the superrich. The entire chain of people involved in high-end real estate deals—lawyers, accountants, title brokers, escrow agents, real estate agents and condo builders—operates almost blindfolded.

In some parts of the world, the chic real estate market has become less and less transparent—and more tempting for those abroad with assets they wish to keep anonymous.

Another way to launder wealth is to use the ultra-secretive world of art through use of shell companies with hidden owners. A pair of Russian oligarchs with ties to Russian President Vladimir Putin allegedly seized on the confidentiality of the art industry by making over $18 million in expensive art purchases. The $64 billion global art world is considered to be the largest legal unregulated industry in many parts of the globe. Secrecy, anonymity and lack of regulation create an ideal environment for laundering money.

The art sales instance highlights that unlike selling shares or making bank transfers, art deals through auction houses are not subject to anti-money laundering provisions and are usually far away from public scrutiny. When an artwork is sold, sellers are not required to confirm the identity of the buyer nor to make sure that the art is not being used to launder dirty money.

A nice way to hide the identity of the owners of ill-gotten wealth is the use of shell companies. These firms take various names such as phantom companies, personal investment firms, international business corporations and simply mail box or letter box companies.

Shell companies are fake enterprises. They exist mostly for no other reason than to launder money. They route dirty money as 'receipts' and 'payments' for businesses they are supposed to do, like buying, producing and selling. However, in reality they do nothing.

Tax havens are normally the heavens for shell companies. Countries with low or no taxes, together with laws against disclosure of banking information, are the heavenly homes.

Tailpiece

Inconspicuousness provides protection. Secrecy assists in escaping taxation. Shell companies are wonderful ways to fool the law enforcement agencies, acting as an attractive accomplice to launder wealth.

Shell companies simply create the appearance of legitimate business dealings through fake transactions, documentations and highly doctored financial accounts.

Sadly, splitting the shell of secrecy on shell companies is seriously strenuous.

Working of Shell Companies

Setting up a shell company is like taking a stroll in a mall—walking around, doing some window shopping and dropping in at a vantage point for buying a coffee. Similarly, you can go to places like the British Virgin Islands, Delaware, Panama or even London, and request a local lawyer firm to get you a shell company for a price which may not be too much.

In case you need more credibility behind your shell company structures, you could pay a bit more and set up your vice company in Nevada, a western state in the USA.

Each of these places, which are popular for setting up shell companies, would provide obscurity to your beneficial ownership of assets there.

The shell structure helps to own properties in the name of covert companies rather than named people. It is nearly impossible to establish with certainty the source of money behind shell companies.

What is more, ownership of shell companies can be shifted at any time, with no indication in property records. This means that when a property was bought by a shell company, say Xylo & Co. purportedly owned by Alexander, the ownership could be transferred in a jiffy to say Ben with Xylo's property ownership record remaining unchanged. However, the beneficial owner would have shifted from Alexander to Ben without any government registering authority getting to know. The property owner's name, Xylo & Co., just remains on paper, without the traceability of its real owner Ben.

Shell companies could be floated in the names of accountants, lawyers, friends or relatives. And you could be the beneficial owner without anyone getting to know about it.

The existence of shell companies hurts any government's attempt to get access to a foreign jurisdiction to crack down on their own citizens who would have moved money offshore to avoid taxes or launder wealth.

For the really well-heeled folks, interlocking companies is a good way to hide wealth. Company X owns company Y which owns company Z, which in turn owns an aristocratic real estate property.

Sometimes buyers of prized properties use LLCs to hide the identity of the properties' owners.

In 2016, *The New York Times* journalists caught lawyers on hidden camera offering to help move funds with questionable origins through a maze of shell companies.

Strange as it may sound but several countries that target extremist funding and banks that evade economic sanctions still allow the creation of anonymous entities which can hide the real source of funds. Narrow objectives of attracting funds have converted many jurisdictions into tax havens, providing shelter to shell companies.

Tailpiece

Anonymity is the hallmark of shell companies. Legal immunity is its plus point—a possible vehicle for illegal acts.

Raison d'être? Companies after all cannot be locked up in a jail; hence, shell companies are a boon to the money launderers.

Shell Shocked Shell Stakeholders

Investors in India were shell shocked in 2017 when they woke up to the news that stock exchanges had been directed by the market regulator SEBI to initiate action against over 300 suspect shell companies and ban them from trading. Such is the problem with shell companies where regulatory activism can strike suddenly without prior notice.[17]

From the dingy flats in Bara Bazar of Kolkata to the 'chawls' in Kalbadevi, Mumbai, hundreds of shell companies are being opened and deployed to do shady deals of benami transactions, hiding fund source, evading tax and making ownership details ambiguous.

In India, shell companies are sadly not defined. This obviously adds to the mess when it comes to these companies.

The Securities Act in the USA has defined a shell company as one that has no or nominal operations and assets. If at all these companies have assets, it would normally be cash and cash equivalents with very little other assets. The predominantly European organization of OECD has defined a shell company as a firm that is formally registered but does not conduct any operations other than the pass-through capacity.

In order to accelerate its crackdown on money laundering, the Indian government is working on defining a 'shell company'. The lack of a proper definition is impinging upon investigating dubious firms. In essence, a shell firm would not normally have any active business operations or assets.

Wealthy individuals in India and elsewhere sometimes establish shell firms. These exist only on paper and do not have an office or employees. It is used to disguise the ownership of assets or to transfer funds illicitly and avoid taxes. They are structured in such a way that they prevent officials from identifying the actual beneficiaries of transactions.

In view of numerous instances where individuals and businesses have abused shell companies, either to avoid tax or to use them as conduit for money laundering, the regulators generally view these companies as dubious.

In late 2019, the Indian government came down heavily again on companies which appeared to be shells—de-registering over 3.4 lakh companies.[18] Some of these were possibly used for money laundering, tax evasion or other fraudulent activities.

The market regulator sometimes does come down hard on suspect shell companies to protect the investor's interest. Investors tend to lose money while investing in companies practising financial juggleries and set up by wayward promoters for the purpose of money laundering. In the past, many investors have burnt their fingers with companies which have suddenly disappeared into oblivion. Many companies which were listed in India during the IPO boom in 1994–1995 have vanished into thin air. No wonder that the market regulators are reticent on promoters floating companies with the intent to defraud investors.

Tailpiece

Need has now arisen to provide a guideline and identify a uniform set of traits that are common to 'only-on-paper' firms. Or else, many unsuspecting investors could keep getting shocked when their invested companies turn out to be dubious shell outfits.

Legitimate Shell Shelters?

Shell companies may not always be illegitimate.

Multinational business corporations or wealthy individuals may need to set them up for legitimate purposes.

Let us take an example. Many countries permit land to be owned only by citizens or locally registered companies. Hence a foreigner seeking a retirement or vacation home would set up a local shell company to purchase the property. So law-abiding people can own shell companies for limited liability or purchase an asset in a foreign land, or for other boring reasons.

Taking another example, a business wanting to establish a joint venture away from a country with dishonest legal system may need to do so through an offshore company based in places like the Seychelles or Luxemburg. This will entail the venture to gain access to a healthier legal system and stronger courts.

Many shell companies share the same address—and this phenomenon does lead to suspect presence of shady activities. But let me tell you that just because an address is shared between several companies, it does not necessarily mean illegality. For instance, a lot of start-ups opt to work from the same room or location.

However, most shell companies are indeed designed.

Tailpiece

While some shell companies take birth due to genuine reasons, the attraction of secrecy provided by shell companies makes it easy and enticing for many to wander into laundering wealth and tax evasion.

Smart Smurfing

Smurfing is a shrewd move to break up large amounts of cash into smaller parcels. This enables it to become less suspicious while depositing in the banking system. Breaking a larger cash lot into smaller chunks, such that it is under the threshold levels of banking radar so that the deposits are not reported by the banks to the government.

In India, when the limit of reporting is ₹50,000, the launderers would normally break its cash deposits into smaller amounts, and then deposit it into one or more bank accounts. This objective can also be met if curtailed deposits are made by multiple depositors or by a single person over a period of time.

In the USA, the deposit limit is $10,000. This becomes the cut-off limit for deposits by launderers who are trying to escape identification.

Let me give you an example of smurfing which got reported in the Indian press.

A report was submitted against a stock-broking firm suspecting that a large number of cash deposits were made into the company's account and that it was subsequently transferred to another entity of the same company. It was found that both companies had multiple bank accounts, a common address with common persons operating the bank accounts. There were substantial cash transactions among the bank accounts.

The information was passed on to the Central Board of Direct Taxes. They unearthed an all-India network of money laundering through 236 bank accounts. The companies were set up by a chartered accountant to conduct share-broking activities, though there were no such business activities.

The modus operandi involved movement of cash between different companies in small chunks to provide a cloak of legitimacy to ill-gotten wealth. The firms also prepared fake sale and purchase of shares to claim speculative loss or gain of income tax benefits for customers. Smurfing and tax cheating were the games the tricksters were playing.

In another instance, dozens of Barclays bank accounts belonging mainly to Chinese students at UK universities had to be frozen in early 2019, when the regulators observed that millions of pound sterling were flowing through these accounts. It is completely feasible that the students were not even aware what was happening through their bank accounts.[19]

In many instances, payments were made at various cities or towns often several times in one day, even though the students concerned were studying in faraway locations. All of the accounts were with Barclays, which identified the activity as consistent with money laundering.

Most of the payments were purposely kept small to evade activating the bank's anti-money laundering alerts—'smurfing' was the ploy. It could be informal money transfers by criminal groups to get the money out of the country of origin and into the banks of the UK and then use the black money banked for legal purposes routed through the accounts of the unsuspecting students. A similar tactic was used in India when demonetisation took place in 2016. Poor people's bank accounts with almost nil balances were used to deposit small chunks of black money. Then new notes were withdrawn after paying some commission to the account holders.

Tailpiece

Billions of dollars of dirty money are being split into smaller parcels and getting washed through the banking channels every year. It's another ploy to beat the system. Corporate crime is simply getting dirtier and smarter, in spite of thousands of government officers trying to unravel the mystery of missing taxes and establish the trail of dirty money.

Swindlers are skilful and supple. Smurfing is a smart scheme to beat the system.

Offshore Banking

Just imagine that you have loads of money but would not like to subject it to tax so that you can enjoy the spoils in full. Would it not be wonderful if you can somehow send the money to a lovely foreign destination and park it in a bank account which keeps your name secret and the wealth untaxed? The bank account will typically be accessible to you whenever you want either for your ensuing exotic holidays or to make fat investments in friendly geographies. This foreign anonymous bank account is known as offshore bank accounts.

As the name suggests, 'offshore banking' involves having bank accounts located outside the home country in a country where there exists a lax banking and taxation system. They allow for the establishment of accounts from non-resident individuals and corporations. The countries where these bank accounts are opened are usually nil or minimal income tax regimes. These geographies are commonly known as tax havens.

These banking practices are facilitated by many countries allowing anonymous banking. Willy-nilly, the banks located in certain countries having well-developed offshore banking system follow loose anti-money laundering regulations. Fraudsters take advantage of these laxities. Money launderers often send money through various 'offshore accounts' to countries which have banking secrecy laws.

Clients operating through offshore banks sometimes practise hundreds of complex bank transfers to and from these banks, so as to help erasing, as much as is possible, traceability of fund sources.

The prime purpose of tax havens is to allow the super-wealthy people to keep their money in offshore accounts for tax avoidance and other purposes.

These are also known as offshore financial centres. These tax shelters are often small geographies, low-tax jurisdictions in remote locations, like the Caribbean islands. In these places, wealthy individuals often hold money within shell companies and anonymous entities.

Switzerland and the Cayman Islands are the most popular destinations for offshore banking. These names follow a rather long list of tax havens, such as the Bahamas, Barbados, Belize, Bermuda, the British Virgin Islands, Cyprus, Curacao, Dominica, Gibraltar, Ireland, Jersey, Liechtenstein, Luxembourg, Nauru, Malta, Macau, Mauritius, the Marshall Islands, the Netherlands, Panama, Taiwan, Samoa and the Seychelles.

It may be noted that when someone's money is nicely stacked in a tax haven, it is keeping itself outside the tax net. Tax laws in most countries insist that their country residents need to report any offshore bank accounts they may be holding. However, offshore banking institutions are generally not obligated to declare any bank holding to foreign tax authorities because they are protected by banking secrecy laws of the jurisdiction where the bank is located.

Offshore bank accounts thus tend to provide financial and legal benefits and serve the purpose of 'layering' of funds. These benefits include less controlling legal regulation, protection of secrecy regarding bank details including ownership name and amount lying therein, easy fund accessibility and protection against local financial or political instability. Most of these accounts also provide interest income to the depositors. It is a win-win for the money launderers.

Enhanced activism for keeping strict KYC norms is making matters difficult for some. In 2019, Britain's largest retail bank by market share, Lloyds Banking Group, was forced to take action to meet the money laundering rules in the beautiful island of Jersey, where the bank's international business was based.[20] The bank froze the accounts of about 8,000 offshore banking customers as part of a crackdown on money laundering. This action was carried out after failing to receive responses from the bank account holders, in spite of providing them with time of over three years to prove their identity.

Things are getting tougher as the times go by. Those hoping to park their surplus wealth in tax havens and money laundering shelters in offshore accounts will increasingly find that old rules no longer exist. The regulations of offshore banking are changing.

As part of the global fight against tax evasion, tax authorities have developed broad powers to capture information held by financial institutions. These regimes place considerable compliance burden on financial institutions and their customers.

To combat the problem of offshore tax evasion, avoidance and stashing of unaccounted money abroad requiring cooperation among tax authorities, a Common Reporting Standard (CRS) on Automatic Exchange of Information has been developed.

The reporting standard will facilitate the automatic exchange of financial account information across more than 100 participating jurisdictions.

The CRS information to be exchanged relates not only to individuals but also to shell companies and trusts. If you are a tax resident outside the country where you bank, then the bank may give the national tax authority information relating to your accounts. This may then be shared between the tax authorities of different jurisdictions. This means that you may try to get away from the clutches by not being a tax resident in a particular jurisdiction.

The International Monetary Fund is increasingly monitoring the developments in the tax haven banks. The enhanced focus on anti-money laundering initiatives in different countries signify that banks are encouraged to report suspicious transactions to the local authorities, despite the prevalent banking secrecy laws. Police authorities are also working on heightened international cross-border cooperation.

Tailpiece

Offshore banking has traditionally been notorious for money laundering, tax evasion and a possible conduit for organized crime. Increased regulation is however making these acts more difficult to execute.

Unfortunately, there are enough clever people who keep coming up with new ideas to bypass restrictions. Hence, a dogged battle is often being played between the governments and the recalcitrant wealthy.

Offshore banking cannot be taken off from the 'to do' list of many rich and famous, though regulators' tussle will continue to try and leash the so-called unleashable!

Offshore Can Be on Shore

Beautiful and tiny islands, located in far-off lands, need not be the only places to tuck away your murky money. There are onshore locations too, where cash can be comfortably camouflaged.

Dubai and her six emirate sisters are well known for housing rich people's bank accounts, where income tax is virtually non-existent. Ireland and the Netherlands also being low-tax regime countries attract many.

Wealthy Americans need not leave the shores of their home country, with the state of Delaware providing all that an offshore account holder is looking for—low tax and secrecy. Nearly two-thirds of the Fortune 500 companies and over a million companies are incorporated in Delaware—a big reason being its low-tax regime. The states of Wyoming and Nevada, in the western part of the USA, offer Delaware-like facilities. Ownership information may only be obtained by a court order.[21]

Switzerland is, of course, the all-time favourite, though the secrecy around banking is getting penetrated by popular moves by many countries. Hong Kong and Singapore, the low-tax regimes, are attracting some of the accounts of the dismembered Swiss bank account holders.

The heaven of tax havens, in terms of popularity, is, however, the city of London. A relatively low tax rate of 20 per cent has attracted nationalities virtually from every country around the globe. A cosmopolitan setting, great banking structure and well-established legal system provide comfort to many.

Tailpiece

Many tried-and-tested onshore locations providing the facilities of offshore sites are nice and liveable cities. So next time you want to hide some murky money, look at these great places to do the business of veiling (though these thorny theories are best snubbed).

Panamanian Scammer Mossack Fonseca

Discussions on dirty money and money laundering cannot be completed without the mention of the famous but now-defunct Panamanian firm **Mossack Fonseca**.[22]

The business of money laundering involves a lot of players. These are known as the 'professional enablers', who in exchange for a fee will turn a blind eye to the source of cash and who really own it. The key players here are usually the lawyers, bankers, accountants and a loosely regulated but vital part of the chain—fiduciary service providers, like the unscrupulous firm Mossack Fonseca.

This Panama-based law firm was licensed by tax havens to incorporate offshore companies. Its employees acted as nominee directors and shareholders, signing on the paperwork and bank accounts of companies over which they had no real control. This was the way to mask the real owners.

The world's fourth largest offshore law firm would create companies and sell them off, which many criminals comfortably used as a mask for their ill deeds. The firm helped some of the world's wealthiest people establish offshore bank accounts and was the source for a trove of leaked documents known as the 'Panama Papers'.

In essence, these papers exposed how some of the most powerful people of the world may have used offshore bank accounts and shell companies to disguise their wealth or avoid taxes.

In 2016, somehow over 11 million files with 2,600 GB of data, providing information on some 214,000 hidden offshore companies, leaked, creating huge uproar across the globe, putting search lights on some of the rich and famous.

The data included emails, spreadsheets, passports and corporate records, revealing the secret owners of bank accounts and companies in over 20 offshore jurisdictions, from Hong Kong to Dubai to the British Virgin Islands.

The leaked confidential papers point at politicians, business leaders and celebrities. Thousands of entities and shell companies connected with over 200 countries appear in the exposed papers—all involved in webs of suspicious financial transactions.

These disclosures have raised serious questions on covert corruption in the global financial system.

Who were involved?

People named are the who's who of global personalities.

Among many others, the documents named close associates of President Vladimir Putin of Russia, the father of former Prime Minister David Cameron of Britain and relatives of President Xi Jinping of China and members of the Chinese Communist Party's Politburo Standing Committee. Various articles reporting the felony also named King Salman of Saudi Arabia; Sigmundur David Gunnlaugsson, who resigned as the prime minister of Iceland after the revelations; and President Mauricio Macri of Argentina.

The scandal also named several sports personalities linked to firms incorporated offshore through the Panamanian firm. These included the soccer idol Lionel Messi, one of the world's richest sportsperson; officials from FIFA—soccer world's governing body; and UEFA, the governing body of European soccer. Incidentally, the underbelly of dirty money is such that an investigative journalist in Ghana, who worked on uncovering of a high-ranking FIFA official taking bribes, was shot dead by gunmen on a motorbike in early 2019.

As is expected, most of the named people have vehemently denied that they broke any laws. In fact, Putin unabashedly pronounced that it was an American plot to undermine Russian unity when allegations were made that his friends moved a mammoth $2 billion among various shell companies.

Even Britain's ex-Prime Minister Cameron weaved stories when it was found that his father was a client of the Panamanian law firm. Initially, Cameron denied that any benefits were derived from any 'offshore funds', only to confirm later that he and his wife had profited from sale of shares in an offshore trust for £30,000 ($42,000) in 2010, the year he became the prime minister. (It so happens that Cameron avowed that the dividends earned were declared and taxed.)

Did India have its Panama connects?

Wherever there are revelations of shady practices, India willy-nilly gets connected in many cases. The India connection in the Panama Papers leaks may not be substantial but did show glimpses of some wealthy stacking away their wealth in offshore tax havens.

Famous names such as actors Saif Ali Khan, Kareena Kapoor and Karisma Kapoor, along with industrialist Venugopal Dhoot, got linked with an unsuccessful bidding through an offshore consortium, for an Indian Premier League franchise.[23]

Not to end the controversial Bollywood linkage with fame and fortune, the Indian media splashed names of superstars Amitabh Bachchan and Aishwarya Rai being directors of companies in Panama.

The information seepages included the name of the controversial corporate lobbyist Ms Niira Radia, who made headlines for her leaked taped conversation for ministerial portfolios with her clients, including Ratan Tata.[24]

Several industrialists who are large bank defaulters have featured in the leaked documents. Vijay Mallya is alleged to have links with firms mentioned in the Panama Papers; Vijay Choudhary, promoter of Zoom Developers, and Umesh Shahra, promoter of loss-making and highly indebted Ruchi Group, have got their names inked on the Panama Papers. Is it that loans taken from the Indian banks were laundered to the offshore locations? Investigative agencies' show cause notices in many cases point to such mischiefs.

As if 'Panama' was not the only happy haven that 'Bahama Papers' cropped up sometime in September 2016, naming 475 India-related people, trusts and companies registered in the tax haven. Unless a few big guns are included, it does not make big news. Some big fish did get hooked up: Vedanta group's Anil Agarwal, erstwhile Baron Group's Kabir Mulchandani and Fashion TV India promoter Aman Gupta.[25]

Tailpiece

Panama Papers disclosures were all about the efforts of global elites to avoid tax on their wealth and to launder it into offshore locations mainly through shell companies. In spite of the 2016 largest-ever leakage of shady records, unfortunately both sides of *The Atlantic* are yet to make failproof regulations and legal framework to discourage and desist laundering by the superrich.

The last words on money laundering, offshore hideouts and shell companies are yet not spoken. We can still expect to hear about and encounter a lot more on tax avoidance and laundering—sadly though!

Turn Black Money into White

Messy money has a dirty problem. How to use unaccounted for wealth when investing in a fairly large asset? Small expenses like settling restaurant bills in cash is not a problem. The challenge arises when you want to buy a home or a car. The full payments are difficult to settle in cash.

Thus, you need good money to make payments through the banking channel, like issuing cheques or through bank transfer.

Black money is nothing but undeclared cash on which no tax has been paid. How to convert the ill-gotten wealth into accounted money, commonly known as white money? Some popular methods used are cited below.

- *Temples tamper truth:* It is understood that many temples in India are willing to convert black money donated in hundis or donation boxes into white money on deducting a nice commission. Say you deposit cash of ₹50 lakh ($67,000) with a temple. They may be willing to give you back ₹40 lakh ($53,000) by means of a cheque.

  You will need to issue a bill on the temple for either rendering a service or supplying some goods. It is easy if you are a consultancy firm. You can easily raise an invoice for providing consultancy to the temple trust. And the rest is cool—bad money turns into easy money through divine intervention!

  Let me cite an example. ABP News reported a sting operation in which the priest of Govardhan Temple in Mathura was willing to convert ₹50 lakh of black money into white for a

20 per cent commission.[26] The Almighty was perhaps in an obliging mood!

- *Giving advances to the needy:* A nice way to convert black money is by giving loans to the poor. On the garb of helping the destitute, these poor people would return the money after keeping a small portion for the services rendered. On receiving the money back, it is banked showing receipt of accounted funds.

- *Bogus loans:* Showing fake loans is a popular method. Black money can be given to a friend or relative. This can be taken back by way of a loan through bank transfer or a cheque. This amounts to a bogus loan entry to convert black money to white. Sometimes, the loan taken is also repaid by giving back cheques, just to show more credibility behind the counterfeit transactions.

- *Money laundering shells:* There are several shell companies across India and most famously in Kolkata, where money can enter and move out in a jiffy. In local language, it is also called *jama-kharchi* or *pad-pedi* books. The shell company could have a business-like look (say a restaurant) and logistics to back, where cash is the king. Deposits of cash can be made in these accounts by people holding black money. The shell firms will then make investment or expenditure bookings, transferring funds into your allotted company. These investments can be taken by you as white money, as there is a source identified.

- *Handy farmers:* Agricultural income is not taxed in India. Unaccounted for money can sometimes be easily attributed to farming sources. The only requirement is that there should be some agricultural land somewhere in India, whether generating income or not. It is reported that a lot of politicians' wealth is attributed to agricultural income, which necessarily remains untaxed.

- *Uncharitable charity trust:* Charitable trusts could sometimes be a wonderful way to tell lies. In these cases, the trustees would normally consist of family members or friends including drivers and servants. Black money is distributed to these friends and relatives, who in turn will give it back to the charitable trust as contributions for a social cause—all sham and bogus. A lot of black money gets converted into white this way.
- *Jeweller's helping hand:* Black money can be handed over to your friendly neighbourhood jeweller. He would in turn give you a purchase bill and a cheque, subtracting his commission, showing that you have sold him your personal jewellery. Of course, in India there will be a levy of GST (Goods and Services Tax), a small price to pay for the conversion. Black money gets transformed into white smoothly.
- *Gift from relatives:* Black money can be handed over to your friends and relatives. They would in turn transfer money through the banking channel as gifts to you. Clearly, you now have official money in your bank account, ostensibly because your relatives love and respect you.
- *Bank accounts for relatives:* Open bank accounts in the name of your family members. Deposit your black money in these accounts—not large sums, as it may attract attention of the taxmen for them to raise alarm on the source of income of your relatives. The money now lying in the bank accounts of your relatives will be treated as squeaky clean!
- *Good investments through bad money:* Dirty money can be used to make investments such as insurance policies, public provident fund or fixed deposits. Needless to mention that deposits in cash over ₹50,000 will attract the necessity to produce the PAN (taxpayer identification card) and thus do not work for depositing a large quantum of black money in India. Hence, this method can be useful by making multiple deposits over several days of small amounts.

- *Real estate is really good:* The hot bed of hiding black money is the real estate, especially in India. Thirty–forty per cent of contractual price is often paid through black money. Good tangible assets get created by using bad money.
- *Use black for small white reasons:* A good way of using some portion of your black money accumulation is by using it for your daily needs—shopping, eating out, holidaying and travelling. This will help to reduce some of your black money aches.

You have understood how many turn their black wealth into white money, using some popular modus operandi. But what is the recommended way to convert bad dough into good money?

The best method to clean up your dirty stable of unaccounted for wealth is to declare the black money being held and pay the applicable taxes, together with interest and penalty, if payable. In addition, the government from time to time declares amnesty schemes to come clean with the dirty money—a great opportunity to take advantage of declaring untaxed money and pay taxes on it—a wonderful way to become a good and responsible citizen of your beloved country.

Tailpiece

For unaccounted money stackers, it's often a game of piling currency and jewellery in offices and homes, hidden in secret chambers in walls, inside idols of gods and in bathrooms, or just laundering it elsewhere.

For the taxmen, black money hunting is like looking for the 'Yeti' (the Himalayan snowman) where the footprints are there but the subject is elusive.

Governments keep trying to plug loopholes to stop the obstinate from illegitimately converting bad bucks into white wealth. On the other hand, some wealthy folks keep playing tricks to hide wealth from the snooping taxmen.

Unfortunately, the cat and mouse game is likely to go on forever!

White Money into Black Money

Recently, a Pune-based automobile parts manufacturer was found to possess ₹13 lakh ($17,000) in new notes—converting legitimate business income into black money.[27] His Kalyani Nagar posh residence, when raided, had cash stashed up. The company's purchase agent used to raise bills for supply of auto parts, which the industrialist used to pay for through banking channel. The agent would then withdraw the money from the bank accounts and hand over the cash to the businessman. It was found to be a ₹200 crore ($27 million) scam. One does not know why the entrepreneur was collecting so much cash—maybe to pay big bribes (₹20 crore or $3 million of illegitimate duty drawback claim was also found to have been collected by the industrialist).

Corporates may sometime need black money. It is usually needed to pay bribes to connected persons including bureaucrats and politicians. Black money could also be required for buying a real estate, where the builder insists on receiving a portion in black to avoid stamp duties.

How does a business dealing with proper invoices and taxable funds convert a portion of the money into black?

- *Proper expenses for cash payback:* A popular method is to get an invoice from a service provider, say a customs house agent or a training company. Banking channel will be used to pay the vendor bill by the company wanting to gain some black money. The service provider will return the amount in cash after deducting commission, which could be 5–15 per cent. Here, the white money gets converted into black. It works when the other side (the service provider in this case) possesses black money, which it wishes to convert into white. Money to be interchanged in this method is unlikely to be large.
- *Ponzi or multilevel scheme, money laundered:* You have heard of the common scam where many get sucked into the lure of making quick money. It is the Ponzi or pyramid schemes. In this instance, people contribute to a phantom scheme, where

the organizers would conjure up a credible story with the bait of high interest or dividend rates.

The money collected from the commoners, which mostly will be white, could then be laundered abroad. The white money in one jurisdiction could become black in another offshore location, say Dubai or the British Virgin Islands. The money could either be used by investing in assets like condos or be layered into the banking system through shell companies to make it white for onward use.

- *Set off loss against profitable business:* Some entrepreneurs have several businesses, with one or two making profits and others incurring losses. While paying taxes, most jurisdictions will allow to set off losses of one business against profits of another.

Say one business earns a profit of $10 million and another incurs a loss of $12 million, then the group as a whole does not have to pay any tax, as at a group level, there is a loss of $2 million. This overall loss can incidentally be carried forward for setting off against next year's income from businesses.

In this instance, though there is white income, declaring losses enables them to generate funds without paying taxes—sort of extra money, though legal.

- *Exports underpriced:* Underpricing invoicing is a nice way to generate black money in a foreign location. Say a firm exports stainless steel goods worth $100 million. The exporter prices these at $90 million (it is difficult often for the customs or the country's central bank to establish exact price of goods due to their varied specifications).

The exporter enters into an understanding that out of the reduced price of $10 million ($100 million actual price less $90 million invoiced), $8 million will need to be transferred into an offshore bank account and the rest $2 million can be retained by the importer as his commission.

This white transaction provides several benefits. The importer pays lower customs duty while importing the goods, earns a commission and the exporter generates unaccounted money overseas. Not an uncommon practice in the world of business. Reverse also happens when imports are under invoiced.

Black into white or white into black, the reasons for converting money depends on the type of fraudsters involved and the reasons for doing so. The bulk of the con game however is played to create more tainted money—income escaping the tax net by misleading the taxmen.

These con jobs are getting weightier and burlier, with corporates and their managers continuing to delude the system to make some extra bucks.

Few Last Words

The world of tricksters has figured out methods to carry out illegitimate ways of making money. The ways and means are too many. This book is not intended to delineate all types of wrongful practices. My purpose is to provide you with a glimpse into the world of business crimes, which is moving furiously fast—be it money laundering, hiding behind shell companies or converting dirty money into white.

Knowledge is power; and if you can recognize some of the illicit practices going around, it should enable you to remain more careful and cautious. Or is it helping you to be complicit in these grimy games (pun intended)?

It must be hastened to add that I would definitely not recommend anyone to practise the conversion of hard-earned white money into polluted cash, and vice versa. Nor would I advise anyone to launder money and move it to shell companies and tax havens for illicit purposes. This is not the purpose for anyone of us to exist.

Chances of getting caught in the vortex of illicit acts are bright. With police exchanging information, using AI and analysing big data, their net is getting wider and larger. While many swindlers will perhaps continue to follow dishonest means to hoodwink the state and its people, the crooked practices are avoidable and not worth the risk.

Will the world ever get free of the obnoxious human behaviour of the wealthy and their connivers? Unlikely, as many would continue to harbour the desire to get rich by hook or by crook.

CHAPTER EIGHT

Ponzi Schemes

A very popular show 'Hamilton' won the Tony Award for best new musical in 2016. It set a record for the most money grossed in a week by a Broadway show. The ticket price skyrocketed, with seats particularly hard to get.[1] The demand created a robust resale market, with tickets regularly listed at thousands of dollars. And crooks took advantage of the situation.

Two New York men, Joseph Meli and Matthew Harriton, conjured up a scheme built on a false promise to buy and resell tickets in high-profile events like the 'Hamilton', to gain millions of dollars by conning investors.

The men apparently raised about $80 million from at least 125 investors in the USA, who were told that their money was being pooled to buy large blocks of tickets to be resold for a profit. Instead, what they did was to use the major portion of the money— about $50 million—to repay earlier investors, propagating the mirage of a profitable investment scheme.

In written contracts, the two men promised investors that they would see a 10 per cent annual return on their investments in a country where people may find difficult to get returns of more than 3–4 per cent. It was a typical Ponzi scheme—borrowing from Peter to pay Paul. (The two men were charged by the police in January 2017.)

A classic Ponzi story is fabricated by stitching a believable money-making proposition. More credible the story and more trustworthy the conjurers, more money gets put in by gullible investors.

Ponzi con games are being played for long. The scheme's current name comes from Charles Ponzi, whose investment scam a century ago involved millions of dollars.

It has now been a decade since Bernard Madoff was caught running the biggest Ponzi scheme in history,[2] a scandal where gullible investors were taken for a $65 billion ride! This case became a cautionary story for investors and regulators the world over.

Have things changed? Are people showing less greed and have they stopped putting in money in the fantasizing world of scamsters? The sad news is: No. In the USA alone, according to *The New York Times* analysis, the market regulator has prosecuted 50 per cent more schemes in the last decade than what was detected the decade before. Other geographies will not have a very different experience.

The schemers have altered their falsehood tales. Instead of articulating on great market beating stocks and commodity strategies, nowadays recipes on investment opportunities in cryptocurrencies and natural resources are being baked and marketed.

Recently, widowed Ms Sioux Schaefer, a horse trainer and photographer from California, was wondering how to bequeath an inheritance to her daughter. A friend told her about investing in gold mines with a sociable Cornell University graduate of a Los Angeles investment company, **Christian Stanley Inc**.

As she spoke with Stanley Powell, the founder of the company, on phone, they bonded well over their shared love for horses. He promised her a 10 per cent return on her money, and she gave him $175,000.[3]

Powell's promised dividend payments never arrived. False promises of gold mines, coal leases and a business for which he had trademarked the term 'reverse life insurance' never fructified. Instead, Powell used the new investors' money to pay the old—shaving off healthy cuts to buy an expensive apartment, fancy cars and luxury items like $5,000 cowboy boots.

It was another typical milking scheme by smooth-speaking scamsters who are now trying to wrap in new schemes to provide confidence to new investors—spinning new ideas to rip off investors. Just to make things more believable, scamsters are now announcing modest returns as opposed to promising astronomical returns—fabricating fine fiction!

Ponzi schemes—be it headline making or creating headaches for a few gullible investors—the contours are the same: They use new investors to pay the old ones.

The ploy has always thrived on the principle of pulling in an initial group of investors, large enough to attract attention but not too big—then a larger second group, whose investments can be used to pay off the first. It goes on to a still larger third group and so on. If things go well, stories about success of the initial investors will go round, making the subsequent groups eager not to miss the bus of making some fast bucks. This attracts more people. As long as the chain remains intact, sceptics will be silenced. This will go on well until the bluff balloon bursts abruptly. And it eventually does rupture!

In essence, a Ponzi scheme does not buy anything real. Early investors get paid with the deposits of later ones, while the latter ones see their gains only on paper until they attempt to cash out.

The Psyche

White attire, greying stubble and constant reference to Allah and the Qur'an, Mohammed Mansoor Khan radiated the aura of a decent and devout person. Through various YouTube videos and advertisements where Khan appeared himself, he convinced investors to invest in his various enterprises as business partners.

Over the years, he weaved a web of deceit. With the money he collected, Khan opened large jewellery showrooms, including the ones in the affluent South Bengaluru, opened pharmacies selling medicines at discounted rates and started hospitals—all adding to his image of a successful affluent businessman.

Khan did not stop here to gain investors' confidence. He arranged to pay the depositors exactly on the last day of every month through bank transfers, deducted 10 per cent tax at source and even submitted the Income Tax returns in Form 16. With all these acts, how can anyone believe that a con game is getting hatched!

The story continued. Khan pitched himself to his Muslim clientele that his business is in accordance with the sharia law, with payments coming from business profits and not interest on investments.

He had air-conditioned offices with smooth-speaking executives, promising returns of 3 per cent per month. The old and the young and the poor and ailing travelled great distances to deposit money with his Bengaluru-based enterprise, named **I-Monetary Advisory (IMA)**—a whopping sum of ₹4,000 crore ($530 million) from over 40,000 investors.[4]

Hell broke loose in June 2019, when investors stopped receiving their interest. The IMA chain of fresh investors somehow snapped and Khan fell short of collections to make the sham returns to investors.

It was a typical Ponzi scheme by a soothsayer, spinning religious stories of helping the minorities, gaining confidence through his suave looks, religious utterances, marketing skills, long association with the community and fabricating tales of extraordinary returns—to swindle the naive, looking for the quick buck. (Khan has since been arrested.) It is a typical instance of fooling a large community by a con craftsman.

Mould the malleable clay of human frailty, add greed and dishonesty to it, mix smartness, eloquence and confidence of the perpetrator, and you would have formed the basic psych and structure of carrying out a financial Ponzi scheme.

Tricks to instil confidence, where victims are fleeced over many months by someone they trust, often begin with the con artist offering companionship and compassion to someone who is in distress. The tricksters then convert this trust into gullibility—reposing belief without reasonable evidence.

This is what usually happens in a Ponzi game too. The perpetrators with stories stitched around highly credible business plans gain confidence of investors.

Ponzi schemes would normally prey on close-knit associates of victims or affinity groups, which the fraud perpetrators are either already connected with or can tap into.

Most fraudsters will look good and speak well. The tricksters start gaining confidence of a few starters, who in turn will vouch for the scheme's so-called authenticity, only to lure many more within the con game vortex. Wishful thinking often takes us far astray.

A typical Ponzi scheme also has its subtleties. Everyone cannot pull off one. It requires cleverness, calculation and charisma. It entails using some sort of psychic influence—skill of the scamster's mind to leverage someone else's.

Tailpiece

Ponzi is a game of swindling through sensory subterfuge, trapping the unsuspecting by make believe tale telling. The duping game continues unabated till today. In fact, hoodwinking is mounting in the Ponzi world, with defrauding becoming larger, deeper and knottier.

Swanky Splashy Scamsters

While money was flowing in from investors, Scott Rothstein, a USA-based lawyer, was extravagant in his spending habits. He bought his wife more than $1 million in jewellery, including a lavish 12-carat yellow diamond ring. He lived in a multimillion-dollar waterfront mansion and regularly wrote big cheques to charities and politicians.[5]

But the good life ended in 2009, when the government accused him of defrauding investors of up to $400 million with a Ponzi scheme based on selling stakes in legal settlements. (Both Rothsteins went to jail.)

It's a similar story everywhere. These high-flying lifestyle habits are usually displayed by the architects of Ponzi schemes.

Most of these scamsters display a veneer of prosperity which can be convincing to investors. They are individuals who are very adept in persuading people of the stories they have strung. They live in nice houses, drive nice cars and appear to be very successful. You will hardly find any instance where these success trappings are missing.

A Ponzi scheme organizer, Brian Callahan, who lived lavishly on Long Island, USA, pleaded guilty in 2014 after collecting $118 million from dozens of investors, including a local fire department, who were informed that their money would go into mutual funds, hedge funds and securities.[6] Instead, he invested in a beachfront resort and spent money on lavish houses and cars. (Callahan is facing up to 40 years in prison.)

In another instance, a New York restaurateur cheated investors of over $12 million in a Ponzi scheme involving a fictitious wholesale liquor business.[7] Hamlet Peralta, who owned the Hudson River Cafe in Harlem, used the money he misappropriated to pay off debts to other investors and to fuel a luxurious lifestyle that included expensive clothing, spas and restaurant meals. The restaurateur got caught and pleaded guilty in 2017.

These are rather common stories where the fraudster is able to swindle millions from unsuspecting investors who trust him because of his reputation in the community as a business owner or other activities.

Most Ponzi conspirators will have confidence-building qualities and will be self-assured, showy, suave and smooth-speaking. They would find investors among people they meet at clubs or parties or at religious functions. The game is all about trust factor, which is taken advantage of in these kinship frauds. No wonder that normal verfications is given a pass in these cases by the unsuspecting investors.

Tailpiece

The conspirators of Ponzi and pyramid schemes will normally dazzle the gullible through their flashy lifestyles and persuasive talks. They will paint grandiose business plans, convincing enough to communicate that fabulous returns are plausible.

If due diligence is not done, getting into the honey trap is imminent. If you cannot identify the red flag, then remember what you had heard when you were a child: 'Don't take candies from strangers.'

Scandals Start Small

The unfortunate truth of human behaviour is that ethical conduct may erode over time. Many of the biggest business scandals—siphoning off millions from Tyco International by the bosses, Adelphia Communication's bankruptcy by diverting funds to other family-owned entities, billion-dollar losses by speculative rogue traders at the Barings Bank and the LIBOR manipulations at the Barclays bank—have followed a similar pattern, starting small to explode later.[8]

Most Ponzi schemes are no different. Little transgressions start with small money taken with the promise to be repaid soon. The promised returns are then paid only through fresh money. More faith gets reposed on new investors with emerging stories of earlier players being paid the assured returns. And when this chain snaps, the scheme implodes.

Bernard Madoff, the perpetrator of the largest ever Ponzi fraud, started small. He had two businesses: a 'penny stock' brokerage and a 'wealth management' outfit. He was a highly respected entrepreneur—with the electronic trading software program developed by him eventually adopted by the NASDAQ. He, in fact, became the chairman of this world's second largest stock exchange in 1990. Although an acknowledged businessman, it beats the logic why he conjured up the Ponzi game through his wealth management outfit. He, accepting first small doses of investment, promised investors extraordinary returns. However, he straightaway deposited the investor money received into his personal bank account at the Chase Manhattan Bank. He paid his 'earlier' investors using money from 'later' investors. He fudged clients' trading statements showing attractive profit numbers. He got caught in 2008, after over two decades of fooling the system. (Madoff was eventually sentenced to a 150-year prison term in 2009, breathing his last in April 2021.)

Charles Ponzi, after whom the ill-famed Ponzi scheme is named, also began small with the great idea to arbitrage the postal stamp market. Way back in 1920, Charles figured out the power of 'postal reply coupons', where the letter recipient can send a mail back home, or anywhere in the world. It was a time when millions of European refugees flocked to America, Canada and Brazil, leaving their family behind. Their only solace was a mail now and then, with a few dollars enclosed perhaps. Folks back home longed for the letters, clutching it like sacred paper. Charles conjured up a scheme surrounding these small-value postal reply coupons, promising 50 per cent return in 45 days. He told investors that he was able to take advantage of fluctuating currency values to purchase international postal reply coupons at a discount and then sell them at face value in the USA at a super profit. (Charles Ponzi was arrested in August 1920, spending several in-and-out prison stints. He died penniless in 1949.)

Both started small scale and eventually slipped into gargantuan phony schemes.

The overwhelming desire to get rich overnight has helped the invention of both 'Ponzi' and 'pyramid' schemes.

Both these schemes sit on deceiving the investors from the onset. Phantom schemes and fictitious stories are fabricated up to light the fire of desire in the greedy. The deceit continues till new money is received to pay the old money.

Ponzi and pyramid schemes are somewhat similar. Ponzi collects new money to pay the earlier investors by knitting fake stories, while the pyramids depend upon multiplying members through a chain of new members being brought in by the earlier members.

Both make tall promises about non-existent business models. These schemes usually come to light during tough times when their continuously fooling people, through intoxicating hopes of high returns, dries up. By definition, both the schemes will collapse. The question always is: When will they end?

Despite efforts by the government authorities, these scams still surface with habitual regularity all over the world.

US regulators say that a new Ponzi scheme operator is found nearly every week, and legal actions are brought against about 100 such questionable investment operations every year. Other countries are not far behind, except that the success of catching these fraudsters vary from one geography to another.

The menace just keeps multiplying. In March 2016, the Indian finance minister reported in the Parliament that around 160 companies had vanished after raising public money. India's Parliament (Lok Sabha) member Kirit Somaiya had announced in January 2016 that there were over 200 Ponzi schemes involving a whopping ₹400,000 crore ($65 billion) still in operation in the country.[9]

Tailpiece

Millions have already been siphoned off by weaving white lies of make believe schemes. As you read this piece, somewhere in the world a new Ponzi scheme is getting hatched to eat away the savings of the naive and innocent.

It is a sheer hocus pocus that people get into by harbouring dreams of becoming rich overnight. Just shun it, even if the contribution required is small and the scheme is looking credible and convincing!

Paltry Ponzi Recoveries

A decade back, one of the biggest Ponzi schemes in history started unravelling in the USA. The Securities and Exchange Commission

(SEC) charged Texas native Allen Stanford with 'a fraud of shocking magnitude'. He eventually went to prison for stealing $7 billion.[10]

The deception was built largely on retail investors including teachers, nurses, firefighters and public servants. Enticed by the promise of safe securities that offered robust returns, countless working families and retirees suffered when the story turned out to be a house of cards.

The tragedy is that in most cases, the recoveries made for the victims, many of whom lose almost everything, are anaemic.

Even after 10 years, less than $600 million of the $7 billion have been recovered for the ordinary savers who trusted Allen Stanford.

The trustees pursuing recoveries for investors in the famous **Bernard Madoff**'s high-profile Ponzi scheme have tracked down $13 billion of the $19 billion of approved claims lost, which wealthy investors had entrusted him with starting as long since the 1980s.[11] This recovery is after a decade when the phantom scheme got unearthed during the 2008 financial crisis.

Madoff pleaded guilty. His five top aides were also convicted. As destiny would have it, his sons, who worked for him, are dead—one hanged himself and the other died of cancer. Madoff's wife, Ruth, is living in a rented home in Connecticut, USA. In spite of convictions, only 70 per cent of the lost money could be recovered—and it's an unusually high number.

Another instance of moderate recovery is the infamous **Rose Valley** holiday membership Ponzi scam, which played havoc mostly in the eastern part of India.[12] Out of the ₹17,500 crore ($2.3 billion) lost, the enforcement agencies reported recovery of ₹10,500 crore ($1.4 billion) by the end of 2020, after 6 years of probe and recovery efforts.

Historic experience shows that recoveries in Ponzi schemes range from 10 to 30 per cent, and many victims do not even get anything.

While the Ponzi scamsters have kept changing their tactics over time, one thing unfortunately has remained constant—most victims do not get their money back. Once duped, most remain deprived.

Tailpiece

Ponzi schemes usually get caught when a tough economic situation prevails. A recession is a good time for Ponzis to be unravelled. When people are hard on cash during economic downturns, edgy investors want to encash assets they have. A Ponzi investment is perhaps an early nut to get cracked with redemption requests. When the conniver is unable to raise further money, the scheme crashes, crackling down without giving people much hope for recoveries.

When the greedy put their money invested in a Ponzi scheme in good faith, only grief is what they unfortunately receive!

Blockchain Ponzi

Blockchain, crypto and virtual currency are buzzwords to confuse and attract unsuspecting retail investors. This is especially true when Ponzi scheme stories get stitched around these unduly complicated and opaque propositions.

To cite an example, the Chinese government has warned against such tricks being used to entice depositors, misrepresenting the schemes as innovative financial solutions.[13] The China Banking and Insurance Regulatory Commission and other agencies jointly declared in 2018 that many investment schemes 'are not really based on blockchain technology but are hyping the neo concept to raise funds illegally'. The logic behind the caution was that when financing schemes declare 'value will only rise, never fall' and 'high return, low risk', these are characteristics of Ponzi fraud. (In September 2021, China banned trading in cryptocurrencies and its mining[14]).

In the post COVID-19 era, thousands of forex trading, cryptocurrency and Bitcoin related Ponzi schemes have been unveiled globally, especially in India. Without the mandatory cryptocurrency regulation, scammers keep looting investors by promising huge returns.

Several novel methods have been devised by the intelligent fraudsters to dupe people by using crypto jargon and lure.

The promoters of cryptocurrency firm **OneCoin**[15] defrauded investors of $4 billion by convincing them that their non-existent digital asset was real. This site claimed that it will take advantage of price differences on various cryptocurrency exchanges to profit from what is called arbitrage—simply buying cheap and selling at higher prices. Unfortunately, they took the investors' money and vanished. It wasn't even a Ponzi; it was a loot.

In another instance, a scam web portal **Bitconnect** used a 'bot' (automated software) on Telegram messaging app.[16] The investors could send a balance enquiry message only to receive fabricated messages showing balances climbing by 1 per cent every day. Just think: $1,000 stashed away into Bitconnect investment account could net you more than $50 million within three years, assuming that the scheme lasts as long. With returns looking like that on paper, how could you not have people going bonkers in sharing the golden news with their acquaintances? Another swindle smarter than standard Ponzi.

'Initial coin offering' is another technique to con people. This is a typical way for start-up cryptocurrency companies to raise funds from its future users. In exchange for active cryptocurrencies like Bitcoin, these initial customers are promised discount on new crypto coins. However, several of these have been fake, even renting phony offices and creating fancy publicity materials—a horrible way to fool the unsuspecting!

In another massive crypto scam, Amit Bhardwaj was touted as a cryptocurrency guru in India. He ran a slew of ventures, including **GainBitcoin, GBMiners, MCAP** and **GB21**.[17] Posing as a crypto expert, he launched a book *Cryptocurrency for Beginners*. The publication was promoted on social media by Bollywood actors such as Shilpa Shetty and Neha Dhupia. Bhardwaj held promotional events in Dubai, with celebrities like Sunny Leone in attendance.

Bhardwaj's story was simple. He flaunted himself as a technology expert, gaining confidence of investors with his grasp, glamour and glitz, conning gullible middle-class investors. He suddenly ran away with over ₹2,000 crore ($270 million), leaving thousands in the lurch. (Bhardwaj got arrested at Bangkok airport in April 2018 and was brought to India to face trial.)

If you look at the crypto Ponzi stories, you will observe that most have spun a variant of hope though fake from the beginning. The deception adventures are numerous. Many are the instances where the naive have been ensnared in the unknown of the new known. The crypto universe is usually unfamiliar and ungoverned. Most do not understand the inner workings. It is critical that investors find out who are involved behind the crypto offerings and understand the credibility of the plan for making real money.

Tailpiece

Cryptocurrencies have often been branded a Ponzi, a tax dodge or an economic misadventure—and it's a fraction of the condemnations that some regulators have thrown in.

Whether the aspersions are correct or not, only time will say. Till then, without proper due diligence and the ability to fathom the probable bottomless pit, do not engage yourself into the cryptocurrency's potential black hole!

Pyramidal Pyramids

The 20-year-old nutritional supplement provider and multilevel marketing company **AdvoCare International** was having its Texas sales conference in 2018.[18] To make the proceedings striking, it had a famous face speaking on the occasion: former US President George W. Bush.

But there was more to the nutritional supplement provider than what could meet the eyes. In October 2019, AdvoCare was fined $150 million for operating an illegal pyramid scheme which deceived customers into thinking that they could earn significant income as distributors of its products. The Texas-based company was also banned from the multilevel marketing business.

It has been alleged that for years, AdvoCare recruited thousands of consumers across the USA to market its health products. The company promised 'the average person a financial solution that will enable them to earn unlimited income'.

Apparently, however, AdvoCare pushed participants to recruit distributors rather than sell products, instructing them to make exaggerated claims about how much money people could make through commissions. Most distributors did not earn any compensation.

It is well known that legitimate businesses make money selling products and services. But money cannot be made by recruiting further sales personnel, especially where there is very little to sell in reality.

The drive to recruit, when coupled with deceptive and inflated income claims, is the hallmark of an illegal 'pyramid scheme'.

The AdvoCare settlement echoes a similar sentence meted out by the regulators a few years ago to **Herbalife,** a USA-based nutritional supplement provider. The company paid $200 million to settle allegations that it deceived buyers and sellers of its products. In that case, the regulator however stopped short of labelling the operation a pyramid scheme. Incidentally, the company continues.

The pyramid scheme assumes an ever-growing layer of new recruits to provide gains to earlier investors. It's all about multiplying numbers through a chain of new members being brought in by old members. This is bound to fail sometime as it is not possible to assume that new members will continue to be brought in for infinite time.

Normally, fraudsters go to great lengths to make their programmes look like a legitimate multilevel marketing one, like Tupperware parties or Amway meets. But the illicit ones use the money coming in from new recruits to pay off early-stage 'investors'. Eventually, the pyramid collapses.

Tailpiece

A pyramid scheme is somewhat similar to a Ponzi structure. Both make promises about non-existent businesses or investment schemes. The returns are paid out of subsequent inflow of fresh funds. As long as fresh funds keep coming in, the fraudulent arrangement continues to dupe the gullible.

The Indian Ponzi Party

The general public often gets enamoured by soothsayers and super stories of quick-rich schemes. India is a hot hunting ground for such crooks.

How good looking and well-dressed brothers can slowly but surely build an empire of fantasized trust—**Goodwin Jewellers**—is a classic example. With 12 fancy outlets in Mumbai, Pune and Kerala, the scamsters Sunilkumar Mohanan and Sudhirkumar Mohanan were gaining customer confidence over two decades.[19] They would arrange lavish opening ceremonies for their flashy retail shops with star personalities attending. They promised 16–20 per cent return on deposits, with money being returned during Diwali. In 2019, just when Diwali season arrived, one fine morning the shops were found shut. How can a jewellery shop close without prior notice at the peak of the festive season? Complaints to police made no difference. Seven hundred depositors were duped of ₹20 crore or $3 million! (The brothers were arrested in December 2019.)

'Gold is golden forever' is the Indian psyche. Taking advantage of this mindset, whether it was Mumbai's Goodwin Jewellers or Bengaluru's IMA jewels, they all took advantage of the golden weakness for gold. A lot of people keep investing their hard-earned money with their goldsmiths to get good returns.

Regular gold schemes encourage depositors to deposit certain amounts monthly. After a year, gold equal to the value of the deposits are handed over usually with a bonus, which could typically be the thirteenth month's instalment being free. While these schemes look innocuous, scamsters misuse the trust bestowed through this long-practised business structure.

Let me tell you another story of a huge heist. Avva Venkata Rama Rao wanted to get rich fast. He had some wonderful assets—his seven brothers! All joined hands to fool the general public with a promise of providing developed plots and farm lands. They promised depositors to withdraw their investments whenever they wanted at a high return. They even set up over 150 companies and named them as the **AgriGold Group of Companies**.[20]

Rao and team spread themselves wide. They spun their counterfeit tales in a very wide catchment area, including states like Odisha, Tamil Nadu, Maharashtra, Andaman and Nicobar Islands and Chhattisgarh. They engaged thousands of commission agents for hefty commission. And lo and behold, they managed to collect about ₹6,400 crore ($850 million) from over 32 lakh investor accounts. However, investors neither got their plots nor their money back—a typical Ponzi payback.

You may not be surprised to know that the perpetrators' names figured in the 'Paradise Papers' exposures (global data on offshore holdings of various entities that leaked in 2017). The fraudsters took help of the infamous law firm Mossack Fonseca to register their massive web of shell companies in the Cayman Islands to launder the ill-gotten wealth. (Three of the promoters got arrested in December 2020 and properties worth ₹4,000 crore [$530 million] were attached.)

High-profile Ponzi frauds continue to get breaking-news space and yet people keep forgetting it when the next scheme gets floated by another con artist. The egregious **Sahara**,[21] which for years sponsored the flamboyant Indian cricket team spending millions, purportedly swindled ₹36,000 crore ($5.5 billion) through perhaps a heady mix of money laundering and Ponzi.

Schemes like **Speak Asia** (₹2000 crore or $265 million), **Saradha** (₹4,000 crore or $530 million) and **Rose Valley** (₹17,000 crore or $2.2 billion) are all under investigation and yet none are anywhere near closure. In fact, when Saradha scam investigations were on, West Bengal Chief Minister Mamata Banerjee went to the extent of staging a sit-in protest against the questioning of former Kolkata Police Commissioner, Rajeev Kumar, for his alleged involvement in the scam.[22]

Get-rich schemes attract Indian people like honey bees to flowers. It is said that over ₹5 lakh crore ($67 billion) have been siphoned off by the crooks in India over the past few decades. Yet nothing seems to have changed in terms of Indians' enduring fascination towards conjured up stories of becoming rich quickly.

Tailpiece

India is a hot bed for Ponzi. With millions looking to eke out some extra income, the shrewd and skilful masqueraders are forever spinning stories of hope, though they are all bluffs. Swindle stories keep getting sewed—make believe business plans, promise of high returns, gaudy business infrastructure and slow building of trust over time.

The Indian fraud opera contains potent Ponzi parties with golden beats of con artists and heady mix of hope plus promise.

Top Red Flags

When a business scheme sounds too good to be true, alarm bells should ring. The top warning sign is the promise of high returns with low risk, or suspiciously consistent returns. Markets will always sway up and down. No business scheme can ever give high returns consistently with low risk. If any scheme is claiming to the contrary, in all probability they are fibbing.

The person who will perhaps be selling you the phony schemes will be unregulated or unregistered. To depict authenticity, the defrauders would normally ask you to furnish KYC documents and fill up elaborate forms. Do not be impressed by the quantum of paperwork or the various letterheads, stamps and seals you see on the docket. Simply ask whether the agent and the investment scheme being peddled are registered under any government bodies like SEBI (market regulator), IRDAI (insurance regulator) or PFRDA (pension regulator).

When you are being promised a particular return, say 20 per cent, there should be publicly available evidence that the scheme is indeed giving these sorts of returns. If you are investing in a public deposit of a reputed company, there would be independent websites carrying the interest figures. The same should be applicable to the scheme being offered to you. No anecdotal evidence works—do not accept the examples of your neighbour receiving the returns.

Keep yourself away from high-sounding profitable investment schemes, howsoever credible stories it may have unless you are satisfied with your the queries from your careful analysis. Remember that any financial scheme promising over 15 per cent return in India is a potential red flag structure. The threshold promised return will vary between countries and regions.

Ponzi schemes are alive and kicking. Beware of smooth-talking storytellers with a promise of high and consistent returns.

Few Last Words

It is now 100 years since the Italy-born Charles Ponzi, one of the most renowned conmen in history, became infamous for swindling millions of dollars of investors' money by launching a scheme which promised unthinkable returns, without even having any business. Eventually, such swindle games came to be known as Ponzi schemes.

Even after a century, nothing has changed. People are still falling into the trap of make-believe quick-to-get-rich schemes. Unfortunately, the intensity, depth and nature have become more nasty, unsafe and treacherous. This type of fleecing is taking new shapes and sizes routinely!

Appetite for easy money, peer pressure of someone known investing, trusting somebody looking reliable, immaculate market-ing gimmicks and short-term memory of recent losses from decep-tions are the usual recipes for people falling into the swindler honey traps.

As long as greed in mankind will remain, Ponzi and pyramid type of con games will keep doing the rounds. We will need to be cautious, conscious and controlled.

CHAPTER NINE

Stock and Commodity Market Swindles

When we have some money to spare, a popular avenue is to invest in stocks. Buying gold, land or properties, for many, is passé. Investing in stocks is a sign of modernity. Shares and commodities like crude, gold and coffee are often invested in, assuming that the price of purchase is fair and not doctored, with the main objective of selling it dearer at a later date.

What if I now tell you that the markets (exchanges, as it is called) for both stocks and commodities can be rigged.

One such story involves Jignesh Shah, a middle-class kid from Kandivali, Mumbai, dreaming since his childhood of being a billionaire by 40. He albeit made it—*Forbes* World's Billionaires List in 2008 featured him, when he had a 47 per cent stake in **Financial Technologies India Limited (FTIL)**, a technical solution company for online trading. But crooked were his means. FTIL floated a subsidiary **National Spot Exchange Limited (NSEL)**, the company which eventually was at the centre of a ₹5,600 crore ($750 million) scam.[1]

Spot exchange is a physical market, where assets are sold for cash and delivered immediately. It necessarily implies that the commodities need to be in warehouses for delivery once someone pays for them. The same process applied to NSEL, which provided an electronic platform to farmers and traders for spot trading.

In 2013, it was found that commodities which were traded through NSEL were not in the warehouses. In other words, trades were being done in futures or forward contracts. The exchange defaulted payments to about 13,000 investors and had to be eventually shut down. Jignesh Shah was arrested, and the money of many innocent investors stood lost. The commodity exchange collapsed.

Another sad instance of an exchange defrauding was found at the **National Stock Exchange (NSE).** It was set up in 1992 to check the near-monopoly of Bombay Stock Exchange, which itself had several scams. However, gross governance failures in the so-called 'trusted' NSE shook stock market investors.

What NSE did was a downright defraud. It is understood that NSE was giving preferential treatment to some traders by helping them connect to its servers ahead of others. High-frequency traders use sophisticated computer algorithms to exploit minute price differences within seconds. It means that traders having servers located closer to the exchange will have a minuscule time advantage over those located farther, as price information takes that much more time to travel over communication networks. When a lot of rumblings were heard in the public domain with whistle-blowers squeaking in shrilled voices, NSE's managing director (MD) Chitra Ramakrishna resigned in end 2016 citing personal reasons.[2] (Both NSE and its ex-MD have since been penalized.)

It is a grave mistake for any stock or commodities exchange to compromise its governance. When insiders cheat and gain undue advantage, the goodwill earned or trust reposed on exchanges by commoners comes crashing down.

If exchange prices are manipulated and lack transparency, whom do we trust when we buy our next equity share or take a position on any commodity?

Insider's Insidious Income

Insider trading is a crime, but not extensively defined in law. Receiving classified information not made public yet and trading in a company's stocks is an unfair game. The trade would be illegal.

Adversity often brings the best in human valour. As the hitherto unknown coronavirus spreads its devastation in 2020 throughout the world, countless people stepped up to perform acts of heroism and compassion, large or small, to aid neighbours and their nation. But then came to light the not-too-inspiring behaviour from two members of the US Senate.

Richard Burr, Senator of North Carolina, and Kelly Loeffler, Senator of Georgia, played the awful game for personal benefits.[3] While they were overtly placating people that all is well on the health front, these two lawmakers unloaded major stock holdings during the same period. They took the step after receiving closed-door special health briefings in February 2020 about the impending pandemic, as its jaws started getting perilous.

When the people at large were grasping with the nuances of the coronavirus, Burr and Loeffler played down the threat and sold much of their stock portfolios worth millions of dollars in a complete betrayal of public trust. The stocks did collapse in a few weeks thereafter, when the news of the pandemic attack became widespread.

While it is unclear precisely what information about the pandemic the two Senators would have received during the health briefings before their suspiciously timed stock sales, the use of any non-public information in guiding their actions would not only be illegal but also unethical—a typical instance of public servants generating extraordinary income from insidious insider information. This behaviour is unfortunately widely prevalent in most geographies and also within the hallowed corporate corridors. (Incidentally, both the Senators refuted the charges)[4]

This practice of taking advantage of certain information which others are not aware of, and then to make profit out of the knowledge, is illegal. In the corporate world, this is often practised when listed companies' shares are traded by the chief executive, its employees or their relatives, when only they know of some developments. This applies when the relevant information is not publicly known.

Let us say that the CFO of a publicly traded company inadvertently discloses his company's quarterly earnings to his friend while having coffee together. The friend takes this information and trades on the company's shares. This is termed as insider trading.

The market regulator is often able to monitor insider trading by looking at the trading volumes of any particular stock. Volumes often increase after material news is issued to the public. But if no such information is released by the company, but volume of shares traded rise dramatically, this can act as a red flag. The regulator can then investigate to figure out who is responsible for the unusual trading and whether or not it was insider trading.

Trading based on inside information will get more and more used by using AI and data analysis. The data mining is now reaching such levels including tracking everything from satellite imagery of car parks to voice recognition software on analyst calls. The difference between big-data and insider-data scams will get fuzzier, unless exposed in the open in some form.

Let me tell you about a very famous so-called insider trader—Steven Cohen, the founder of the former hedge fund **SAC Capital.**[5] This was the biggest Wall Street insider trading scandal since Ivan Boesky (famous for proclaiming 'greed is healthy', making millions betting on corporate takeover insider information, appearing on *Time* magazine cover in December 1986 and getting jailed shortly thereafter in 1987).

Many do not trust the stock market. They regard these markets as money-raking machines and not for the primary purpose of broader societal benefit to garner capital for business. Sceptics identify Steven Cohen as their mascot.

SAC Capital came to dominate share trading in the US stock market before it pleaded guilty to insider trading charges in 2013 and paid $1.8 billion in penalties. Cohen himself escaped criminal indictment, though he was the firm's heart and brain (outfit's name came from Cohen's initials). (He now runs another multibillion-dollar hedge fund.)

Although Cohen could not be nailed by the regulators, they did try hard. The closest they got was to jail Mathew Martoma, a close aide to Cohen, who garnered inside information about an Alzheimer's drug from a doctor who was running its trial. Cohen escaped indictment, though SAC made huge profits by trading in shares of the involved companies.

In Sheelah Kolhatkar's book, *Black Edge,*[6] the author mentions Cohen building a vast machinery which relied on a web of data, some of it illicit. Even the way in which he gained legal insight leaves a foul taste in the mouth. He paid big commissions to banks to let him know first of any new information, so he could beat other hedge funds and investors to the trade. These guiles provided Cohen an 'edge' over the competitors. There were various edges: 'white edge' involved insights into legitimate trading opportunities; 'grey edge' when a company executive dropped hints about its results—a nod or a wink that did not quite amount to illicitness—then there was the 'black edge', milking from information not available elsewhere.

Shrewd were the ways Cohen exploited inside information. He insisted his traders produce an 'edge' but avoided knowing what shade it was. He demanded trading strategies accompanied by a 'conviction rating' of 1–10, rather than an explanation of where they came from. Incidentally, Martoma gave his Alzheimer's edge a 9 marking. This shielded Cohen from getting indicted.

The clever Cohen hoodwinked the regulator, made tons of money and yet played with insider information. His ingenious methods were music to many insider traders' nosey ears.

Moving to India, the market regulator SEBI of late is taking insider trading seriously. There is an increase in the number of cases being scrutinized for apparent violations.

For instance, SEBI took up 50 cases for investigation related to insider trading in 2019–2020—a fivefold increase over five years.[7]

In the last couple of years, several who's who of India Inc. have settled allegations of insider trading with SEBI.

To cite an example, a renowned couple in India—the promoters of the popular business TV channel NDTV, Prannoy Roy and Radhika Roy—were penalized by SEBI in 2020 for their alleged illegal gains of ₹17 crore ($2 million) for indulging in insider trading.[8] The company was under reorganization since September 2007, but the developments were made public only on 16th April 2008. The power couple sold some of their holdings the following morning, immediately on opening of the stock market, that is, within 24 hours of the organizational restructuring information being made available to the public. This is contrary to insider trading norms. Early advantage of information was taken by the promoters to make some private gains. (In 2020, SEBI restrained Roys from accessing securities market for two years and directed to disgorge illegal gains with 6 per cent annual interest.)

Insider information advantage is a lure for many. It attracted even India's Warren Buffet, the stock market guru, Rakesh Jhunjhunwala. In early 2020, SEBI started probing for his alleged stock market dealings in the listed education firm, Aptech. It is said that he had inside information about Aptech's finances and expansion plans and had made trades on the basis of this information.[9]

This is not the first time when Jhunjhunwala, the billionaire investor, had come under the market regulator's scrutiny. He was questioned in 2018 for suspected insider trading in the engineering services company Geometric, which is now a part of HCL Technologies, the Indian IT major. Jhunjhunwala settled the case through consent filing by paying ₹2.5 lakh or $3,400. ('Consent' is a mechanism through which alleged violations can be settled by paying a fee to the market regulator without admission or denial of guilt.)[10]

When one becomes a big investor, can the person be devoid of using classified internal information? Think about Rakesh Jhunjhunwala and Steven Cohen—the two supremely successful stock investors and both alleged to have taken advantage of hush-hush information.

Violations of insider trading norms in listed companies can take various shades and sizes. These infractions could include executives or directors and their immediate relatives being in possession of unpublished price-sensitive information; trading in shares by individuals known to be friends with the company's MD; or an executive director passing on unpublished information to analysts who in turn publishes research reports making recommendations on the scrip to their clients. Possibilities are many.

The insider trading regulations in India have evolved over the years. The SEBI (Prohibition of Insider Trading) Regulations, 2015, provides the statutory base for prohibiting the wrongdoings, with the regulations made more stringent in 2019.

To counter the menace of insider trading, the Indian market regulator SEBI has been armed with widened information access rights. These privileges include access to call data records (phone tapping not yet allowed), scouring social media information and access to records of personal information of employees.

Tracking insider trading is a difficult task. It involves a lot of data mining for building evidence. But remember that the fight is against smart crooks who are usually well versed with the tricks of the trade.

Tailpiece

The core of a healthy stock market is to ensure that all investors have equal access to the rewards of participation in the market. All members of the investing public should be subject to identical market risks, all having access to the same information base for taking the decision to buy or sell shares. It cannot be that only a few have some data which others don't—helping a few to happily trade and pocket gains.

Laws are placed to make stock markets functioning impartial and smooth. But tricksters are ever evolving their tactics to bypass these basic tenets of fairness.

Brokers Break Belief

Most of us buy and sell shares in companies. It is a nice way to partake in the economic wealth creation and make our savings grow. For dealing in shares, many of us use stockbrokers or middlemen—professionals who execute buy and sell orders for stocks and other securities. They would usually be associated with a registered brokerage firm and handle transactions for retail and institutional customers alike. Trust is the main element of these deals, as we would believe that our brokers, who will get commission from us, will act in our best interest.

Let me give you an example which saddened my heart on hearing it. Since the days I remember in dealing with shares, **Karvy Stock Broking** was the 'go-to' financial services company with the credibility of helping clients with their investments since the early 1980s. But the company took advantage of the trust reposed by its customers. They played with its clients' assets. The stockbroking firm (or persons within it) pulled off an elaborate heist.[11]

Can you accept the notion that your broker confirms about your stock holdings but it happens to be a piece of toilet paper—the confirmations being fallacious! Does it mean that you should worry that the market intermediary (i.e., your broker) may take possession of your investments, the stocks bought on your behalf, sell them off and appropriate the proceeds? According to the SEBI investigation, that is what Karvy Stock Broking did with shares belonging to over two lakhs of its clients.

What Karvy did was preposterous. It transferred the shares out from their clients' depository accounts, pledged them, took money against the shares pledged and moved it to its real estate business. All this without client consent and amounting to about ₹1,100 crore ($145 million). How can a share broking firm use 'your' stocks for their 'own' purpose? This is a massive deception, reneging on trust vested—a murky corporate crime. (The brokerage firm was expelled in late 2020 from stock exchange membership.)

Let me give you another instance of a stock broker reneging on investors' faith. **Anugrah Stock and Broking,** a leading Indian financial broking house established in 2003, ran an unauthorized derivatives advisory service.[12] It amassed over ₹1,300 crore ($175 million) from 500 naive investors. The stock broking firm, in reality, ran a Ponzi scheme, announcing high assured monthly returns from its derivatives trades, and eventually failing to meet its settlement obligations. (In late 2020, NSE expelled Anugrah from its membership.)

These types of episodes do lead to the key question: Are my investments through my stock brokers safe? If you ask an expert, then logically it must be answered by a counter question: 'Safe from what?'

When you make any investment, you are aware that there could be two types of threats to its safety. One, its inherent investment value may decline as it would be subject to market risks. Two, someone else could dupe or run away with your money. The latter is deception. With all the checks and balances put up by the government nowadays, it is reasonable to expect that no one can swindle your money invested. But truth seems to lie elsewhere!

Stories of stock market frauds in India and their linkage with brokers will remain incomplete unless the famous **Harshad Mehta**'s, popularly known as the Big Bull, is told.

It was 1992—with the stock market both exploding and then imploding—when Harshad Mehta, the poster boy of Indian stock market, ruled the roost. Mehta did a lot of hanky-panky and played the market to his advantage.[13]

Simply speaking, among many swindling actions, Mehta borrowed money from the Indian banks against its own receipts which were often forged. He used these bank receipts (or BRs as it's colloquially called) to borrow. The borrowed money was then invested in stocks. The market took off as Mehta kept pumping in money, fraudulently obtained. In the period between April 1991 and April 1992, the Sensex (Bombay stock market index) went into a frenzy, returning 275 per cent, moving from 1,200 to 4,500 points—a record.

The scam came to light when the State Bank of India found a big hole in its government securities account, some of which were ostensibly given to Mehta for selling, but he did not. He used these securities to borrow more to play in the market. On investigation, it was found that Mehta had systematically manipulated and pumped around ₹3,500 crore ($1.3 billion) in the stock market system. In August 1992, the scam got exposed. It resulted in market crashing by 70 per cent, leading to one of the biggest falls and a bearish phase which lasted for several years. (Mehta, jailed in 1992, died while in custody in 2001 after a cardiac arrest.)

Around the same time, between 1999 and 2001, another stock broker **Ketan Parekh,** a trainee with Harshad Mehta and with a hoodwinking story similar to that of the Big Bull, borrowed heavily from the banking system to invest and manipulate stock prices. He would normally buy large stakes in companies with small market capitalization.

Ketan Parekh's favourite was 10 stocks, which ultimately came to be known as K-10. Among many ploys, Parekh would prop up share price through round tripping. He would pump money into his targeted stocks and start fictitious trading within his own network of companies. The average person in the stock market would start believing that the stocks were rising, leading to more people investing in these stocks, driving the prices even higher. Then, as the prices started climbing, Parekh would slowly liquidate his holdings without making much fuss, contrary to the practice of his flashy mentor, Harshad Mehta.

By the end of March 2001, Parekh's game was up, and it was established that he was responsible for rigging the prices of 10 stocks over at least 5 years. (Parekh was jailed and debarred from trading in the stock market for 15 years, which expired in 2017.[14])

Harshad Mehta and Ketan Parekh will remain in the annals of Indian stock market as brokers who manipulated the system to their own advantage, bumping up some stock prices but only to have them crash later, leaving many investors especially the retail segment in the lurch.

Can stock brokers be trusted anymore? What recourse does an investor have if holdings go missing? Can any safeguards be taken against such scams?

After the Karvy storm, the Indian NSE woke up from its slumber. It has issued an advisory to the investors on how to keep their stocks safe. It has advised the following:

- Ensure that payout of funds and securities is received in your account within one working day from the date of payout.
- Be careful while executing any power of attorney (PoA)—specify all the rights that the stock broker can exercise and timeframe for which PoA is valid. It may be noted that PoA is not a mandatory requirement.
- Register for online applications, namely SPEED-e, provided by the depositories for online delivery of securities as an alternative to PoA.
- Ensure that you receive contract notes within 24 hours of your trades and statement of account at least once in a quarter from your stock broker.
- Securities provided by you towards margin are not permitted to be pledged by your stock broker for raising funds. Take note of this.
- If you have opted for a running account, ensure that the stock broker settles your account regularly and in any case not later than 90 days (or 30 days if you have opted for such settlement).
- Do not keep funds and securities idle with the stock broker.

- Regularly login into your account to verify balances and verify the demat statement received from depositories for correctness.
- Check messages sent by the stock exchanges on a monthly basis regarding funds and security balances reported by the trading member and immediately raise a concern if you notice any discrepancy.
- Always keep your contact details like mobile number and email ID updated with the stock broker.
- You may take up the matter with your stock broker or the stock exchange if you are not receiving the messages from the bourse and the depositories regularly.
- If you observe any discrepancies in your account or settlements, immediately take up the same with your stock broker and if the broker does not respond, then approach the stock exchange or depositories.

It is sad that stock brokers, like Karvy, whom we have trusted so far with our life savings, turn out to be not always trustworthy. An important conduit in our quest for wealth creation—some of our stock and commodity brokers—has taken for granted the trust we repose on them. The problem is not with all, but it's the few bad apples which negate the confidence in the basket's content.

Tailpiece

Can stock brokers—people whom we trust—steal our money? While it would be rare that they would physically pilfer, but theft could happen through fraudulent violations of securities laws or misusing our money. The broker trickery could include unauthorized trading, omission of material disclosures, excessive trading, improper investment recommendations, non-disclosure of personal conflict of interest and neglectful portfolio management. Unfortunately, stock broker dishonesties are more common than what most of us would think.

'I am not dismayed that you lied to me; I am sad that I cannot trust you anymore' summarizes perhaps the feelings of many towards the broking community. It is for the fault of a few that the larger community could be under duress.

Penny Stocks

Many of you may have seen the award winning film *The Wolf of Wall Street*, a 2013 American biographical crime comedy movie based on the 2007 memoir of Jordan Belfort, who played dirty games in penny stocks.[15] The movie recounts Belfort's perspective on his career as a stockbroker in New York City and how his firm, Stratton Oakmont, engaged in rampant corruption and fraud on Wall Street in the penny stock market, which ultimately led to his downfall.

The middle-class boy Belfort tried and failed to establish himself on Wall Street in a more traditional way—receiving tutelage in the late 1980s at a blue chip firm but got laid off in the market crash of 1987. He reinvented himself by taking over a penny stock quintessential 'boiler room' and giving it a credible sounding name, Stratton Oakmont, to gain the confidence of working-class investors.

Essentially, 'boiler room' means an outbound call centre marketing dubious investments through telephone calls. It is a room where salespeople work using biased and deceitful information, selling penny stocks or committing outright stock frauds.

Belfort and his company specialized in 'pump and dump' operations, artificially propelling the value of nearly worthless stocks and then selling it at fat profits. Ultimately, the stock value drops with investors losing money. (Belfort was indicted in 1998 for money laundering and securities fraud, spent nearly two years in federal prison and was ordered to pay back $110 million to the investors he had deceived.)

This real-life story of penny stock fraud became the backdrop of the famous movie about Wall Street manoeuvres starring Leonardo DiCaprio. Such is the lure of penny stocks!

The cardinal principle of stock market is: buy low, sell high. It's common sense. Would it not be wonderful to spot shares that are going cheap, say US 7 cents or ₹5 or less, and then make a killing when the stock price goes up? Only if the life was so simple!

Small-priced stocks are often termed as penny stocks or micro-cap stocks. Unfortunately, it has a long history of trickery and untrustworthiness. And yet it attracts new investors every day. It is all about the bait to get rich by spending the minimum.

There is an innate desire for many to buy a lot of shares with less money. For example, ₹5,000 ($65) will buy 50 stocks if each is priced ₹100 ($1.3), but it will buy 1,000 shares if the price is ₹5 (US 7 cents) for every penny stock.

Many inexperienced investors prefer 1,000 shares of dubious value over 50 shares of real value. They have the false feeling of excitement with every penny of share price increase, as it will apply on a large number of shares bought.

The bad news is that penny stocks suffer from two fundamental glitches that make them ripe for rackets.

One, being low value, seldom will any legitimate analyst make coverage or the press scrutinize these stocks. This results in minimal information availability. Con artists find it easy to gravitate to places where there are lesser searchlights.

Two, usually there is low liquidity, due to low prices, small daily volume and trifling floating stock. This makes fraudsters or unscrupulous promoters to control the stock and artificially manipulate prices.

Penny stocks suffer from two common forms of deception.

- *Pump and dump:* Crooks acquire large quantum of certain company's stock and pump up the price by providing false information, encouraging rumours, fabricated press releases, deceitful discussions in social media—all leading to more investor interest creation. This results in pumping up the price further. Once the price moves up, the scamsters would dump the stocks, causing the price to collapse.
- *Fake facts:* Information will be floated on some unverifiable breakthrough technology or forthcoming large contract

announcement. Often, the company may have no earnings or latest audited financial statements. Creating an aura around fake facts, the stock prices will be manipulated to the advantage of the tricksters.

The greed to make fast bucks enthralled many in the COVID-19 years of 2020 and 2021 when governments were pumping in money to prop up economies. Retail money started chasing the Indian penny stocks. Believe it or not, the frenzy over small stocks reached such extremes that shares of some companies that were not even booking any sales, let alone profits, went through the roof.

To cite some examples of this insanity, a fruit-jam maker **Transglobe Foods Ltd's** stock price skyrocketed over 4,300 per cent within the year of 2020, and the real-estate services firm **Shree Precoated Steels's** share jumped over 1,000 per cent. The worst part is that both companies have reported no sales and obviously no profits for the last several years.[16]

Similar instances of speculative frenzy in penny stocks are aplenty. The US market regulator SEC caught a frenzy in February 2021 and suspended trading in **SpectraScience, Inc.** The shares had surged 630 per cent in 2021 to just over two-tenths of a cent before the halt. You will be surprised to know that the company hadn't filed reports in years, and its phone number doesn't even work! Such is the madness sometimes created by some penny stock.[17]

Euphoria when the market is on fire is value destructive. Penny stock prices get stoked by poor sense of judgement, speculation or sheer fraudulent intent. It is the amateurs and retail investors who end up at the losing end in the game of beating the market. 'Bulls make money, bears make money, pigs get slaughtered' – goes a saying!

Do not touch penny stocks to become penniless unless you are in the know of specific developments of the sector, industry or the company.

Tailpiece

The psyche of penny stock market: Cheats will first load up on ultra-cheap share of a small stock hardly anyone trades. This will be followed up by 'pump'. They will pitch the stock with bright prospects, spreading positive information to push up its price. Finally comes the 'dump'. After the price spikes, the fraudster sells the shares, leaving the new buyers holding an empty bag.

The mindset of penny stock traders: As long as they do not lose too much, the perpetrators often continue to be a force; it's only when the con traders start losing more than they can afford that they start exiting the penny stocks.

Small value stocks—with little interest among the larger investor community and scant information in the public domain—make it a darling for the scamsters. Manipulating the price becomes easier. It is thus a recipe for impending ruin.

Short Selling Scams

Strange, but it's possible that you profit when the stock price falls!

While common sense says that when price rise, you make profit by selling stocks bought earlier at a lower price. But the reverse could also help you pocket gains. Sell at a lower price on a future date hoping the stock price will fall.

Let me explain how it could work. If you sell something which you don't own on the assumption that the price will fall, with the aim of buying them back for less, you make a profit.

A few examples may help to explain the phenomenon better. In September 2020, suddenly shares in the American truck start-up **Nikola Corporation** fell more than 14 per cent after a short seller's report claimed that the business was an 'intricate fraud'.[18] It squeaked that the electric truck group had exaggerated its technology prowess and forged product launch videos.

The accusations came just a few days after General Motors announced a $2 billion deal with Nikola. It so happened that the start-up got touted to be the next Tesla, despite having no planned sales until 2022. The report containing the allegations was issued by Hindenburg Research. It claimed to have 'extensive evidence' that Nikola's 'proprietary' technology was procured from another company, and the electrical inverters were bought from a supplier while claiming it had made them in-house. Nikola's managers apparently hid the real manufacturer's brand name with a tape, during a demonstration video.

In another accusation, the short seller Hindenburg Research said that Nikola faked a product video in 2018 by rolling its Nikola One truck along a downhill stretch of a highway, to disguise the fact that the vehicle had no working engine, and filming it to appear as if it was being driven.

Whether Nikola had the technology to sell or it was faking its expertise, only time will tell. But short sellers do concoct stories giving negative spiel to a company's prospects to force a price decline. In the hope the company share price would weaken in the future, traders can take a position to sell the shares at a future date at today's price. A game of short selling could many a time be a con game—from research reports to analyst commentaries.

In essence, a short seller makes money by identifying stocks that are felt to be overvalued and then betting that the stocks' price will fall once the market figures it out. A short seller accomplishes this by borrowing shares from an investor-lender and quickly selling them at their current inflated price. Later, when the stocks' price goes down, the short seller purchases the stocks and returns them to the lender. This will help to close the seller's short position.

Short sellers make profits by hoping that the price of the share betted on would fall. Normally, short sellers would target companies which they feel are overvalued for reasons other than fraud— say poor strategy, uncompetitive quality, emerging competition or imports playing havoc, factors which short sellers could have picked up earlier than others. However, of late, many short selling are taking place, claiming that the stocks are overvalued as the financial statements are doctored and fraudulent—a game professional short sellers often play. Whether these bets turn out to be right or not is another story, but short selling could often be a wagering game for many.

There is another type of short selling which is popular—'naked shorting'—nothing to do with the way a short seller could be dressed though! It is the illegal practice of selling shares without having arranged to borrow or procure the shares being sold.

While short sellers and bears have been scoffed at and censured since the early 1600s when the modern stock exchange took shape, these players have played positive roles in identifying fraud and excess in the market. A good example is the battered German fintech company **Wirecard AG,** which filed for insolvency in June 2020, days after revealing that more than $2 billion in cash were missing from its balance sheet.[19]

This was a startling instance from the then Europe's shining tech star with a market value of $14 billion, which just evaporated into the celestial space. Wirecard, once the darling of Germany's financial technology scene, became the first company from the DAX-30 (Germany's premier stock market index) to slip into insolvency.

It is a classic case where the whistle-blowers and the media (*Financial Times*) were at the heart of uncovering the fraud in early 2019. Wirecard's head of international finance, based in Singapore, was suspected of cooking books to boost sales and profits for various entities in the Asia Pacific. Short sellers smelled blood, shorting the stocks in February 2019.

Large stock price swings prompted BaFin, Germany's financial watchdog, to announce a two-month ban on bets against the share price, citing risks to the German economy. It was the first use of a crisis measure to protect a single company. Wirecard continued to defend its business model with *Financial Times* carrying on its investigations on the company's illicit methods of doing business and fraudulent accounting. Come June 2019, the ploy could not be hidden further, with the auditor revealing about the missing cash.

Short sellers sensed profits. They believed that the stocks were overpriced. Had these punters like the hedge funds (which employs alternative investment approach to protect against market volatility), not pursued and investigative journalism not taken place, it would have been difficult to foresee how long the Wirecard would have continued its tricks.

At the end, the short sellers were proven right. (Incidentally, short sellers made a handsome gain of over $2 billion off Wirecard's collapse.)

Is short selling common? Yes, but lesser than what some market regulators think. It is still a minority sport. Hedge funds are known to play big and perhaps were the original shorters. As the name suggests, hedge funds go 'long' buying stocks, but hedge their positions with some 'shorts', so they could at least offset losses, irrespective of market price swings. Short selling is all about selling shares which one does not own.

Sometimes short positions can be very painful. When Volkswagen shares were shorted in 2008, Porsche suddenly revealed that it had quietly lifted its stake in Volkswagen. This radically shrank the pool of available shares with which shorts could repay their loans, pushing Volkswagen shares up 150 per cent in a day. Things just went the other side!

Stock market manipulation and information distortion often instigates those holding certain stocks to sell. This can happen even if it means taking a loss by selling the stock for less than its original purchase price. Concurrently, the short and distort fraudsters cover at the low prices and lock in their potential for profits. This tactic can be shattering for a company, creating catastrophic losses to investors who could fall for these slur campaigns.

Few Last Words

Many a time, we would receive a tip to buy the so-called potential hot stock by investing just ₹50,000 ($675)—and some of us will put our money quickly, not to miss the opportunity. However, when we have to buy a television for a similar sum, we would do endless research to figure out the best buy. This is the dichotomy that stock market sharks take advantage of. The belief of making a fast buck, not missing out on a potential multi-bagger stock or a plausible hot tip, hoping it contains some insider information, often leads us to the snake-infested marketplace.

The bright spot is that the market regulators are now better trained, laws getting sharper and the obstinate being punished. This should make this marketplace more credible.

Stock market is one bazaar, where fortunes are made and lost with equal measure. Unless fundamentals of the company, industry and management are researched, this marketplace is not the right place to do bargain shopping.

Beware, stock markets are full of sneaking swindlers ready to swoop on the susceptible! Rip-offs are practised recurrently in these seemingly unsuspecting souks.

CHAPTER TEN

Insurance Imposture

A 30-year-old businessman Sumeet More from Maharashtra ran out of money. He was in dire straits due to his accumulated debts. Desperate to pay off his loan liabilities, he hacked a macabre plan of murdering his friend (who was physically structured like him), passing him off as himself and claiming his life insurance money of ₹1.5 crore ($200,000).

Sumeet asked his friend Tanaji Aawale whether they could go out together for a nice holiday. Tanaji loved the idea of a weekend break to Sumeet's native town. The unsuspecting Tanaji went in Sumeet's car for the trip. On the way, Sumeet hit Tanaji on his head with a stump. Then he set ablaze the car. He waited till the car was completely gutted before leaving the place.

The Pune police found the charred body in the car. The vehicle was registered in Sumeet's name, and it was easy to trace his residence. The police handed over the burnt body, which was beyond recognition, to Sumeet's family, assuming that it was his.

However, the police suspected that something was amiss. When the body was handed over, Sumeet's family did not show grief as expected in such situations. On keeping a continuous watch, the police observed that the family was not heartbroken. The cops questioned Sumeet's elder brother. On sustained enquiry, he confessed that his sibling was hiding in Jejuri town, not too far away. Sumeet was arrested a few days later.[1]

Such are the horrific stories in the world of insurance, where money can be made without any physical injury or assault to the claimant.

In another instance of insane behaviour for the lust of money, a man murdered his wife two days after taking a life insurance policy in her name. An Uttarakhand resident alleged that five men had entered his house one night to abduct him and his wife.[2] The abductors shot his wife dead when she resisted. But the man failed to disclose the reasons for attempted kidnapping, or name any person who tried to kidnap him and his wife. No physical description of the culprits could be provided by the man.

The Supreme Court convicted the man for murder and imprisoned him for life, 18 years after the crime took place. What the court found was the suspected person initially complained that three men entered his home at midnight for abduction. Later, he changed the version to five persons. If the intruders had come to abduct him and his wife, shot his wife dead, then why did the gangsters not take the suspected man away? No cogent explanations were given. The false claim of recovering insurance money was put to rest.

Insurance is a contract of indemnity. It involves an understanding between two parties where one party called the 'insurer' undertakes, in exchange for a fixed payment called the 'premium', to indemnify or pay the other party called the 'insured', a fixed amount of money on the happening of a certain event covered by the contract, where an actual loss takes place.

The business of insurance rests on the idea of knowledge, which is mostly imperfect. Various classes of risks are being covered by the insurance companies since the concept's inception in the 17th century. The risks are spread into various buckets, working on the laws of large numbers. Insurers do not know exactly where or on whom the risks would lie. By insuring a cluster of risks, it spreads the same over a wider base. It does not matter ultimately which one goes bad. And this is where fraudsters try to take advantage of.

The con game starts here—obtaining compensation if somehow someone can prove a loss where an insurance policy exists. Money would flow from the insurance company, even if no real loss would have happened, say no one died but life insurance money was claimed or no loss in fire occurred but fire insurance claim was filed.

The Economist magazine commented in January 2020[3] that for healthcare sector, it is a scandal that the treatments offered are mostly for the wrong ones. Take an example: Doctors are far too quick to prescribe magnetic resonance imaging (MRI) scans in case of back pains. In rich countries, perhaps 80 per cent of MRIs for back pain are unnecessary. Surgery is suggested, but it is common to see that it does not work.

Cigna, an American insurer, found that 87 per cent of customers who had spinal-fusion surgery for wear and tear of spinal discs were in a lot of pain even after two years of surgery, needing more treatment. For most back pain, the best treatment is non-medical. Some stretching exercises will mostly work fine. But the medical world does not always work the rational way.

It is easier and financially rewarding for doctors to prescribe painkillers, scans or inoculations than to explain to the patients that lifestyle modifications may just as well work. Hospitals and doctors go happy; insurance bills pile up; patients bear a portion. It is a money-making machine working with insurance companies bearing the brunt!

To top it all, it is estimated that 1 in 10 insurance claims are fraudulent, with insurance impostures having field days.

Tricksters' Tricks

A group of thugs roped in some labourers in Rajasthan. They got their details, gave them some money and purchased heavy vehicles in their names. Then loan was taken against the purchase. Although these labourers were the vehicle owners, they had no control over the asset. The insured, that is, the labourers, were promised payment of monthly EMI for the vehicle loan. After about a year, these vehicles were transferred to Northeast India. Insurance claims were filed for vehicle thefts.

On investigation, the insurance company observed that while the owners of the vehicles were different, only one advocate had registered the first information reports (FIRs filed with the police) for the so-called stolen vehicles. Further, it was found that the vehicle owners were all labourers who could not have afforded such heavy vehicles. The claims got rejected, and the fraud got unveiled.

The insurance market is where money keeps flowing—from the insurance companies to the ones who are supposedly insured. The basic reason for fraud is because the financial claims are not backed by definitive supply of goods or services. Hence, the audit trail for services rendered or goods delivered is missing. It thus becomes a hotbed for the tricksters to trick the insurance companies to settle bogus claims.

It's a cat and mouse game. As the insurance companies keep evolving their control mechanisms, so do the fraudsters keep devising newer methods to cheat.

Let me now cite some common ploys employed in the insurance world to make some fast bucks.

- *Insure terminally ill:* The favourite method deployed is to obtain a life insurance against a terminally ill patient. As death is likely to take place sooner than later, it is a nice way to pocket some big claim amount. Rural India, where the infrastructure is inadequate, is a hot bed for these lies. The doctor who checks the person having some pre-existing illnesses is either bribed or threatened. For instance, patients having even cancer are certified as fit cases for insurance. Nice fat cheques can then be collected by the nominee on the death, which could happen rather soon.

- *Accidental accident:* Many a time, insurance policies have a rider, stating that should there be an accidental death, the claim amount is doubled. This is a great provision to be misused. Natural deaths are sometimes passed off as accidental ones. Doctors could either be involved or are sometimes threatened into certifying fraudulently.

- *Disaster distorted:* Chaos ensues when a disaster strikes, creating a big canvas for fraud. A large volume of claims prevents insurance companies from checking the minor details, usually due to lack of manpower. For example, a single home may escape the catastrophe in the mid of a ring of destroyed homes. Data (namely assets, belongings, quality of construction, etc.) from such unaffected home, which could be fudged, may be used to settle claims of the other affected homes. Inflated claims filed are another swindle. Homeowners may knowingly sign inflated claims for repairs done or not done. It is a common practice to bill the insurance company for higher quality materials which are eventually switched for poorer versions.

- *Misrepresented motor cover:* Theft in motor vehicles is ripe for constructing frauds around it. Feign theft of vehicles. File an FIR with the police, stating that the vehicle has got stolen. Lawyer, police, fake insured, all of them could conspire to take the insurance company for a ride.

- *Unhealthy health insurance:* Some hospitals work hand in hand with the fraudsters to make fake bills. Over-invoicing, non-existent treatment, improper medicine bills, incorrect doctor visits and many more could be the methods to cheat the insurance companies.

- *Finance fudging:* The financial market is full of crafty people. Making money on the sly is sometimes the objective. Let me cite an instance which will make the matter clear—how the intent of some insurance products are played with to make money. Codere, a Spanish multinational gaming company, owed money it could not repay. *The Economist* reported that Codere company's bonds were trading at about half the face value.[4] Blackstone, an American private equity firm, offered it an inexpensive $100 million loan. However, there was a catch. Blackstone had bought a 'credit default' insurance (it helps to transfer credit risk) on Codere's debt, which would pay out about €14 million ($19 million) if Codere missed a bond payment. So Codere delayed a payment by a couple of days to trigger a 'technical default'. Blackstone received the pay-out, and Codere got its loan. The company got saved from bankruptcy.

Credit risk is the possibility of a borrower failing to service or repay a debt on time. On payment of a premium, that is, say credit default swap, an event of default by the borrower can be protected. This instrument was turned around by Blackstone in the example cited to make a fat sum of money. This was not a fraud but borders on unethical use of an instrument intended to protect a non-payment and not a 'managed' default.

Tailpiece

Globally, insurance is a $6 trillion industry. With that quantum of premium changing hands in a year, and with half of the premium belonging to the life insurance sector, the business numbers make it ripe for deception and forgery.

Insurance claims, by their nature, involve someone filing for a privilege, with the other party accepting the prerogative. This should happen when something has gone wrong. But what if nothing is amiss or the claims are boosted? This is the root cause for enhanced insurance tricking.

Travel Trekkers' Tricks

When you go on a holiday, and that too into the cool climes of some quaint mountain range, the last thing that comes to your mind is: 'Will I be fleeced?'

An avid German trekker, Gerhard Fischer, when heading towards the famous Mount Everest base camp in Nepal, felt an intense chest pain. His Nepali guide, without much ado, immediately called for medical evacuation, saying that it is a case of severe mountain sickness.

But after a few hours, Fischer started feeling better, with his oxygen level getting back to acceptable levels. His travel companion, Isabelle Schneider, suggested to the guide that if they could just rest for a day, things should get better, or maybe just walk down slowly, as many do.

That's when the guide saw an opportunity!

He shoved aside the tourists' suggestions and pressed for an expensive helicopter evacuation. Things got worse when they landed in a hospital usually catering to foreigners in the Nepalese capital city, Kathmandu. Fisher's passport was confiscated for several days, probably to gain some extra hospitalization days. The doctors and hospital bills kept rising. In fact, a doctor suggested that Fisher's symptoms would need to be exaggerated to enable the insurance company pay for his stay.

The whole episode was just a scam to suck money out of the insurance companies. Millions of dollars are being fraudulently claimed as insurance compensation, where the Mount Everest trekking companies, guides, helicopter evacuation companies and hospitals are conspiring to push up superfluous evacuations, bumping-up medical symptoms and forcing needless hospitalization.[4]

The fraud could get weirder! When Olivia Brown's, a Canadian trekker, mountain flight back to Kathmandu was delayed due to bad weather, she got immensely worried that she could miss her connecting flight to Toronto. That was a brilliant opportunity for the locals to make some extra bucks. The trekking company came up with an alternative.

They suggested that the trekker say that she was suffering from severe food poisoning, so as to enable the insurance company to pay for a helicopter flight—another plan to dupe the insurance company.

Lot of hush-hush goes on, though the locals seem to covertly know the fraudulent game plans. The Nepalese government has published some new rules for trekking companies. Whether these will arrest the ill practices, time will only tell. A government report did point accusative fingers at the service providers: **Flight Connection International** and **Swacon International Hospital,** Kathmandu, for making false invoices and fleecing insurance companies.[5]

Certain tour operators thriving with political connections have turned the subterfuge into a bloated rip-off. Sadly, the golden tourism geese are being slaughtered by the greedy few, like the Himalayan deception at the foothills of the world's highest mountain range, the bountiful Himalayas.

Tailpiece

Tourists beware, when local touts go out of their way to assist when you are in some trouble! Exercising caution and care could prove useful. Thankfully, not all vacation destinations display dishonesty.

Bogus Claims

Let me tell you a story which I recently heard about how fake life insurance claims are typically structured. In the register of deaths in a Maharashtrian village, Sanjay Kolatkar was entered as one who died by drowning on 25 May 2017. A doctor's post-mortem report certified the death. But there was a twist in the tale. Sanjay had died in 2012. Dinesh Kolatkar, Sanjay's brother, filed a life insurance claim for natural death in July 2017 for ₹10 lakh ($13,000), citing the reference of a life insurance policy of Sanjay. The insurance company started investigating the death, only to find that the gram panchayat's record showed that the accidental death took place five years back.[6] The claim got rejected owing to fraudulent statements.

This is not an isolated instance. There are innumerable instances of death claims citing gram panchayat or village records, only to spin tales on lives which may or may not have departed from the mortal world.

Ghost applications are a major area of fraud. Claims on behalf of terminally ill or mentally imbalanced persons is another cheating method. Normally, these involve a team of racketeers and low sum insured.

Deceitful claims are often filed to fool the insurance company.

Let me give you another example. A motor vehicle accident claim was filed, claiming that the driver of a truck rammed into a tree, leading to the helper seating next to the driver dying. While investigating, it was found that the truck driver fled the scene and was absconding. The accident's major impact was on the driver's side. How come the helper died but the driver was safe? On further investigation and reconstructing the event, it became clear that the helper, who did not have a driving license, was driving the vehicle when it met with the accident. The helper got head injury and it tallied with the post mortem, as it stated that he died out of profuse bleeding from the forehead. The claim was rejected.

Bogus claims abound all over. Fertile minds keep churning up fraudulent schemes.

The warm summer months are usually pleasant for the hospitality industry, in many geographies. Pricing soars, giving lovely bottom lines to hotels and airlines industry, in places where the sun shines bright and clear. However, *The Economist* magazine reported in July 2017[7] that tour operators and hoteliers get apprehensive in these times. To cite an instance, they got hit by a sweeping incidence of food-poisoning claims mostly from British tourists.

The rate of illness reported by all nationalities at resorts across the sunny region of the Mediterranean was fine. But the number of sickness claims made by Britons after eating at all-inclusive hotels peaked five times the normal since 2013. Claimants typically demanded £5,000 ($6,500) in compensation and up to £100,000 in lawyers' fees. To cite an example, the hoteliers in the popular Majorca Island in Spain reported claims costing them a whopping €50 million ($58 million) ever year.

It came to light that most of these claims were fake. No nationality other than the British were as ill. In 90 per cent of the claims, the symptoms were self-reported. In most of the cases, the medication proof was the payment receipt for diarrhoea-relief tablets. It so happened that many of the claim letters were identical, with just names, dates and hotel names changed. Many all-inclusive resorts were up in arms due to the fraud claims!

The fallout has been significant. The travel industry launched a media campaign, warning tourists of imprisonment if false claims get detected. Hotels commenced monitoring tourists more closely, with some even forcing customers to wear electronic wristbands tracking their movements.

Had these claims been genuine, it would have normally been covered through insurance policies which hotels would take to cover customer claim risks; and holiday makers would be covered for their medical costs through their travel insurance policies.

While the ill-tummy syndrome may have got exposed, the fraudsters are unlikely to give up on their machinations. Can mental distress or phony tourist-raucous be the next cause to con claims? Cheaters are unlikely to check out so coolly! Fake claims after all have been a money-making scheme for some.

Tailpiece

It cannot be too tough to fake an insurance claim. Push your car off a cliff, call the police, report your car as stolen, bribe the cops, get a police report and file for a theft insurance. But beware, though apparently easy, most get caught. Weeding out the wheat from the chaff is the inherent nature of this multibillion-dollar industry, where the truth has to necessarily be separated from sham.

It does not mean that some will not try to scam the insurance system—the battle of wits is unlikely to end in the distant future.

Mala Fide Medical Indemnification

Strange is the way the connected insurance world behaves. Frauds happen as if it is a routine. *The New York Times* in December 2019 reported a story of medical insurance claim, which, though legal on the face of it, was phony in nature.

Andrej Rosenthal met with an accident while riding his bicycle on a Sunday, hitting a pothole at high speed in Washington, USA. He fell unconscious, lying on the pavement, till he was picked up a few minutes later. He was diagnosed to have suffered a few broken ribs, a broken finger, a broken collarbone and a broken shoulder blade.[8]

The treatment he got via paramedics and in the emergency room and intensive care unit were great. The trouble began when the medical bills started arriving.

It was all crazy high charges: $182 for a basic blood test, $9,289 for two days in a room in intensive care and $20 for a pill that costs pennies at a pharmacy.

The bills contained things that either did not happen or just sort of happened. Let me give you some billings that looked ludicrous to say the least.

- *Medical loot:* In the trauma room, someone tied a hard brace around Andrej's neck until scans confirmed that he had not suffered a grievous spinal injury. It was removed within an hour. The medical equipment company that provided that piece of plastic billed $319. The insurance company later paid $215 (90% of its discounted rate of $239), with Andrej having to bear the rest—$24—as patient share. It is like attending a seminar where you are given a hamper for which you are billed $100. But there, at least you take home something. But in the case of Andrej's neck brace, not only did he hardly wear it, but he could not even take it home as a souvenir.

- *Cover charge:* The biggest single item on Andrej's bill was a $7,143 trauma activation fee. What was that for, since every component of his care had been billed and billed handsomely? Among the line items: $3,400 for a high-level emergency recovery visit; $1,030 for the trauma surgeon; between $1,400 and $3,300 for five purported CT scans. What purported was that Andrej went for just one trip into a scanner to examine his skull, upper spine and maxillofacial bones but was billed as three separate things. There was also an administration fee of more than $350 each for four injections. It is like being billed in a hotel for sitting in the lobby as if a suite was used.

- *Masquerader billing:* Bills were made for doctors which Andrej did not even see. Some of these bills were understandable, like for the radiologist who read the scans. But others were for bedside treatment from people who never came anywhere near the bed to deliver the care. Andrej had a small finger fracture with a cut which needed some stitches, which a trainee doctor did. But the $1,512 bill came in the name of a senior surgeon, as if he had done the work. It is like being billed for a senior partner's time, when only an assistant spent time and gave the advice, in a law firm.

- *The drive-by:* The day before Andrej left the hospital, a physical therapist visited and asked a few questions. From that brief encounter, the therapist noted 'ambulation deficits, balance deficits, endurance deficits, pain-limiting function, and transfer deficits.' That translated into a bill of $646. The therapist said that he was there for 30 minutes, but he was not. The therapist claimed that he walked Andrej up 10 steps with a stabilizing belt for assistance. He did not. There was no significant health service given, just an appearance and some boxes checked on a form. It's a phenomenon called 'drive-by doctoring'.

- *Enforced elevation:* On Monday, when Andrej was in pain and out of pills, the trauma doctor suggested that he be examined in the emergency room, because the trauma clinic was open only from 8:00 to 10:45 a.m. on Wednesdays and Thursdays. So the trauma doctors were met in the emergency room, and they talked to Andrej, who remained in his street clothes. They gave him a prescription. Arising of the interaction—which could have happened in the lobby—but happened in the emergency room, it translated in an emergency room visit charge of $1,330. But when the trauma clinic is open less than six hours a week, billing for an emergency room, which did not use any emergency resource, feels like a scam. Is an emergency room visit determined by the content of the services rendered, or merely by the location? It is like being booked for a deluxe suite room in a hotel when you have clearly asked for an ordinary single-bed facility.

The insurance company ultimately paid for most of these questionable charges, though at discounted rates. But even a discounted payment for something that never really happened or did not need to happen or that were not agreed to by the patient is simply a scam.

Does the content of the above story sound familiar? Many of you may have had a similar experience. The degree of over-charging may however vary. There is a portion of the billing which needs to be self-borne by the patient, which is known as deductibles. Overbilling of medical expenses, though perhaps insurance covered, has become a big con game, and it's ballooning in most healthcare centres.

Tailpiece

Why do insurers pay inflated bills of hospitals and doctors? Perhaps the insurance company is too busy to check the veracity of billings. Or is it that the insurance companies are used to overbilling by hospitals, who in turn push up the insurance premium for you and me (the insured) to bear? Or is there a booty sharing mechanism between the doctor–hospital–insurer trio?

Data, Big Data and Defrauders

Throughout childhood, I loved reading detective storybooks—the way sleuths would unravel the clues, put them together in some logical fashion and identify the conspirator. The fun was not the crime per se, but how the culprit was detected by the detective.

The insurance companies are also going through a metamorphosis—trying their very best to unravel the perpetrators of deceptions. However, with the development of technology, most detectives are not humans any more. Fraud detection software and forensic techniques are used to comb through millions of data and transactions. It looks for patterns and make predictions. Dishonest activities get identified faster.

Fake claims are as old as the insurance industry itself. The world of insurance and finance is getting shaken up through machine learning. The industry is excited with the possibility of using big data and AI, as they see a huge potential to understand risk behaviour and, more importantly, how to tick-off tricksters.

Insurance actuaries (risk assessors and managers) are hoping to exploit decades of data to predict how things may pan out. The risk managers and auditors are enthused with the possibility to predict fraud trends—identify fishy-looking claims for further investigation.

Machine learning is getting extended not only to dishonesty protection but also for finding new business strategies like product mix and risk profile. These smart devices have changed the way businesses will function, especially insurance, where risk forecasting and falsehood unravelling are big game changers.

The big data can possibly be used in the following two ways:

First, ease in buying insurance, by quick form filling with a lot of preloaded information available on the forms based on customer data accessible from the cloud domain will prevent cheaters from filling up falsified information.

Next, and perhaps the most potent one, is to find out the risk profile of the insured. Insurers will have access to more and more information about their customers—income profile, past claims and earlier behaviour pattern—thus predicting potential perils. This will enable proper pricing of the insurance covers. The positive fallout of course would be to prevent scammers from cooking up unclaimable claims.

Insurance business runs on the concept of risk pooling, in which large groups share risks of each other, say healthcare scheme of an organization, where any employee's sickness cost is supposed to be recovered from the premium of healthy co-employees. However, there are negative fallouts of data mining—it may lead to more precise risk segmentation, with pooling concept getting discontinued. This would necessarily mean that high-risk customers will end up bearing higher premium. Pricing of insurance products will get more custom-made.

Auto insurers have begun to determine premium based on how a particular driver behaves while driving. 'Telematic' trackers show how often accelerators are getting pressed or brakes getting employed. Many health insurers require customers to wear fitness bands and offer discounts when healthy lifestyles are being followed.

The Economist magazine, quoting an article in the Technology Quarterly, gave some instances where fraud detection software could identify red flags.

Let us take the instance of car insurance. Monday-morning insurance claims are likely to be more fraudulent than on other days, since weekends make it easier for policyholders, who stage accidents, to assemble friends as fabricated witnesses.

If a claimant was injured due to an impact near the driver's seat, for example, the accident is less likely to have been stage managed and the claim less likely to be a sham, even if it is being filed on a Monday.

Drivers of cars with low resale values are proportionately more prone to file fraudulent claims than the ones owning a luxury car.

If the insurance on the luxury car has expired, the possibilities of foul play drops, since this increases the likelihood of the person driving a cheaper but properly insured car or the person not driving at all.

German insurers, for example, noticed that claimants who call back shortly after filing, angrily demanding speedy settlement, are disproportionately more likely to be cheaters.

And there could be quite a few combinations of mala fide human behaviour which a software can identify much easily. It is humanly impossible to sift through and identify the staggering number of combinations of fake activities. Fraud–detection software have the ability to evaluate a vast number of permutations and deliver a fraud-probability score.

AI use is not without its drawbacks. Machines may take time to learn how to use the algorithms from a plethora of historical data. Even without deliberate fraud, machines may incorrectly work out their conclusions and fail to distinguish which claims should be paid out in full and which should not.

Let me give you few examples of machine faux pas.

Lemonade Inc., an American property and casualty insurance company, in its early years of 2017 and 2018, had very high payouts.[9] In fact, payouts as a proportion of premiums for 2018 were about 150 per cent. It meant that they were paying out claims more than their premium receipts. However, the average loss ratio for US home insurers should have been around 75 per cent. It was suspected that AI could have played havoc by approving high payouts. Once the company made enhancements to its systems, the payouts fell to about 90 per cent in early 2019.

Contrary stories on AI insurance settlements also exist. Some say that there could be a sinister move in using big data. Optimization programs could lead to paying lower settlements, which needy customers may accept without any complain. Not a happy news, but intelligent programs could map customer profiles and offer quick lower settlements to optimize insurance company profits— not an impossible thought. This is cheating.

After all, intelligence, especially of machines, can be used advantageously or adversely.

Tailpiece

The fraud-finding intelligence software are getting smarter, with fresh claims providing more data to help tune the algorithms or computational logic to detect deceits. With insurance infamy blowing full in the insurance world, the machine intelligence is making the swindlers sweat more than what its human counterparts were doing so far.

Machines are the Sherlock Holmes of today's insurance industry.

Pointless Premium

Can you imagine to pay one-fifth of your annual income as your car insurance premium? This is indeed the scenario in Detroit city, where a car insurance could cost you as much as $5,400 per year, where a typical household income could be as low as $26,000 per annum, reports *The Economist* in July 2018.[10] In this US city, cars are an inescapable necessity, as the city lacks a robust public transportation system. The outcome of this outrageous insurance premium is that residents flout the law by registering outside the city limits with half the insurance costs or by driving without any insurance at all. It is estimated that over half of the residents drive without an auto insurance.

Why does Detroit have such excessive insurance premiums? Basically, there are two broad reasons.

The basic reason for high premium is the rampant fraud practice, usually through overbilling by hospitals for accident patients. And the other reason is the benevolent nature of the State promising to pay lifetime medical expenses, rehabilitation services and lost wages after a car accident, irrespective of who was at fault. This is an unbelievable generosity. The outcome is hefty insurance premium, leading to more fraudulent practice by the residents of trying to avoid taking the rightful auto insurance cover.

This is not an atypical experience. There are many geographies which face high insurance premium from time to time—the outcome of fraudulent behaviour by either the medical fraternity or the insured.

Let us take another example of frauds leading to higher premium. Insuring Italian drivers is fraught with business risk. About 1 Italian car in 12 is involved in a motor claim each year, compared with 1 in 23 in France, which has similar numbers of people and cars.[11] While fewer than 200,000 Frenchmen claim injury in accidents every year, can you imagine how many Italians do so? One million!

The result is over-the-top premiums in Italy. At an average of €407 ($515), Italians pay well over twice as much for their annual car insurance as French drivers, reports *The Economist*. Premiums increased by 18 per cent in Italy between 2002 and 2009, against an average of 7 per cent in Europe. Even so the insurance business does not make enough money in Italy. Fraud is the reason for this disproportionately high premium.

Tailpiece

Insurance premium is the cost you pay to buy your protection. For every service, there is a fair price. So is for insurance. But fraudsters could con by extracting some extra claims. Plus, frequent fraud results in higher premium. It cuts both ways—heads or tails, we lose when sharks swing. That's what you need to be cautious about— imposters in the insurance industry are not infrequent.

Catch Me if You Can

Fraudsters are lurking around to make money from the remunerative insurance trade.

Take for instance India—a massive ₹20 lakh crore ($300 billion) insurance market. But a major problem is that the scams keep cropping up. Every year, over ₹40,000 crore ($5 billion) of insurance frauds are caught. In life insurance, frauds take place mostly in the segment where the sum assured is between ₹2 and ₹12 lakh ($2,500–$15,000).[12]

In Europe, detected and undetected insurance frauds are around €13 billion ($16 billion) every year. The worse is that up to 10 per cent of the claims could be dubious.

In the USA, the insurance industry consists of over 7,000 companies, collecting over $1 trillion in premiums annually.

The massive size attracts swindlers in hordes. Over $40 billion every year is lost through insurance fraud (non-health insurance). That means insurance fraud costs an average American family between $400 and $700 annually in the form of enhanced premiums.[13] This is a colossal number!

Suspicious claims are the starting points to identify the problem areas. Statistical analysis, complaints from claim adjusters, grumbles from insurance agents, whistle-blowing or tips from the public and law enforcement agencies provide useful red flags for suspected duplicity.

Some common methods implemented by insurers to tackle the racket are as follows:

- Cross-checking and investigating documents
- Using data analytics
- Running through special investigation of doubtful claims
- Appointing private investigators

Suspicion of cheating obviously leads to delay in claim settlements, and claim rejections in certain cases. Unfortunately, the brunt falls on the honest insured.

A potential fraud case can involve up to 45 days of investigation time, but can take far longer depending upon complexities. Hence, it is difficult to specify a time frame for deceit examination.

Scams obviously lead to enhanced cost of policies and adversely affect the claim ratio for the insurers, arising from a large quantum of claims filed being disallowed due to suspected fraud.

Insurance is an attractive area for defrauders to dabble in. The industry will continue to play the cat and mouse game, with insurers putting up every possible trap to catch the con artists. Unfortunately, the guile game is unlikely to end soon.

Few Last Words

Insurance con and chicanery is one constant challenge facing the industry worldwide. A fraud survey report of 2017 by RGA[14]

(Reinsurance Group of America) on life and health insurance businesses brought out some startling findings.

Insurance deceits could be organized, deliberate or opportunistic.

'Organized' criminals could attempt to profit from deceitful schemes; 'deliberate' actions could involve policies bought with express intent to deceive; and 'opportunistic' policies involve misrepresentation made while taking policies, say false declaration of sound health in case of health insurance.

While insurance companies continue to garner capabilities to fight fraudsters, the survey singles out challenging facts, which include that 3–4 per cent of all claims are fraudulent with higher fraud claim incidence in the Asia-Pacific region; the bad news is that of the fraud identified, less than 2 per cent result in prosecution; claims under fraud investigation can take up to 8 times the normal settlement time; and there is a 50-50 split between optimism and pessimism in the industry's ability to prevent cheating in the future.

Nearly half of the companies surveyed have identified fraud being assisted by agents. Insurance business is largely dependent upon brokers, and if this group is dishonest, then it is a cause for deep concern.

There is another bad news. Life insurance fraud is well fitted for a crime, with low risk and high reward potential. Even when the scam is detected, there is low possibility of actual punishment. What an ideal turf for tricksters!

Identifying artifice before claims are made is the best answer to the malady. Strengthening internal controls, identification of insured risk while selling a policy, using machine learning and continuous data assessment of claims filed can be some of the answers to fight the horrible virus.

Insurance is all about risk management. However, hoodwinking and hoax by some are playing havoc, enhancing the risk for the insurers and making the life of the honest insured more challenging by raising premiums and delaying settlements.

Strangely, the most popular risk management tool—the insurance—may turn out to be risky!

CHAPTER ELEVEN

Accounting Artifice

It was 2007 when the editorial team of the revered *Fortune* magazine sat together to decide the 'most admired securities firm' of the year. They overwhelmingly came to the conclusion that Lehman Brothers, the global financial services firm, could be the only one which fits the bill. It's an organization that could do no wrong.

Come 2008, the most venerated 158-year-old firm goes belly up!

Lehman Brothers generated the spark that turned the sub-prime debt crisis into a global financial meltdown. What went wrong? Lehman Brothers used accounting sleight of hand to mask bad investments which led to its eventual collapse, though there were several other reasons for its death. The company practised 'materially misleading' accounting gimmicks for concealing the perilous state of its finances.[1]

The investment bank's executives went to extraordinary lengths to conceal the risks they had taken by practising financial engineering. Lehman's ability to convert securities and other assets into cash resulted in a new term entering the financial lexicon: 'Repo 105'.

Lehman's problems primarily stemmed from its huge holdings of securities based on subprime mortgages and other risky debt. As the market for these securities deteriorated in 2008, Lehman began to suffer huge losses and a plummeting stock price. Rating firms downgraded many of its holdings, making it difficult for Lehman to borrow.

When bankruptcy was looming round the corner, Lehman worked hard to make its financial condition look better than it was—and one way was to push out of its books the poor quality assets it possessed.

What they did was to carry out the 'Repo 105' manoeuvres—an accounting jugglery. They twisted standard financing method known as a repurchase agreement and warped its depiction. Lehman first used Repo 105 in 2001 and became dependent on it till its bankruptcy.

Repos are typically used to convert securities and other assets into cash needed for a finance firm's activities. The basic idea is that you sell the security to somebody and they give you cash, and then you agree to repurchase it the next day at a fixed price.

Essentially, this is a short-term borrowing using the assets as collateral. As the period is short, there is little risk for the collateral to lose value. The lender—the firm purchasing the assets—therefore demands a very low interest rate. The repo method allows firms to borrow cheaply than it could on a long-term basis, which is riskier for the lender.

Under standard accounting rules, ordinary repo transactions are considered loans, and the assets remain on the borrowing firm's books. But Lehman found a way around so it could count the transaction as a 'sale' which removed the assets from its books. This Lehman would do just before the end of the quarterly financial reporting period to show a good quarter-end picture. The move temporarily made the firm's debt levels appear lower as funds would come in, although for a few days only, to help offsetting certain liabilities.

Two things therefore happened: One, the bad assets were hidden by hiving off, and two, the liabilities showed lower as temporary funds moved in. The trick was used for some time with impunity. About $39 billion was removed from the balance sheet at the end of the fourth quarter of 2007, $49 billion at the end of the first quarter of 2008 and $50 billion at the end of the next quarter, when Lehman's luck for creative accounting ran out! It was window dressing the books to look better temporarily but could not propel it into permanent prop-ups.

The Financial Accounting Standards Board (FASB; which laid down accounting principles in the USA)-approved rule Repo 105 contained a provision, saying that the assets involved would remain on the firm's books so long as the firm agreed to buy them back for a price between 98 per cent and 102 per cent of what it had received for them. If the repurchase price fell outside that narrow band, the transaction would be counted as a sale, not a loan, and the securities would not be reported on the firm's balance sheet until they were bought back. It was window dressing the balance sheet to expressly help bring down the bank's reported leverage—the ratio of assets to equity—the very reduction which the bank was externally promoting.

This provided the opening for Lehman. By agreeing to buy the assets back for 105 per cent of their sales price, the firm could book them as a sale and remove them from the books. But the move was misleading, as Lehman also entered into a forward contract, giving it the right to buy the assets back. The forward contract would be on Lehman's books, but at a value near zero. It was not just financial engineering but also cooking of books.

Very clearly, the one-time largest bank's long-term assets were being funded by short-term debt, for example, repo agreements, with borrowings of billions of dollars each day in the overnight wholesale funding markets in order to keep operating. By early 2008, most institutions refused to accept Lehman securities as collateral or demanded more collateral for a given level of financing, eroding Lehman's ability to raise funds and continue to honour its short-term obligations.

The people inside Lehman were very much aware of the accounting shenanigan they were practising. One Lehman executive wrote of Repo 105: 'It's basically window-dressing.' Another responded: 'I see ... so it's legally do-able but doesn't look good when we actually do it? Does the rest of the street do it?' The first executive replied: 'Yes, No and yes.'

It must be understood that Lehman intentionally manipulated accounting with the goal of deceiving investors, rating agencies and possibly their regulators, leading to the largest corporate bankruptcy in the US history.

Lehman was not about what you could actually see on the pages; it was about what wasn't there. In September 2008, when Lehman went belly up with roughly $450 billion still owed by the bank, it had just $65 billion left to settle creditors' claims. The latter could only accept 14 cents for every dollar Lehman Brothers owed them. 'Thieves', people mumbled about the once most commended bank.

Lehman's story is one of the numerous instances of company management broiling books, showing significantly 'better than reality' picture and misleading the world in believing feigned stories.

Financial accounting forms the key for everyone including investors, bankers, creditors and employees to gauge how enterprises are performing. Accounting is largely based on certain principles and practices but involves some exercise of judgement and subjectivity. That does not justify playing into grey areas.

Window dressing of financial results—showing non-existent revenue, creating fictitious profits, eliminating portions of debts, overstating assets and understating liabilities—is a means by which holier than thou images are presented through financial information and presentations. Accounting chicanery is one of the many modes by which the world of business cheats.

Given that financial information is the basic document on which everyone relies, the tendency to justify playing with numbers by some corporate finance teams is very worrying. The situation should have been reverse—it should have been the finance team driving anti-corrupt practices—but that does not seem to be the inside story in many cases!

Famous Few Fraudsters

Think of accounting fraud, and **Enron** perhaps will pop up first in your mind. It may be worthwhile spending a few minutes on how these guys perpetrated the game-changing scam. Within just 15 years, Enron grew to be one of the largest American corporations straddling over 40 countries employing 20,000 people. However, its achievements were made under the garb of carefully crafted string of scams.

The American energy giant had formed over a dozen illegal partnerships with other group companies, allowing the company to conceal debt off its balance sheets, bury its losses and generate fictional revenues. Partnerships were formed with subsidiaries housed in tax havens like the Cayman Islands, helping to avoid paying taxes in four of the last five years of its existence. To top it all, the biggest banks like Citigroup and JPMorgan helped Enron to structure the shady partnerships.[2] It eventually led to Enron's insolvency in 2001 and also the decimation of its auditors, Arthur Andersen.

Quickly thereafter in 2002 came the scandal of **WorldCom,** the American telecommunications company which inflated assets by a whopping $11 billion.[3]

WorldCom cooked its books by capitalizing operating expense items (resulting in increased assets and underreporting costs), and entered fake accounting entries to generate bogus sales, to meet its profit margin goals. The discrepancies were discovered by an internal auditor during a routine check of the capital accounts. The auditor could not find adequate backup documents to support the amounts mentioned in the accounts, a suspicious clue which ultimately led to the discovery of the shifting of expenses.

Tailpiece

Consequences of accounting fraud could be severe. Companies have gone belly up (like Wirecard AG), businesses transferred (like

WorldCom), entrepreneurs arrested (like Satyam) and audit firms destroyed (like Arthur Andersen). These were either intentional manipulation or misrepresentation of financial numbers, all leading to dreadful outcomes.

What Prompted These Accounting Frauds?

The massive accounting chicanery by Enron and WorldCom had the world sitting up and taking notice of what corporates can do to take any system for a ride.

But why did these companies carry out the monumental scams?

Enron wanted to keep pace with their eye-popping growth. *Fortune* magazine polls had been declaring it as the most innovative company in America for four consecutive years—a company which was fundamentally bankrupt by 2001. Although Enron did many other things, it was essentially buying and selling energy. The company was mainly involved in natural gas and electricity, converted these into contracts—called derivatives—which were sold to investors for millions of dollars based upon 'future' cash flow possibilities. Most of these contracts failed to deliver the promised returns.

In order to keep its mystique alive and stock prices growing, Enron swept its losses under creative accounting hiding slots. Those were the days of digital technologies and globalization. Esoteric stuff like 'derivatives' were cool but asset-based deliveries were old-fashioned. Enron management tried to take advantage of get-rich-super-fast cult. They were incapable of managing it. They took recourse to lies and damn lies. But ultimately the truth came out. The company went bust. (Post-bankruptcy, Enron was rechristened as Enron Creditors Recovery Corporation, with the sole mission to liquidate assets for creditors' benefit, paying about $22 billion from 2004 to 2011. Its last creditor payout was in May 2011.)

In the case of WorldCom, its CEO Bernard Ebbers became rich through the ever-increasing price of his holdings in the company. The Internet debacle of 2000 put pressure on WorldCom stock prices. The company was unable to maintain its otherwise aggressive growth.

Ebbers had borrowed for his other businesses by hypothecating his holdings in WorldCom. But with falling share price, his security with banks became inadequate, leading to the requirement of topping up his shares pledged. Ebbers along with his CFO fudged the company accounts between 1999 and mid-2002 to retain high share price, avoiding the necessity to either give more shares for security or return the loans taken on the back of the shares pledged. In July 2002, WorldCom's bluff was called and the company went for the USA's largest bankruptcy protection. (On emerging from bankruptcy, the company was renamed as MCI in April 2003, which was later taken over by Verizon Communications.)

A similar story got repeated in India during 2001–2008 by Satyam Computers, an Indian IT outsourcing company. They mis-reported non-existent cash balance of over ₹5,000 crore ($1 billion) along with overreporting of sales, profits and receivables, with understatement of liabilities.

The gigantic chicanery was committed to show customers, the stock market and the outside world that the company was very large and growing at a fast pace. The main motive was to impress global customers and incentivize them to give new orders to Satyam and not to its competitors such as Infosys, Wipro and TCS, who were also growing rapidly in a highly competitive environment. (The scandal played havoc to Satyam; it was bailed out by the Mahindra Group by merging Satyam with its IT arm, Tech Mahindra, in April 2009.[4])

Greed overtook rational business practices. When the management found promises unfulfilled or business performances lagging expectations, they practised hubris. Truth caught up sooner than later, leading to disastrous consequences to the much-hyped organizations of seemingly high repute.

Tailpiece

Corporates have cooked books of accounts throughout history. Irrespective of the reasons, it's all about making it appear that the business's financial health is better than what it really is.

Accounting Deception Drive

The motives for creative accounting could be quite complex and diverse. It is difficult to conjecture every conceivable thought process behind the book-keeping bluffing game. The following reasons may generally lead to shenanigans in the books of accounts.

- *Enticing excuse:* Management bonus and incentives could be linked to achievement of business results. This could be a good reason to push the boundaries of accounting principles to show better-than-reality business results.
- *Peer pressure:* If the other companies in the similar industry are doing well, while the company in question is struggling, there could be an inherent desire to fudge books to show colourful business performance. This competitive pressure led to the infamous Satyam scam, where the company wanted to outperform its peers.
- *Past promise:* Commitments to analysts or investors made earlier could lead to manipulating results, if the actual business performance is shoddy and sketchy. Even not being able to meet prior period performance could lead to fudging. Failure to meet banking covenants could be a raison d'être for fiddling books.
- *Occasional opportunities:* While accounting does involve use of sense of interpretation and estimates, sometimes circumstances could provide the leverage to carry the accounting judgements too far. Having a friendly auditor could prove advantageous to get little more adventurous in accounting elucidations.
- *Accounting approach:* Committing unethical acts is often a matter of attitude. The thought process of some entails stretching things a bit too far. Management could rationalize depiction of higher-than-actual profit to borrow from banks, only to rationalize that such acts were required for the organization's good. Rationalizing a dishonest act is sleazy.

Accounting chicanery are getting bigger, nastier and loathsome. Let me give you an instance where the auditors found the largest corporate scandal in South Africa. A forensic audit carried out over a 14-month period revealed a huge accounting chicanery at **Steinhoff International,** a South African international retail holding company, dealing mainly in furniture and household goods.[5]

The executives of the company recorded €6.5 billion ($7.4 billion) in fake transactions to inflate the value of Steinhoff before the international retail group collapsed in 2017. Over a period of eight years, the company had been overstating profits and asset values involving a small group of top executives and outsiders. An investigation by PwC revealed that the transactions were supported by documents including legal documents which were mostly backdated.

South African investors lost billions, as the company's equity got wiped out in the accounting swindle. This included the country's richest man Christo Wiese, who was the Chairman and the largest shareholder. After resigning in light of the scandal, Wiese sued the company to claw back billions of dollars in his share purchases. (Steinhoff is battling the accounting fraud fallout facing billions in legal claims, with the business struggling to find its feet back.)

Tailpiece

Cooking of books are instances when businesses make minced meat of accounting ethics. This would typically involve falsification or manipulation of financial information to provide untrue and unfair view of actual business performance.

The reasons for the accounting unscrupulous acts are not just one, but would normally be a complex set of motives leading to book-keeping trickeries.

Figure Fudging

In the greater Noida region, if you wanted a nice home, Amrapali properties would have been a choice, considering their massive enticing advertisements all over. The acclaimed Indian cricket team captain M. S. Dhoni was Amrapali's brand ambassador. With the help of celebrity endorsements and rosy pictures, the group sold thousands of residential units. They collected flat buyers' hard-earned money but did not use it for construction.

Amrapali Group, with the help of their statutory auditor Anil Mittal, doctored the financial accounts between 2008 and 2015. Showing great financial numbers, the company took large loans from banks fraudulently.[6] The promoters siphoned off over ₹3,000 crore, leaving in the lurch over 40,000 flat buyers without constructing their dream homes. (The auditor was arrested in June 2020, as he had apparently connived to prepare the doctored accounts; earlier, even the company chairperson had got arrested.)

The Amrapali story is a classic case where doctored accounts and dream ads duped investors. If financial figures are falsified, a lot can be achieved to carry out dishonest acts.

Similar questionable accounting was practised by the yesteryear serial winner of the most admired company in America, **GE**.[7] The manufacturing conglomerate faced questions on its shady accounting for its legacy insurance business. Doubts have been raised over the company's accounting for reserves related to its insurance business which it has been trying to wind down for years.

Accounting problems surfaced in late 2017, as GE was struggling with declining profits and cash flow. The company in January 2018 disclosed that it needed to bolster its insurance reserves by $15 billion and booked a $6 billion charge.

Investors were taken aback by the insurance business scenario, as GE had been declaring that the company had shed its insurance risk. GE had already in 2004 spun off or sold its insurance holdings.

But apparently, GE kept the risk for a bloc of 'long-term-care' insurance policies, written by it until 2006. Such policies are supposed to pay for nursing homes and assisted living services. Unfortunately, it proved to be an expensive proposition as the company underestimated how much the policies would need to pay out.

GE had removed the 'long-term-care liabilities' from its 2012 annual report and did not account for it till 2018, when it put it back. This is when GE reported insurance liabilities of $38 billion, up from $11 billion the previous year.

Internally, the GE employees were acknowledging that a bloc of long-term-care policies were toxic and sufficient reserves ought to have been booked in the accounting books. It was only in 2017 when the accounting folks apparently realized worrying trends in its insurance books. They then had no option but to shore up the reserves after the liabilities suddenly swelled.

Being upset and angry, pension funds brought a shareholder lawsuit in 2017, alleging that the improper insurance accounting fuelled a fraud in inflating GE's results.

(GE was fined $200 million by SEC in December 2020 for allegedly misleading investors on various issues including improper accounting for future liabilities in the old insurance business.)

Even **Mattel, Inc.,** the maker of Barbie dolls and Hot Wheels cars, was suspected to have doctored its accounts.[8] The toy maker announced in October 2019 that its CFO would be leaving after an investigation found shortcomings in the company's accounting and reporting procedures. Strangely, the company declared that the actions did not amount to fraud.

Creativity in accounting is also sometimes known as earnings management racket. It involves intentional manipulation of accounting policies, estimates and entries, to show a rosy financial picture.

Tailpiece

The stimulus for figure fudging could be numerous. It could be to secure funding from financial institutions or better management bonus or to meet expectations projected earlier or sheer desire to project a glowing financial position.

Modes of executing the false picture are abundant: improper revenue recognition, understating expenses, capitalizing revenue costs, fraudulent accounting entries, improper asset disclosures, incorrect valuations, and the possibilities are endless.

Sham Sales

If you wanted your coffee in a cosy corner in China, the choice for many shifted from Starbucks to the country's new-found high-flying **Luckin Coffee,** which took the market by storm.[9] Floated in 2017, the coffee house grew at a blistering pace, opening stores faster than Starbucks, doubling its valuation to $12 billion, eight months after going public.

But bad news struck when things seemed to be going well. Suddenly, in April 2020, the company announced that much of its sales were fake. The three-year-old juggernaut suddenly came to a screeching halt, with stock exchange moving to delist Luckin.

What went wrong?

It transpires that Luckin sold vouchers redeemable for tens of millions of cups of coffee to companies which had ties with the company's chairman and controlling shareholder, Charles Lu. These fake sales helped the company to book significantly higher revenue than its coffee shops produced.

The company also showed corresponding payment of $140 million to a procurement employee under the name Ms Liang towards payment for raw materials such as juice, delivery and HR services. The twist was that Ms Liang was fictitious.

The size and audacity of trickery were humungous. The ability to fake financial results prompted the promoters to take the company public within two years of its establishment—a classical story of painting a picture of hope and achievement based on false numbers of revenue and costs.

The attractiveness of misleading investors with higher sales numbers even charmed the automaker **Fiat Chrysler**.[10] The Italian–American company inflated its monthly sales numbers by paying dealers to report fake sales between 2012 and 2016. The auto giant boasted about a streak of year-over-year sales increases into 2016, when in reality it had faltered since 2013.

Not to be outdone, even the famous German car manufacturer **BMW** was investigated in 2019 for dubious sales in the USA.[11] In this instance, it was suspected that some on-trial vehicles delivered to dealers were reported as wholesaler purchases to improve sales figures.

Accounting fraud's favourite stallion is to show non-existent sales. Propping-up sales figures serve the purpose of showing business growth and concomitant higher profits. If a company's sales are growing, the investing community gets a high and looks positively at it. Investors have a thirst for fairy tales.

Tailpiece

The most commonly used yardstick to judge a company's business performance is to review its sales growth. And if this number can be fudged through accounting jugglery, lying about business's image gets easier.

Channel Stuffing

We would normally believe when big corporates announce healthy growth numbers. 'Revenue showing upward trend'—these words are music to the ears of investors. This development is often followed by enhanced stock prices and bolstered company goodwill.

But let me tell you that the sales figures may not always be as authentic as it sounds. Many could include 'forced' sales made—only to prepone a particular month's sales or to have an understanding that the sales made in a month can be returned in the month following. While this is not exactly an accounting jugglery, it adds to the doctoring efforts of a company's financial numbers.

Many big names have practised inflating sales by dumping goods with buyers. It is all about timing differences—recording revenue in improper periods.

The American pharma major **Bristol Myers Squibb** was found to sell excessive amounts of pharmaceutical products to its wholesalers ahead of demand, effectively overstating its revenues by $1.5 billion.[12]

A similar channel stuffing was practised by the anti-virus software maker **McAfee Inc.,**[13] inflating its revenues by over $600 million.

Window dressing the accounts can take many forms, ranging from the relatively benign to outright deception. In manufacturing companies, for example, a manager might engage in 'channel stuffing'—filling products into sales channels just before quarter end, even if they have not been expressly ordered—to help meet targets and boost reported sales.

This is not far removed from the retail store manager who, knowing monthly targets have been achieved in the current month, delays recording sales for a couple of days to the following month, to help meet the sales targets of the following quarter.

Tailpiece

Perhaps the oldest trick to fudge numbers, channel stuffing is rather common with only a few instances getting out in the public domain to raise our eyebrows. It makes things look good in the short term, but in the long term it is a sort of internal Ponzi scheme, eventually collapsing with the truth catching up.

Circuitous Connections

Round-tripping transactions involve circuitous business between two or more companies without economic benefits to the companies involved. The sole purpose usually is to inflate revenue or provide impression of strong sales growth. The round-trip transactions could involve the same amount within a short period, or it may involve a loan made to a customer who can use it to purchase goods. Actual payments could have been made, but settling dues does not legitimize the revenue generated if there is no economic benefit resulting from it.

Let me cite an example how round tripping can be used for a multibillion-dollar fraud. A three-carat yellow-orange cushion-cut diamond was shipped at least four times between fraud-accused **Nirav Modi**-controlled shell companies and the infamous jeweller for over five weeks in 2011. The price of the large gem alternately shrank and spiked by a million dollars as it moved across the globe. This practice of trading goods repeatedly to give the appearance of distinct transactions was central to the largest bank scam in Indian history. The circuitous sale was the master plan in which Nirav Modi and associates borrowed through PNB, about $4 billion between 2011 and 2017. Nirav Modi structured sham transactions supposedly to 'import' diamonds and other gems into India. He used a web of more than 20 secretly and indirectly controlled shell companies.

Tailpiece

'Ring-a-ring-a-roses', the nursery rhyme sung in a merry go round ride, is what circuitous sales involve—the same set of merchandise going round and round among a set of entities, to depict a false image of high volume and business prosperity. Several large names have practised it. Some get caught, many escape. Unfortunately, it's a common deceitful act being played by several businesses.

Bill and Hold

Bill-and-hold transactions occur when the seller records a sale, but the goods or services have not been delivered. Say a seller produces the products, does not deliver them to the customers, but records the sale in the year end. The customer takes delivery only in the following year and not earlier. The transaction may involve legitimate customer orders but the customer may not be willing to take delivery. The transaction could also involve fake orders and sales booked to boost revenue numbers. The swindling steps could entail seller holding goods in its facilities or dispatch to different sites, including third-party warehouses.

The American ATM maker **Diebold Inc.** manipulated its earnings from at least 2002 through 2007 to meet financial performance forecasts, misstating the company's reported earnings by over $125 million.[14] The list of fraudulent practices included improper use of 'bill-and-hold' accounting. 'Diebold's finance executives borrowed from many different chapters of the deceptive accounting playbook to fraudulently boost the company's bottom line,' complained the director of SEC, the US market regulator.

Tailpiece

Bill and hold is a typical hocus-pocus accounting. It is not often easy for the auditors to catch the hoax—and hence it's rather attractive ruse among many.

Contingent Sales or Sell-through Agreements

Sales agreements could include contingent terms which are based on some future performance of the buyer (could be distributors or resellers). The terms would impact revenue recognition by the seller. The 'contingent' terms may not be shown upfront in the sales agreements and may be provided in side agreements.

'Sell-through' agreements are similar to consignment sales and can involve shipment of goods to a party who agrees to sell them onwards to third parties. Revenue cannot be recognized until the goods are sold to a third party with no further ifs and buts.

To cite an instance of a blatant accounting fraud, in March 1997, **Sunbeam Corporation** headquartered in Florida, USA, improperly recognized revenue on a 'contingent sale' to a wholesaler.[15] The household appliance-manufacturing company booked $1.5 million in revenue and $400,000 in income from a purported sale of barbecue grills to a wholesaler. The wholesaler held Sunbeam merchandise over a quarter end, without accepting any of the risks of ownership; the agreement provided that the wholesaler could return all of the merchandise if it did not sell it, and that Sunbeam would pay all costs of shipment (in both directions) and storage. Incurring no expenses in this transaction, the wholesaler in fact returned all of the grills to Sunbeam during the third quarter of 1997. Sunbeam cooked its book massively by incorrectly booking contingent sales.

Tailpiece

Under a consignment arrangement, there is no sale until delivery is made to the ultimate buyer or further conditions to sale are met. When the selling company records sale as soon as goods are delivered to the consignee, this is falsified acceleration of sale. How can revenue be shown when merchandise is not really sold?

Missing Money

Just imagine a company preparing its accounts and getting it audited for years showing that substantial cash is in its coffer, but in fact the fund position is just an illusion. Things can't get worse from this perhaps!

The German fintech company **Wirecard AG** had to file for insolvency proceedings in June 2020, days after revealing that more than $2 billion in cash were missing from its balance sheet, which probably did not even exist.

It is suspected that the likely fictitious cash balance corresponded to all the net income Wirecard had misreported over more than a decade. It basically meant that the asset side of the balance sheet showing a comfortable cash balance did not exist at all! The hole in the balance sheet exhibited that the much touted fast-growing online payments business was a mirage than a miracle.

Misrepresenting cash in the balance sheet is not a new trick. This falsehood is employed by many organizations to project a holier than thou image.

The Indian tech giant **Satyam** played a similar trick several years back. This led to an analogous consequence. The company had to be forcibly merged with an existing software company under government intervention.

Tailpiece

Cash is the most significant business asset providing instant liquidity. A good cash and bank balance provides the greatest strength to any business. And if that number is shown to be higher than what it actually is, the quality of the balance sheet enhances overnight.

Hide Expenses and Liabilities

Adelphia Communications, the fifth largest cable television operator in the USA, had to file for bankruptcy in 2002, when it was found that the company concealed loans to its controlling shareholders, the Rigas family, of over $3 billion. It also hid several other transactions between the company and the Rigas family. Incidentally, the company also overstated its equity by $0.4 billion and improperly netted related party receivables and payables, hiding proper disclosures.

The easiest way to conceal expenses and liabilities is to simply ignore recording it; dump bills from vendors into your drawers, and let it overflow! Cost concealment is easy for services, as it is difficult to cross tally. When it amounts to goods, it may get difficult to ignore an invoice liability as circumstantial evidence would show goods received but not accounted for, unless the receipt of goods itself is hidden.

Sometimes liabilities are hidden with an idea to show it in the future, hoping enhanced income in the later period will be able to absorb the costs.

Capitalization of revenue expenses is a widespread method of enhancing income by not charging to the P&L account. It is another way of hiding expenses, by showing cost items in the balance sheet as an asset, though the incorrectly accounted asset value will be subjected to depreciation.

The high-profile fraud by the USA's second-largest long-distance telephone company **WorldCom,** unearthed in 2002, adopted the method of reducing its operating expenses by characterizing them as capital costs. What they did was simple. The company being a telephone company paid 'line cost' fees for the right to use the lines and networks of third-party telecom companies. These fees are an expense under accounting principles. But WorldCom capitalized around $3 billion of these line costs between 2001 and 2002, inflating the company's profits by the same amount.

Products, when sold, sometimes are backed by performance warranty. Say an air conditioner sold could have five years' warranty for compressor performance. If problems are encountered in the quality, the seller needs to estimate the likely cost to be incurred to rectify the ill-performing air conditioner. Warranty costs are provisions that require an accounting adjustment if they originate from any present obligation. Accounting shenanigans are executed by omitting to record the liability that would in turn reduce the expense, and overstate profit.

Tailpiece

Many are the ways by which accounting information is decorated to show a false picture—hiding or capitalizing expense is a popular technique to bump up profit or reduce loss numbers.

Inventory Inventions

Manipulating inventory value has two clear benefits. One, it helps to alter profits. Two, it enables working capital funding enhancement due to higher inventory availability or to meet debt covenants.

Modifying methods include moving inventory between locations and varieties to deceitfully inflate quantities, postponing and underreporting of write-downs for obsolescence, manipulating inventory valuations and improper inventory capitalization.

Companies may 'create' inventory by fabricating journal entries, goods receipt reports or purchases orders.

To show improved profits, **Comptronix Corporation,** an electronics parts manufacturer, fraudulently increased the value of its inventory between 1990 and 1992. When its false inventory figures became too high, the company's executives freaked.[16] They converted a major part of it into 'purchased equipment' or 'fixed assets' through phony purchase orders and accounting entries. Cheques for the amount of fictitious purchases of fixed assets would be written by the company. It was here that the plan boomeranged. Comptronix got caught and had to restate its accounts.

Many tricks can be employed to misstate inventory. Creating phantom inventory is a popular ploy. When inventory-backed financing is sought, possibility of adjusting inventory higher exists. If stocks show a trend of the revenue rising faster, a deception perhaps is taking place. Many could be the ruse.

Tailpiece

One of the simplest ways to commit financial statement fraud is to distort the value of the assets of the company. Investors and auditors would do well to keep their sharp eyes on the inventory numbers, they are evaluating or examining.

Refreshed Receivables

Bad and old customer receivables can be 'refreshed' to show the outstanding amounts being current and not aged. This would avoid creation of bad debt provisions too.

For showing phony sales, the most logical implication is to show corresponding higher receivables, which would then need to be tampered with, as the debtors would remain unpaid. The receivables can be refreshed by exchanging transactions with customers, where customers can receive 'credits' to their accounts and are allowed to repurchase goods, howsoever small it could be.

Let me give you an instance of how phony receivables were created to get bank funding, only to get caught after two years of fudging.

An Indian-American CEO and part-owner of a now-defunct New Jersey-based marble and granite wholesaler **Lotus Exim International,** Rajendra Kankariya, conspired with other employees to obtain a credit line of $17 million by fraudulent means.[17] The bank believed that its funding was secured by the company's accounts receivable. In reality, the company fabricated, inflated and refreshed many of the accounts receivables. This ultimately led to the company defaulting on the line of credit.

To conceal the lack of sufficient collateral, the company's employees created fake email addresses on behalf of its customers, so that they could pose as them and answer the bank's and auditor's enquiries about the debtors. (Kankariya pleaded guilty in September 2020 for committing the fraud.)

Tailpiece

Accounts receivable is not real money in the bank. Businesses can fake or misstate invoices, carry out the accounting shenanigan and yet it may be difficult to figure out the truth. Debtors' deception is an attractive mode to doctor accounts.

Deceitful Disbursements

Trickery has many ways: Recording non-existent costs, false billing, sham procurement, ghost employees and fake expense reimbursement. A popular phony procurement pattern is to set up fake vendors in the accounts payable. Putting across falsified expense vouchers for reimbursement is an old game often practised.

Payroll falsification is a popular mode to make fraudulent payouts. It can include falsification of hours worked, creation of fictitious employees, failure to remove leaving employees and diversion of payments to employees, managers or co-conspirators.

The Association of Certified Fraud Examiners' 2016 report[18] examined over 2,400 instances of fraud across the world. It discovered that payroll fraud and cheque tampering popped up in one in five cases.

Tailpiece

Fake expenses, reimbursing personal expenses, multiple reimbursement against the same cost incurred and overstated expenses are modes of showing less profit by businesses to avoid paying corporate tax.

Playing with Promotional Paybacks

Rebates, incentives and discounts are often offered to customers as promotional avenues to purchase products. Such incentives are often based on fulfilment of future events like meeting threshold volumes in a specified period. As it's a giveaway based on future estimates, it could be subject to manipulation or bias. Frauds could arise in booking the benefits upfront as an income for the buyer, even when the right to accrue the benefit could be some time away. Falsehoods arise in improper financial reporting and misclassification of credits in income statement.

Let me cite an instance. **Sunbeam Corporation,** the American appliances company, made improper accounting treatment for supplier rebates. During 1997, Sunbeam began recording as income rebates obtained from suppliers which related to later period purchases.[19] Under accounting principles, a rebate should normally be recorded as a reduction in cost of sales in the period in which its associated sale is made. However, the company fraudulently accounted for future volume discounts upfront.

Tailpiece

Goodies likely to be received in the future cannot be assumed to have already earned. And when this happens in accounting books, infraction gets involved.

Dipping into Cookie Jars

A popular method to project a false sense of comfort is through the creation of excess or 'cookie jar' reserves. It is accounting used to create cash reserves in good years so the amounts can be used to offset poor earnings in bad years. The effect is to give the impression that the company is consistently achieving earnings goals and meeting investor expectations.

Let me cite an example. The spell of invincibility was broken for **Dell Inc.**, the darling of the financial markets as it displayed the magical power to drive down costs and enhance efficiencies from its supply chain.[20] In 2010, the huge financial illusion was shattered. What Dell did was this: The computer company made an agreement with Intel Corporation in which Dell used Intel microchips exclusively in return for payments by Intel. Dell did not disclose the special payments to investors. Dell failed to meet earnings targets every quarter from 2002 to 2005. It used the undisclosed exclusivity payments received earlier from Intel, to make up the shortfalls. In essence, the computer company maintained 'cookie jar reserves' to cover shortfalls in its operating results quarter after quarter for three years. By releasing the reserves it had created in an earlier period, Dell created an illusion of well-being converting losses into profits through the accounting magic wand.

Tailpiece

'Cookie jar' is a business colloquial for undisclosed cash balance or funds reserved for a liability which does not currently exist. This rainy day reserve is a tactic resorted to by many enterprises, though it amounts to doctoring of financial numbers.

Off-balance-sheet Liabilities Hiding

Off-balance-sheet entities or transactions can be used to conceal bad news such as debts and liabilities. This could also help to improve the income statements by understating liabilities and pushing out costs.

Enron's failure to disclose billions of dollars of debt held by off-balance-sheet entities ultimately prompted its fall from grace when the non-disclosures got unveiled in 2001 through an internal whistle-blower. It so happened that the *Fortune* magazine named Enron 'America's Most Innovative Company' six years in a row prior to the scandal.

Tailpiece

Balance sheets provide statement of assets and liabilities on a particular period end. And if I can push out bad assets or higher liabilities on to some other company, my balance sheet would look cleaner. Many accountants take this stratagem through intercompany deals or related party transactions—a beautiful way to beautify an ugly balance sheet.

Improper Investments

In order to prop up assets and earnings, businesses can deliberately inflate investments or create fabricated ones. Deliberate misclassification of investments can take place in order to show improper recognition of gains or failure to recognize losses. Dishonest schemes can also be structured to hide or defer losses from sale of investments or prevent impairment and write downs.

Writing off of useless goodwill is a common method to impair investments. 'Goodwill' means the premium a company pays to acquire another, over and above the acquired company's book value. This extra payment is deliberate, either to win against fellow suitors or to entice the shareholders of the bride. Technically, it is an asset, though an intangible one, with the assumption that the extra payment is buying something significant and worthwhile— business goodwill to be precise.

Now for goodwill 'impairment', when extra buck was paid in the purchase price but turns sour, makes the value of the acquired company worth a whole lot less than what was paid earlier. And this is where con games can be played to hide the inevitable, refusing to take write-downs of the intangible 'goodwill' asset value and impact results adversely.

Tailpiece

Investment is an asset. If it's of poor quality but depicted as if everything is hunky-dory, it will be an accounting infraction.

Improper Disclosure

Accounting information together with its notes, schedules and explanations, is to be made in such a way that readers are able to take a view on the company's financial position and performance.

It is obligated on the management to divulge all significant information in the financial statements, without misleading anyone. The management should communicate all significant events which could have some bearing on the financial position or results of the company. If a material fraud had been discovered, the implication needs to be disclosed. Similarly, if a court judgment or a regulatory decision could have a bearing on the reported numbers, the matter needs to be divulged in the annual report.

Materiality is pertinent to the presentation and disclosure of financial statements. The accounting statements should disclose the information which is relevant to understanding an entity's 'financial position' on the reporting date and its 'financial performance' during the reporting period. Care should be taken not to reduce the understandability of the financial statements by obscuring material information with immaterial data. Information that are not material need not be specifically disclosed.

Another crucial matter for disclosure is related party transactions. If any business is undertaken with another entity whose management can be influenced or controlled by the company, then it needs to be revealed. Doubts can exist about the arm's length nature of these transactions, ruling out economic harm on the company. Unfortunately, disclosures in this area are often dicey.

Tailpiece

Any business corporation's health can be judged by the disclosures it makes usually through its periodical financial statements. If these documents are not truthful or are mixed with hoax and chicanery, then hoodwinking the users becomes easy. Unfortunately, many financial statements contain hubris.

Accounting Scams: Any Positive Fallout?

While dodges and dupery are daily occurrences in the business world, some are so shrewd, sizable and stunning that they etch stretched scars on the society. Governments have woken up, regulators changed systems, watchdogs becoming more active and laws getting altered. The business world has also sat up to witness some changing paradigms.

Enron and WorldCom accounting scandals shook the US government out of its slumber and made it turn the governance knobs on corporate America. In India, the Satyam swindle made the authorities wake up from their stupor.

Post the Enron and WorldCom fiascos, three broad changes came into existence in the USA. First, Sarbanes–Oxley Act of 2002 was enacted to make elaborate reporting requirements and improve accounting disclosures; second, FASB tightened accounting standards; and lastly, companies were made to have majority of independent directors to question company management and auditors.

The fallouts were also felt in several other countries, with governments enacting regulations with tougher disclosure and internal control requirements on the corporate world.

With the changing nature of corporate frauds, the UK enacted the Corporate Governance Code effective from January 2019. It brought in focus more high-quality reporting with less importance on ticking boxes, and use explanations to communicate with stakeholders.[21] For instance, when more than 20 per cent of votes have been cast against a resolution, companies will have to explain the actions they intend to take and publish an update within six months after such a vote.

Canada, Germany, Japan and many others have made life tougher for the corporates to doctor books of accounts and play mischief.

India saw the introduction of Clause 49 in the Listing Agreement for stock market-listed companies in late 2005. It brought in some basic corporate governance practices[22] and disclosure requirements. The changes included specifying minimum number of independent directors, setting up of an audit committee, a mandatory preparation of management's discussion and analysis (MD&A) section and the report on corporate governance in the annual report.

The Satyam accounting scandal in 2009 led India to overhaul its corporate oversight laws. The Companies Act, 2013, got enacted. It revamped accounting and auditing standards, imposed stiffer penalties for fraud and created more government oversight over corporates.

To prevent Satyam-like scandals from resurfacing—where the auditors failed to notice several inconsistencies despite auditing the company for years—the new legislation introduced mandatory rotation of auditors. It targets corporate governance and ensures more transparency for all companies doing business in India, irrespective of its size, structure or ownership.

The new 'Companies Act' and 'Listing Obligations and Disclosure Requirements Regulations 2015' for listed entities have tightened the screws and bolted several nuts on corporate India.

The governance process will always be evolving and cannot ever be treated as final. Every time legislations are made to plug some potential loopholes, ways to dodge them are figured out, which leads to a fresh set of controls to rein in the business world.

To catch the recalcitrant, most geographies are periodically bringing in checks and balances in assuring proper accounting practices, at least for the stock market-listed entities.

In India, some accounting related regulatory developments are significant. They include: the setting up of accounting and auditing regulator National Financial Reporting Authority (NFRA) since

November 2018; need to report since April 2018 on key audit matters (KAM) which auditors believe are important to be disclosed; and the several stringent disclosures from April 2021 through Companies (Auditor's Report) Order (CARO) 2020 report. These are all attempts to make the accounting reports credible, and the auditor–auditee ecosystem accountable.[23]

Whether these changes are enough to prevent business frauds getting larger, deeper and wider, only time will tell, as we all know that old habits die hard!

Tailpiece

Legislations will need to keep pace with the economic offenders, whether they commit accounting fraud or other misdemeanours. For instance, of late, many high-flying wilful-defaulting entrepreneurs have run away from India, leaving large loans behind them. Kingfisher Airlines' Vijay Mallya, diamantaire Nirav Modi, Winsome Diamond's Jatin Mehta and Sterling Biotech's Sandesara brothers are a few who have left behind a stack of bad loans. All of them showed flowery financial data, both past and future, built lenders' confidence, but then reneged on the trust reposed on the businesses.

While corporate defrauding is striding fast and furious, the regulatory and policing frameworks are trying to adjust themselves to the growing financial menace.

Auditors: Watchdog, Bloodhound, Sniffers or German Shepherds?

Whenever a fraud comes to light or an accounting deceit gets revealed, the most common questions that get asked are: Where were the auditors? What were they doing?

The key question is: Are auditors at all responsible for unearthing chicanery?

The accounting world's most popular phrase perhaps is: 'An auditor is a watchdog, not a bloodhound.' This was said over hundred years back, in the famous Kingston Cotton Mills Co.'s case (1896), where Lord Justice Lopes further said, 'The auditor is justified in believing tried servants of the company in whom confidence is placed by the company. He is entitled to assume that they are honest and rely upon their representations, provided he takes reasonable care.'

Echoing a similar sentiment recently, the President of the Institute of Chartered Accountants of India reconfirmed in March 2021,

> An auditor's job is not to become a bloodhound and should not be seen as an investigator. An auditor can be a little bit of a watchdog and at the most what one can expect them to become is a sniffer dog—which smells and passes on the feeling to the audit committee.[24]

If these statements are to be followed, then auditors are definitely not responsible for detecting frauds. But should it be so?

Times have changed. The world of business has moved on significantly since the days when auditors were not expected to be detectives. Auditors are, in fact, the only 'third parties' who have the right to look into the business transactions of an auditee enterprise. There is no one else who has as much access as the auditors have in the normal course of business.

Things in the business world are also not the same anymore, as the auditing standards have got tightened. The current standards setting out auditor's responsibilities expect the auditors to exercise professional scepticism. The focus is on assessing the risk of fraud. In the absence of suspicion, the auditors may still accept records and documents as bona fide.

Unfortunately, despite the tightened regulations and lessons learnt over time, audit slippages are still taking place. For instance, the infrastructure development finance company IL&FS (with doctored accounts and possible fund diversion of ₹13,000 crore) and PNB (where Nirav Modi, the borrower, defrauded over ₹11,000 crore for 7 long years) are examples to suggest that some auditors could have been sloppy. Sometimes, they still accept the management's assertion, missing in making basic routine checks.

As news keep pouring in of corporate frauds, business blow-ups, banks not repaying their dues and cybercrimes wiping out savings of many, the expectations from the auditors are enhancing. While the auditing community focuses on 'true and fair' view certification of accounting statements, the society expects the 'accuracy' of the financial numbers to be endorsed. And that's the dichotomy to be bridged.

Thousands of audits are conducted around the world without concerns—the result of auditors' independent verification, judgement and objectivity. The accounting profession has by and large reformed itself to address glitches, adapt and improve. But it is the few audits which falter that leads to instigate doubts about their veracity and fairness.

Let's not miss out that the company management is primarily responsible for fraud detection and control. However, when the company accounts which have evidently been examined by the auditors cannot be trusted, the faith of the wider community on the financial reports will stand eroded.

In contrast to the 'watchdog-only' philosophy espoused by some, the Indian accounting and auditing regulator NFRA chairman's recent widely publicized view suggested that the audit fraternity must forget the 'watchdog and not bloodhound' description. He added that this is 'serious misconception' needing 'to be exorcised from everyone's mind'.

Enhanced responsibility and concomitant trust are being placed on the auditing community with the emerging challenged business scenario. More companies are falling sick with millions suffering in lost jobs and vanishing investor wealth. This is more so with the impact of the pandemic, the rise of e-business risks and heightened practice of cybercrime.

High-quality audit requires more than merely adhering to the prescriptive standards and the completion of files. It should move to becoming more informative than ticking the compliance boxes, and one which helps to grow trust in business activities and disclosures.

Historically, auditors were assumed to be invigilators (watchdogs) but not a sleuths (bloodhounds). But the society at large seems to be expecting the audit community to sniff for frauds lying around and to detect the hidden mala fide. It is assumed that if auditors pick up a scent of something wrong, they need to follow the bloody trail: 'smell test' to detect the stink of hidden fraud. Auditors are definitely 'sniffers', if not 'German Shepherds' who are the best in search, detection and rescue tasks.

Auditors are the moral arbiters. They are the carriers of good corporate governance. At the very least, the societal expectancy makes the auditor detect 'material' fraud.

It is time for the auditing community to fundamentally reassess their roles and tasks, in line with the expectations of the society and the governments. Or else a time may come when their invaluable signatures could sink in value.

Few Last Words

Accounting provides information. It is data which helps investors, bankers, creditors, government and the society at large to get an impression of any business organization's financial performance. It is the management of any enterprise which is primarily responsible for preparing and disclosing the accounting numbers. And when these figures are manipulated, it is a no-brainer to assume that there were ulterior motives working behind the scene. This is where the auditor comes into picture to play a role, to assure the society either all is well or there are red flags to be aware of.

The ways to doctor financial statements and disclosures are numerous. Some flavours of the possible phony schemes which are commonly practised have been discussed in this chapter. These should enable you to identify probable fault lines and deceitful disclosures. The instances are not exhaustive but inclusive.

Accounting rules and practices are ever evolving. Not only the principles and practices are getting aligned across the globe, but efforts are also on to account for new developments.

'ESG' accounting is one such area—designing a reporting framework for environmental, social and governance standards, possibly prompting investors to divert more money into the responsible sectors. Another new-era move is 'carbon' accounting. It is primarily used to measure and disclose the climate emissions of financial sectors' investment portfolios.

Novel developments are a welcome change. But when businesses collapse or repayments default, often crooked deeds come out of the closet. This results in doubts being expressed about accounting systems and roles of auditors. Bad corporate news often leads to searching questions on the accounting and auditor fraternities.

Accounting trickery is a complex tapestry of motive and opportunity. Even if more laws are enacted and more regulatory watchdogs employed, the inherent human nature of some to bamboozle others and make quick bucks is not going to be eliminated. It is regrettable the way human nature functions.

Neither are all corporates holy cows nor do all enterprises have poor corporate governance. There are some black sheep which we need to identify through either the colour of their behaviour or the stain on their information. It is both an art and a science.

Financial engineering helps in fulfilling the innate craving of many managements to amplify the positive and camouflage the negative. This is leading to corporate dishonesty. It will be foolhardy to think that it will get eliminated ever. We need to keep our antennas on alert mode, so should there be alarms, we are able to at least start sniffing for snags.

Where temptation exists, dishonesty and dirty deception will often follow. Thus, it is good to know the tricks of the trade which tricksters could use to trick us.

CHAPTER TWELVE

Ominous Omens of Financial Frauds

Nature provides early warning signals, so do historical developments. Sometimes we may ignore the red flags. Dark clouds do send signs of an impending storm, but many a time we hope that it will pass. Even when there is smoke, we may sometimes ignore that there could be a fire. A tragedy could strike if one omits to act on ominous omens.

Let us take a live business example. IL&FS was a highly rated infrastructure development group and one of India's largest nonbank lenders.[1] It suddenly collapsed in mid-2018, unable to grapple with its overflowing debts.

Gory news of management chicanery got out of its closet. India's serious fraud investigator observed a series of accounting and financial indiscretions which eventually led to the group's ruin.

It transpired that the group gave all sorts of bad loans worth ₹91,000 crore ($12 billion). The executives, including former chairman Ravi Parthasarathy, allegedly window dressed financials of the parent company. The apparent objective was to show higher profits which helped to borrow more.

This aided top management to justify their pay hikes. The company doled out perks and stock options to select employees through an employee welfare trust—which incidentally owned 12 per cent of IL&FS. To make matters worse, the top managerial remuneration increased by 66 per cent in 2017–2018. Parthasarthy got the biggest hike at 144 per cent. In comparison, salaries of employees other than managers rose only by 4 per cent.

The main issue involved was that the parent IL&FS and its direct subsidiaries borrowed short-term funds such as commercial papers, intercorporate deposits and bank loans, based on window-dressed financials and high-credit ratings. These short-term borrowings were in turn lent for the long term at high interest rates to its group companies and other borrowers. It was a typical short-term and long-term fund mismatch. (This malady has already been discussed in a previous chapter in much detail.)

The funds moved down the pyramid from the borrowing entities with high credit ratings to its other loss-making project subsidiaries as loans and advances. And these mala fide loans kept piling up. For instance, the parent company IL&FS sanctioned loans of ₹2,500 crore ($330 million) to its subsidiaries in 20172018 (against ₹320 crore or $40 million in the previous year)—an eightfold increase!

The companies also gave loans to its subsidiaries to repay old loans—a scheme which is called 'ever-greening'. This helped the lending companies show interest income generated by fresh loans on its balance sheet. Considering that the lending companies were registered as non-bank financial companies, the lender took advantage of relatively lax bad loan provisioning requirements.

Not stopping here, IL&FS used to charge high fees from its direct subsidiaries as consultation, brand, project management, loan syndication and advisory fees. These fees, deducted upfront from loans advanced, became the main source of revenue and helped the parent and its direct subsidiaries recover a large part of their investments even before a project was launched. That made the parent and key subsidiaries look financially healthy to borrow more. However, these tricks obviously enhanced the financial burden and saddled subsidiary projects with unsustainable debts.

The cycle continued till it became impossible to sustain, ending in multiple defaults and spooking the Indian credit market.

One wonders how the three credit-rating agencies—CARE, ICRA and India Ratings—failed to spot the red flags of stress in IL&FS. They kept granting it the highest ratings till the group somersaulted into debt default.

It so happened that in July 2018, company founder Ravi Parthasarathy stepped down, citing health reasons. In August, there was a default within the group. This rattled all. Believe it or not, the rating stood at AAA (the highest debt-safety rating) till a day before the group defaulted, only to be brought down by eight notches in one day. IL&FS got rated into 'default' status in September.

This escalated into a credit market crisis in India and forced the government to take over the infrastructure group in late 2018 to contain a financial contagion.

Next, it leads us to the role of auditors—Deloitte and BSR (a KPMG affiliate in India). Auditors seemed to have had loads of red flags.

Let me state a few of the ominous signals pointed out by SFIO: negative net owned funds (due to too much of accumulated loss); negative capital adequacy ratio (wiping out of capital); funding of defaulting borrowers through their group companies again and again; suppression of NPAs; non-verification of end use of bank finance; and taking alibi of management representations.

Should the auditors not have got alarmed when they encountered the above tell-tale signs? As the SFIO is alleging, did the auditors 'connive and collude' with the top management to conceal material information and fraudulently falsify the financial statements from FY13–14 to FY17–18? The investigating agency alleges that the auditors 'knowingly did not report the true state of affairs of the company'.

Can the credit-rating agencies be blamed for part of the IL&FS scandal? Why did the rickety financial position spring out only when the group was heading for bankruptcy?

Answers to these questions perhaps will remain unanswered for long. The matter is however rather clear: If red rags shown were paid heed to, perhaps so much mayhem to nation's wealth would not have taken place.

Frauds in banks are just not dissipating. There are too many tricksters trying to milk financial companies.

In a global banking survey[2] by KPMG between November 2018 and February 2019 in over 43 retail banks across the globe, over 60 per cent experienced increase in fraud volume globally. And the bad news is that over half of survey respondents stated that fraud recoveries were less than 25 per cent of the deceit losses. This low rate demonstrates the importance of prediction and prevention efforts.

One wonders whether the number of delinquency account could have been significantly brought down had there been red flags raised and early warning whistles heeded. The huge rise in banking frauds clearly shows that early warning systems in banks are either inadequate, not working or not being noticed.

Tell-tale Signs for Lenders

In ailments like epileptic seizures or prostate cancer, a patient's gradual health deterioration could grow into a sudden catastrophic state. The progression of illness would normally be in three stages: a normal state, a pre-disease state and a disease state. The 'normal state' is a steady state, representing a relatively healthy stage during which the disease is under control or in a chronic inflammation period. The 'pre-disease state' is the limit of the normal state, immediately before the threshold point is reached. The process of illness is usually reversible to the normal state in this stage, if it is appropriately treated. However, the malady usually becomes irreversible to the normal state if the system passes the critical point of the pre-disease state.

Hence, it is essential to detect the pre-disease state so as to prevent qualitative deterioration by seeking appropriate medical intervention. This is the tipping point for a patient—this is where the early warning signal system needs to work. Or else, the patient could make a drastic transition to a 'disease state'.

Similar principles apply to businesses. It is good to anticipate the threshold point where things in business could just start to wobble and then, perhaps, go on to crash! It could just be impending competition, imports playing havoc, flickering customer order intake, frequent customer complains or botched-up production system. Normally, the early signs of financial stress can be sighted when payments to lenders or suppliers are getting delayed or promised disbursements are being skipped.

Some helping hints could enable investors and lenders to foresee businesses brewing financial trouble. If any of the following broad signals are depicted, it should be taken as a matter of concern requiring further investigation:

- *Fund strapped:* The borrower is short of cash and is struggling to meet its liabilities. For instance, the enterprise routinely delays repayment of bank interest or principal.
- *Frosty behaviour:* The borrower is hiding facts and not being transparent, though apparently there are no signs of cash crisis. For instance, the project is set up through a loan, but the borrower is hesitant to provide its progress.
- *Fraud:* The borrower is involved in deceit. For instance, a company uses loans for non-approved purposes or current assets like inventory declared but do not exist.

Keeping the above broad three indicators in mind, some early warning signals for the lenders had been delineated by the Reserve Bank of India (RBI) in 2015. I was part of the RBI 'Early Warning Committee' along with the Institute of Chartered Accountants of India, which looked into the recommended red flags in end 2018.

The pointers should alert financiers about potential fraud, fund shortage or opaqueness, leading to probable borrower default in meeting its liabilities.

The following is the list of 'early warning signals':

- *Undisputed statutory payment default:* Businesses are required to make various payments to the government within stated due dates. But if a borrower is not paying the statutory amounts on time or is frequently delaying the payment of the liabilities, then there is something amiss.
- *Bounced cheques:* When cheques get returned unpaid, especially those of high value and that too frequently, it is a red flag, more so if the cheques issued remain unpaid due to 'insufficiency of funds'. It would show that the borrower is frequently having cash flow crisis but issues cheques perhaps to placate vendors for some time.
- *Frequent project alterations:* Loans are sanctioned for projects based on project reports submitted, but when the borrower makes changes in the project scope after loan approval, in terms of cost, timelines, technology, capex and supplies, it is not a good sign. The afterthoughts in the use of money do not augur well and could involve fund diversion for non-approved purposes.
- *Import payments remaining unpaid:* When imports are made, foreign bills are raised by vendors. These need to be honoured on time. Delays for long time and especially for material amounts indicate cash flow stress for the borrower.
- *Payment delays:* When liabilities are generally not settled on time, the matter needs to be examined. There are, however, companies which habitually do not pay on due dates, though they may have funds. However, many will delay as they are cash strapped.
- *Bank guarantee invocation and LC devolvement:* When bank guarantees are frequently invoked and LCs devolve as the buyer does not honour commitment even after the due date, these are signs of fund shortage.

- *Underinsured inventory:* Continuous underinsurance of inventory, say beyond 25 per cent, could be a sign of weak financial position. This practice cannot always be pointed towards cash constraint and could be due to cost savings mindset of lower insurance premium. There could also be the possibility of inventory shortage, and hence underinsurance.
- *Dispute on securities:* Borrowers are supposed to offer securities to lenders. If there are disputes on primary securities, then it should be a red flag. Collaterals offered need to be free from every encumbrance, unless the lender specifically agrees otherwise. Hence, disputed security is not a good sign regarding borrower ethics.
- *Funds from other banks used to liquidate loans:* Funds received from other banks if used to meet the banking liabilities, unless it is normal course, would need to be looked at with suspicion on financial soundness. Monitoring every inward movement of loans taken and utilization thereof may not, however, be easy.
- *Funding interest through new loans:* Unless it is normal course of business, if the borrower arranges fresh borrowing to repay the old outstanding interest, it is a red flag of financial distress.
- *Import leg non-disclosure for trading activities:* Trading or merchandising would involve buying and selling. But when import leg (buying) is not disclosed to the lender, it may amount to an unethical practice. Appropriate alarm on corporate governance needs to be raised.
- *GSTIN on invoice:* When invoices are devoid of statutory details, there is reason to believe that the invoice may be fake. All registered businesses under GST are assigned a unique Goods and Services Tax Identification Number (GSTIN). Invoices should carry this number, of both the seller and the buyer.
- *Stock inspection not allowed:* If on flimsy ground, a borrower does not allow representatives of the lender to inspect warehouses, it is a sign of worry. Banks have the right to inspect inventory, as it is a normal practice to hypothecate it to the lenders.

- *Exclusive collateral charged to a number of lenders:* If primary or collateral securities are charged to a number of lenders without the no-objection certificate from existing lenders, then it is certainly a fraudulent practice.
- *Concealment of important documents:* Master agreement and insurance certificates are vital documents. If these documents are concealed, then proper intent of the borrower needs to be seriously questioned.
- *Borrowed money used for floating front companies:* If it is found out that the borrowed money has been used for floating front or associate companies, it should be looked at seriously.
- *Stock audit reports showing concern:* If some critical issues are pointed out in the stock audit report, like physical inventory lower than book stocks, the matter needs to be seriously considered a red flag.
- *Undisclosed liabilities in Registrar of Companies (RoC) search report:* When liabilities are found during search of the records with the RoC, but they are not reflected in the annual report of the borrower, then it amounts to non-disclosure of material information.
- *Frequent request for general purpose loans:* Loans requested frequently for 'general corporate needs' would show strain in cash position of the borrower. This could act as a trigger to suspect probable non-payment of bank liabilities in the near future.
- *Frequent ad hoc sanctions:* If loans are given frequently on 'ad hoc' basis, it should be considered a red flag for financial distress.
- *Sales proceeds not being routed through lenders:* When sales proceeds are not routed through consortium of lenders or borrowing banks, the matter is of great concern.
- *LCs issued without underlying transactions:* If LCs are issued but are not backed by underlying transactions, it is deceitful in nature.
- *Payments to unrelated parties:* When high-value bank transfers like RTGS are made to parties unconnected with business for which banking relations exist, it's a red flag.

- *Loan accounts showing large cash withdrawals:* When heavy cash withdrawals or unusual cash deposits take place in loan accounts, the matter should be looked at with suspicion.
- *Non-availability of original vouchers:* If original bills are not produced for verification even after requests are made, then it is a matter of grave concern.
- *Unusual inventory movement:* Significant movement in the inventory, disproportionate to the turnover depicted, needs to be seen with a pinch of salt.
- *Unusual receivable movement:* Significant fluctuation in receivables, not in sync with change in turnover or variation in the ageing of receivables, is a red flag.
- *Fixed assets increase but long-term funding source unclear:* Increase in fixed assets without corresponding increase in long-term sources even when the project is under implementation is a matter to be checked. Plus, if capacity enhancement is taking place but the current capacity utilization is low, it needs to be verified.
- *Disproportionate change in other current assets:* Assets of 'others' in nature could include advances, prepaid taxes, etc. These would normally change in proportion to the turnover and activities. But if the activity levels are not changing, but 'other' current assets are oscillating, the matter needs to be looked into.
- *Disproportionate working capital borrowing:* If there is a significant increase in working capital borrowing as percentage of turnover, then the matter needs close scrutiny.
- *Increase in borrowings even when balance sheet shows cash balance:* This is bizarre! Why should anyone borrow when there is cash in the balance sheet? When there is increase in cash and cash equivalents in the balance sheet, increase in borrowings must be treated as a red flag. Cash balance depicted may be a mirage.
- *Changes in accounting policies:* If the borrower changes or alters its accounting policies frequently, there could be something amiss.
- *Actual project cost significantly higher than projected:* When the project cost is in wide variance with the standard cost of the project installation, it is a matter for further investigation.

- *Claims not acknowledged as debt:* When there is presence of high claims from vendors or lenders but these are not acknowledged as liabilities by the borrower in its accounting books, it is not a good sign.
- *Unbilled revenue increasing:* If unbilled sales value increases from year to year, it is a serious concern. In fact, any un-invoiced revenue, considered in the profit and Loss account as income, needs scrutiny.
- *Substantial related-party transactions:* High number of transactions with interrelated companies and that too not commensurate with the nature of borrower's business is a big red flag.
- *Material qualifications in the annual report:* Material qualifications in the audit report, KAM, matter of emphasis and material weaknesses mentioned by the auditors or disclosed by the management in the annual report are all matters of grave concern.
- *Annual report depicts discrepancies:* An analysis of the numbers may disclose inconsistencies in the annual report. For instance, receivables are going up significantly without significant change in sales numbers may be due to recording of fictitious sales.
- *Materially adverse information:* It refers to poor disclosure of materially adverse information and no qualification by the statutory auditors. For instance, there was a long strike in the factory but neither any implication is disclosed in the annual report nor the sales revenue is showing any dip—an unlikely scenario unless there is traded (not own-manufactured) sales or some fraud involved.
- *Raid by tax or statutory officials:* It would be an area of deep concern if there was any raid by the Income Tax, GST, FEMA, EOW or any other statutory authorities or reporting under anti-money laundering legislation.
- *Promoter holding reduction or increase in encumbered shares:* When there is significant reduction in the stake of the promoters or increase in their encumbered shares, it is an area of concern. It could mean probable business downturn, lenders selling

pledged shares to recover unpaid dues or fund shortage leading to borrowings against promoter equity.

- *Auditor change reason unclear:* When statutory or internal auditor changes or resigns, but the reasons thereof are unclear or not disclosed, the matter needs further investigation. Similarly, if there are no internal auditors though it is statutorily required, it is an area of concern.
- *Frequent deviation from bank's guidelines:* While sanctioning credit, lenders would have given guidelines for utilization of funds, etc. If there are frequent deviations, it is an alarm bell.
- *Non-business generating profits:* If a substantial portion of profits is being generated from non-core activities, then it is a red flag, for instance, a manufacturing company generating profits from non-core activities like share sale. It only enhances the risk profile of the borrower, as any adverse movement in share prices could entail business adversity.
- *Turnover and GST return not matching:* If there is unsatisfactory reconciliation between the GST return and turnover shown in the accounting statements, then it is an early warning signal that something is wrong.
- *Ratio analysis not in line with industry standards:* Significant deviation in turnover and other ratios in comparison with industry benchmarks needs examination.
- *Quasi capital source unknown:* Quasi-equity or quasi-capital are debts which have traits of equity. It could be mezzanine or subordinated debt with probable flexible repayment options or unsecured. If its source is not explained, then it's a red flag.
- *Abnormal share price movement:* If share price movements during the year have been abnormal and adequate explanations are unavailable, it is an area of concern, as it could involve insider or speculative trading.
- *Sudden resignation of key managerial personnel:* Sudden departure of some key managerial personnel is a worrying event. Normally, bunched senior-level resignations take place when things are not going well or during promoter mismanagement.

- *Credit rating downgrading:* Sudden or substantial downgrading of the borrowing company by the credit–rating agency must be looked at by the lender seriously. It would normally mean enhanced risk of repayment of borrowings.

- *Criminal cases filed against borrower:* If criminal cases are filed against the promoters or directors of the borrowing entity, it is a huge warning sign requiring investigation.

- *Adverse information on promoters or management:* If there are detrimental material about the promoters or directors or key management personnel, the lender should investigate further.

- *Adversities in the age of debtors:* During age analysis of debtors, one could observe danger signs, like most debtors are old though not provided for in the accounts. It could mean that both income and assets are overstated.

- *Capital work in progress not being capitalized:* Delay in capitalizing into fixed assets of 'capital wip' could mean that there is desire on the part of the borrower to avoid providing 'depreciation' in the books of accounts and hence show a better profit picture. A similar situation may exist for intellectual property rights.

- *Sales return not shown appropriately:* High sales returns either of the previous years or current year, when not reflected properly, could be shown as prior period adjustment or extraordinary items. These are improper reflection of the factual position. Sales returns are usually worrying signs and could imply reversal of artificial boosting of past period sales, and high return number is a red flag.

- *Non-creation or delay in charge creation:* When loans are taken, assets are offered as mortgage or hypothecation. 'Charges' on these assets have to be created in favour of the lenders. Non-creation or delay in charge creation is not a good sign.

- *Unjustified high GST credit lying unadjusted:* GST credit on inputs is taken while paying GST on output. When there are unjustified large credit lying unutilized, the matter needs verification.

- *Intangible assets to be properly valued:* If valuation of intangible assets is not carried out frequently, the reason could be that the value has shrunk and the company does not want to take a hit in its results.
- *Borrower showing profits but facing fund crunch:* If the borrower is facing fund shortage but the accounting records are showing profits, there is definitely something amiss. There could be doctoring of accounts which would need immediate investigation.
- *Delays in debt servicing:* Frequent delays in debt servicing is a huge red flag. It would be in fact the mother of all early warning indicators.

Tailpiece

In business, brewing trouble provides red flags. The lenders just have to keep their eyes and ears open wider than their heart— potential losses can then be minimized, if not avoided.

It is commonly said that red flags are moments of hesitation which determine our destination; if you ignore it, be prepared to embrace the heartache waiting to arrive.

Ominous Sign of Auditor Quitting

When it comes to batteries, my all-time favourite is **Eveready**—it lasts longer, providing better value for money. Sometime in June 2019, while flipping through the daily economic newspaper, I was surprised to see the negative news of one of my chosen battery maker's auditor calling it a day. PwC resigned as their statutory auditor, citing its inability to analyse the impact of financial support extended by Eveready to its promoter group entities.[3]

An acclaimed name like Eveready Industries joined the bandwagon of companies where auditors lost faith in their client's quality of financial affairs. Investors panicked and share price dropped over 10 per cent on getting the news.

Similar fate would take place in many investors' minds when they get to know of auditors resigning. It is a big red flag.

Auditors are under increased pressure, thanks to tougher legislations, improved investor awareness and public scrutiny.

The introduction of the Insolvency and Bankruptcy Code and National Company Law Tribunal in India, where non-payment of debts is leading to auctioning off or closing of failing borrower companies, has heightened pre-emptive action from bankers. This has lifted good-governance thresholds higher. Debt market defaults and the increased corporate governance scrutiny on defaulting companies are enhancing pressure on the company management and their auditors.

The formation in India of the National Financial Reporting Authority, as a watchdog for audit quality for listed and large companies, has made the auditors further careful of their worthy work. Earlier, it was only the Institute of Chartered Accountants of India which was overseeing the audit quality. The new body—NFRA, acting as a surveillance camera for auditors' work—provides possible deterrents for poor-quality audit and raises red flags on suspected doctored accounts.

Many are the reasons why auditors resign.

KPMG's India arm resigned from **IL&FS** financial services companies because of 'investigation by regulatory bodies'. 'Unsatisfactory response to queries' was the stark reason why auditors in **Reliance Capital** and **Reliance Home Finance** resigned. The market sentiments became very negative on getting this news. 'Lack of transparency' can be quite a black mark on any company. Deloitte stepped down in August 2019 precisely for this reason from **Dewan Housing Finance** after raising concerns about intercorporate deposits. 'Client not cooperating' is another reason for auditors calling it a day. PwC in mid-2020 quit as the auditor of **GVK Power & Infrastructure,** claiming that the company was not cooperating in the audit work for their Mumbai airport operations.[4]

Multiple or back-to-back auditor resignations make matters worse, and it's a huge red flag. Deloitte resigned in May 2018 as an auditor from **Manpasand Beverages,** the maker of mango-based fruit drink, citing the management's inability to share crucial data.[5] Just one year later, in May 2019, the successor auditor, Mehra Goel & Co., put in their papers amid ongoing investigation in GST scam case. The story did not end here. Just after another few months, in October 2019, its next auditor, Batliboi & Purohit, had enough of their client. It cited that the audit team members were not allowed to enter the client's Vadodara factory for conducting the statutory audit. These are serious warning signals for poor governance

Resignations of auditors will normally affect investors' sentiments once the information is available in the public domain. It usually has negative sentiments attached, till it gets clarified that the resignation was routine like personal reasons, health issues or conflict of interest due to non-audit services being undertaken.

The Indian market regulators have started taking auditor resignations seriously and asking for clear reasons. Investors need to keep track of these developments, as these are potential red flags.

Growing number of businesses, dumped like suspecting spouses, are being left for trophy partners. This is because auditors are dropping their corporate clients in droves. The companies which are getting dropped by accounting firms are those considered either not worth the extra effort required for the inadequate fees or being judged too risky to work with, due to tougher accounting rules. It is the latter reason of risk averse split-up that is to be looked at with care, caution and chariness.

Sorry, we want a divorce—screams a note filed by an auditor! This is a red flag. And when the paper of annulment is served without any notice, that's too ominous.

Whatever be the reason, the auditor–client break-up news does not augur well for the business world.

Few Last Words

We go for our annual health check-ups to figure out if there is something adverse brewing in our bodies—to identify some early warning signals to detect any potential threats. A timely diagnosis could save many lives, sickness and agony.

Similar theories are applicable to the banking business. Borrowers could be struggling to repay debts, doctoring financial statements to project incorrect picture, diverting funds for unapproved purposes or just planning to run away with the money borrowed. Many could be the reasons. Several signals could emanate to show possible dark clouds building on the horizon. Numerous are the ways the lenders can figure out in advance the stress signs or impending indiscipline.

Red flags are sometimes ignored hoping that ominous developments will pass or are treated as mere false notes. Whether we like it or not, history is often a great early warning signal. Ignoring it will be perilous.

Corporate frauds are increasing by the day—and the worst part is that these are getting larger, deeper and audacious. But while business crime cases are going up, the proportion of cases reported to the police is declining. Some presuppose that reporting con cases harm organizational reputation. And many businesses believe that the police and the legal system either lack the technological resource to handle financial deceits or cannot always be trusted.

Unfortunately, by not reporting crooks to the police, the former are free to move from one target to another. The system gets more polluted with scamsters on the prowl, and for employers it gets further difficult to discern the ones who are trustworthy at the time of hiring.

Non-reported frauds also arise when deceits and deceptions are structured at the top of the corporate pyramid. It is but obvious that these will neither be complained against nor reported to law enforcement agencies. The society remains oblivious of the malady which could strike from the prevalent unethical business practice virus. Think of a situation that a company works on Ponzi principles— no real business—but takes money from investors under a phantom promise of super returns. Who will complain against this hoax? Perhaps no one, till the scheme fails on its own hubris.

Whistle-blowers can however play an important role in unravelling ongoing scam bugs. In the infamous cases of Enron and WorldCom, women employees helped unravel the huge artifice being practised inside their organizations. Employees are often in the best position to uncover the wrongdoings from within, which otherwise may have remained hidden under the carpet.

The business world is inundated with diverse, sophisticated and perilous con schemes. While organizations very often are quite good at noticing and dealing with predictable, lower-level risks, many however fail to either anticipate or deal with more hazardous threats. Business dishonesty—mostly premeditated—is undeniably a dangerous game in progress.

Conning Unlimited

New York is often known as the city of dreams, and Anna Sorokin, a Russian immigrant, had plenty of it.[1] This middle-class young chic lady had longed to be a member of the upper echelons of the Manhattan society.

Anna elbowed her way into the city's active social scene through clever lies and incredible self-confidence. She tried to raise money to open a members-only arts club on Park Avenue South.

To friends and those wanting to do business with her, there was no reason to believe that she was not the person she said she was—a wealthy German heiress with a taste for the high life—though she was in fact the daughter of a Russian truck driver.

From November 2016 to August 2017, she played the part of a wealthy baroness, and looked it too. She wore designer clothes—Gucci and Yves Saint Laurent—and hopped from one luxury hotel to the next. She doled out $100 tips, treated friends to expensive meals and even chartered a private plane to Omaha for the Berkshire Hathaway Conference, where Warren Buffett was speaking. She also negotiated her way to obtain a loan of $22 million.

These were all fabrications. Anna swindled $275,000 from the rich and the unsuspecting, including friends and financial institutions, to pay for the extravagant lifestyle she so desperately desired.

It is a classic case of human felony where a young con artist went to extraordinary lengths to convince people of a fantasized world around her and that she was a scion named Anna Delvey.

'Fake it until you make it,' her lawyer said. 'Anna had to live by it.'

(Anna was arrested in 2017 on charges of larceny and theft, convicted to spend four years in prison.)

There are some people who are differently wired. Think of a criminal who can commit a cold-blooded murder and yet sleep peacefully, while many of us are unable to even withstand the sight of blood. Think of a gambler who gets pleasure by taking risks, while many of us would detest venturing into casino slot machines thinking of the loss probability stacked against us.

Similarly, there are people like Anna around us, who are trying to paint pictures which could be a figment of their imaginations. It is difficult to make out early the intent of these cheats. Beware of the too-good-to-be-true stories being narrated. Try to do some reference checks, make background verifications and check social media corroborations before you commit your resources to people who are promising great returns. Most of the time, your research may just surprise you!

Do Ethics in Business Help?

Should businesses be run on an ethical manner? Why should our business ventures bother about social purpose, sustainability and environment? Why can't the government take care of it?

Questions like these can come up often to challenge the wisdom of businesses which would like to run on ethical principles and in a fraud-free manner.

What is common between *The Times of India*, Taj Mahal Palace hotel, Shalimar Paints and the Britannia biscuits company? They have all lasted over a century with elan and aplomb. If you go behind their long-sustenance stories, one thing you will figure out is their ethical history. Minor blips obviously would have happened, but any significant duplicity would be missing.

Let me cite some instances of enterprises which have been socially responsible, being ethical in their approach. The sustainable expert consultant GlobeScan's *The 2020 GlobeScan/Sustainability Leaders Survey* report[2] ranks Unilever first among global giants studied. Just to let you know, William Lever, founder of my professional life's alma mater Unilever, had pioneered during the early 20th century the concept of marketing its products with health benefits. This was at a time when disease and malnutrition were widespread. Even today, its mission is no different. And notice the outcome. The company continues to be a shining star of the business world.

The consumer goods British multinational Unilever is followed by Patagonia (manufacturing outdoor clothes), IKEA (ready-to-assemble furniture seller), Interface (a flooring company) and Natura (a personal care cosmetic group). Companies such as Danone, Microsoft, L'Oréal and Tata also find a pride of place in the top 10 listing. Innovation, transparency and sustainable value creation has been their success mantra and will continue to be defining the flavours for big businesses in the times to come.

Do corporations not follow ethical practices for their own benefit? Surely they do. For instance, Unilever and Nestlé run programmes to improve water conservation in cocoa used in ice creams and chocolates. Small farmers are trained by consumer-goods giants like Coca-Cola, SABMiller and Walmart. The purpose of these moves is to improve farming practices, eliminate environmental risks and secure their farm supplies. It's a win–win ethical strategy which enables businesses to thrive and prosper.

While behaving responsibly brings brownie points from consumers and society, poor governance adversely affects market value of organizations. Whenever news on shady practices emerge for corporates, you will notice the knock-off effects on the business valuation.

The erstwhile high-flying Indian housing finance company DHFL's shares went for a free fall of 90 per cent when a whiff of a ₹30,000 crore ($4 billion) fraud emerged in November 2018.[3] The Indian finance market's once darling Yes Bank's shares fell 40 per cent in April 2019 when it became clear that for years the bank was underreporting NPAs and thus overreporting its profits.[4] Same was the story when Kobe Steel, Japan's third-largest steelmaker, who admitted falsifying inspection data on an estimated 20,000 tons of metals shipped to 500 customers in October 2017, and its stock valuation plunged by 40 per cent over two sessions.[5] All these are pure cases of markets giving thumbs down to the corporates failing in their test of non-fraudulent practices damaging their credibility in the eyes of their customers and investors alike.

One way to retain checks on ethical corporate behaviour is to keep your antennas directed towards public opinion. I always believe that if there is smoke, there is some fire. If public impression is smelly, then something fishy could be brewing in the organization.

Tailpiece

The question is: Does ethical practice help businesses? Socially responsible companies have largely shown healthy growth in share prices over the years. The stock price of Unilever doubled in the last decade, so are other well-governed companies like Coca-Cola, SABMiller, Walmart, Mahindra & Mahindra and Wipro showing stellar performances. Look for organizations which have been around for a long time—one attribute you will always find: ethical business habits.

I am reminded of the famous quote: You can fool all the people some time and some people all the time, but you cannot fool all the people all the time. Crooked measures can give businesses a short-term crutch but cannot provide a long-term pillar.

It is said that business ethics is finding the difference between what you have the right to do and what is right to do.

Can Risk Management Eliminate Corporate Frauds?

Whenever some crisis occurs or a breaking-news scam ensues, risk management actions gain a new flavour. For instance, post the 2008 global financial crisis, the recent stream of bad debts in the Indian banking system, or the 2020 pandemic-related business horrors, many banks changed their business models, revamping credit risk monitoring and managing. Among many other steps, overreliance on mathematical models has taken a back seat.

Managing risk is often looked upon as a mystical business function—intended to control losses and meet compliance canons. With more businesses falling victim to intricate intangible risks—from data leaks to skewed accounting—the role of risk management is expanding from protecting business results to promoting ethical and value-based decision-making.

Consider some instances of appalling risk mismanagement: LinkedIn's data of 700 million of its users posted on the dark web in June 2021, impacting more than 90 per cent of its users; Wells Fargo bank creating thousands of fake customer accounts; Karvy Stock Broking surreptitiously using clients' equity-shares as security to take loans and then diverting proceeds to real estate investments; India's infrastructure lender lending for long period on short-term borrowing. These are all failures fuelled mainly by the modern world's devious mix of greed and short-termism. Irrespective of the size and nature, all arising from human failings, a proper risk management ecosystem could have prevented almost all of them.

Many a time, risk management action plans have been interpreted as a drag on the organization or leading to bureaucratic interruptions. It has often been pointed out that risk managers spend more than half their time on financial reporting and legal compliance adherence, even though a significant portion of enterprise valuation gets destroyed by mismanagement of non-insurable strategic risks.

To manage risks better, businesses need to focus on the following three risk steps:

- Risk and reward need to be balanced. We know that higher risks lead to higher returns. Hence, communicating across the business, the organization's risk appetite is important.
- Businesses are made of people and not of bricks and mortar. Hence, the employees need to be trained for risk appreciation. Only then will the decisions taken have the risk ingredients mixed in the culinary outcome.

- Focus on outcome and not the process. Holding quiz sessions on cyber risks will not prevent hacker attacks. Understanding risks involved in decision-making will benefit. For instance, appreciating Internet-related risks will help the company to take appropriate decisions to prevent cyber fraud.

The management teams need to change the way they think about risks and how to deal with it. Do not put in complex risk management systems to counter even more complex risks. These steps will come with their own blind spots. The employees have to be equipped to deal with common levels of risks and value systems.

The tone, tenor and togetherness to the rank and file of the top management deeply impacts its attitude towards risks. A management team which practices what it preaches and not just renders lip service influences ethics and good governance positively.

Management of risk involves taking four basic actions:

- 'Identify' the risks
- 'Assess' its seriousness or otherwise
- Take actions to 'control' downsides, if any
- 'Review' whether steps taken are adequate

Risk, in essence, is 'uncertainty that matters'. Its management is a protective shield, and not a bureaucratic hurdle.

Tailpiece

A single sling from David was good enough to slay Goliath. So are the approach and attitude towards risks. Embracing the tactics of legal compliance or ticking the governance boxes will make no dent in managing risks. A single-minded approach towards ethical ethos with risk agility will help enterprises boost profitable growth and prevent corporate cheating.

What Should We Do?

With swindles from businesses in full swing, the biggest issue always remains what can be done to control, if not eradicate, corporate cheating. In order to understand the possible action plans, it is necessary to recognize the two types of frauds the corporate world is exposed to. They are 'micro' and 'macro' frauds.

Let us first understand what 'micro' ploys are. As the name suggests, it is usually committed by a staff member or someone from inside. Theft by an employee, bribery by the purchase team, cashier running away with cash from the till, and accounts staff siphoning off customer receipts and then practising teeming and lading to hide the mischief are some 'micro' fraud instances.

'Macro' hoax, as the name implies, will usually be committed by the top management, for example, doctoring balance sheets (e.g., Satyam accounting scam), producing products not in accordance with customer promise (e.g., Volkswagen producing diesel cars with significantly higher emission levels and lying about it) and running a dishonest business concept like a Ponzi scheme (e.g., Saradha scam).

It is easier to control the micro deceits. Strong internal controls, management audits and providing incentives to whistle-blowers would go a long way in making the corporate world micro-fraud-ready.

The problem, however, is with the macro deceptions.

If the top management is involved in committing mischiefs, it is difficult to figure out its existence or to rein it in. It becomes tougher, especially for the non-executive board members, lenders and investors, to assure themselves that their company is fraud-free.

Appointing a professional management team, making internal auditor report to the audit committee of the board, asking intelligent questions during board meetings, periodic visits to factories and workplaces, creating a safe ecosystem for whistle-blowers and time-bound investigations when fraud doubts are raised, would be good starting points for the non-executive board members to take.

However, it becomes more challenging for investors and members of the public to identify corporate macro frauds. They will have to depend upon audit reports, information available in the public domain, own analysis of the financial statements and verifying the quality of the management team.

Human mind is a complex tool. Greed will continue to drive many in making shortcuts to wealth accumulation. The desire to achieve success by hook or crook, inspiration from peer defrauders and need to meet promises made earlier, are some of the trigger points for certain business managers giving a short shrift to good governance. Some get caught, many roam free to carry out more harm. The business world is getting more complex, competitive and challenging. Concurrently, corporate chicanery is taking a new shape, size and structure.

With the regulators struggling to bring the recalcitrant to the books, investigative steps are getting more complex in line with the changing nature of the white-collar crimes, and as naming and shaming of the wayward are unlikely to be implemented, it is important to be aware of the maxim 'Knowledge is power.' If you know what can go wrong, you are better prepared to prevent wrongs from happening.

Few Last Words

Corruption and dishonesty is prevalent around the globe. It is the degree that varies. It would be naive to think that deceits and deceptions are going to diminish or disappear. With the growing sophistication of tricksters and digitization of the economies, it is expected that the fraud virus will only enhance the global con malady.

The good news is that with the development of AI, ability to use big data and increased sophistication of machine learning, enhanced capability is getting garnered by the regulatory bodies and the police force to catch the business fraudsters. International exchange of information and cooperation among governments to catch the recalcitrant is also changing the paradigm against the tricksters.

Fraud is a hidden crime. The worst part is that dishonesty reported is only a small portion of the cheating detected, which in turn is a fraction of infractions practised.

The most unpleasant reality is that many people are dishonest and will try to defraud you or your loved ones. This is in spite of the ecosystem getting more sophisticated and regulatory systems becoming tougher for the business fraudsters.

Awareness is the big defence. Anticipation is better than cure. Avoidance is the best remedy.

Notes

Introduction

1 The Economist, 'The Use of Banned Drugs Is Rife in Sport', 10 February 2018, https://www.economist.com/international/2018/02/10/the-use-of-banned-drugs-is-rife-in-sport

2 https://www.businesstoday.in/industry/banks/story/nirav-modi-case-pnb-fraud-11400-crore-scam-ed-cbi-raid-101200-2018-02-15

3 *The New York Times*, 'Goldman Sachs Ensnarled in Vast 1MDB Fraud Scandal', 1 November 2018, https://www.nytimes.com/2018/11/01/business/goldman-sachs-malaysia-investment-fund.html

4 Katherine Reedy, 'Study Explores Why Employees Cheat and How Companies Could Unknowingly Contribute to the Behavior', 10 October 2017, Phys.org, https://phys.org/news/2017-10-explores-employees-companies-unknowingly-contribute.html

5 https://www.nytimes.com/2021/02/03/business/mckinsey-opioids-settlement.html?searchResultPosition=1

6 Lisette Voytko, 'Shell Companies Hide $15 Trillion from Taxes', 9 September 2019, https://www.forbes.com/sites/lisettevoytko/2019/09/09/shell-companies-hide-15-trillion-from-taxes-study-reports/#5d31698e7269

7 https://economictimes.indiatimes.com/magazines/panache/exploring-the-worlds-phantom-fdi-luxembourg-ireland-well-known-tax-havens-destinations/articleshow/71075083.cms?from=mdr

8 James Siswick and Alexandra Will, 'Cum-Ex—An Introduction to the 55 Billion Euro Heist', Bloomberg Tax, 24 September 2020, https://news.bloombergtax.com/daily-tax-report-international/insight-cum-ex-an-introduction-to-the-55-billion-euro-heist

9 https://thefinancialcrimenews.com/wp-content/uploads/2019/11/FCN-GTA.2019.Pub-Final.pdf

10 Experian, *The 2018 Global Fraud and Identity Report*, 2018, https://www.experian.com/assets/decision-analytics/reports/global-fraud-report-2018.pdf

11 https://www.nytimes.com/2020/04/17/your-money/coronavirus-fraud.html

12 https://www.kroll.com/en/insights/publications/global-fraud-and-risk-report-2018

13 https://indianexpress.com/article/business/amid-covid-effect-bank-steps-willful-defaults-rise-rs-38976-crore-7309969/

14 https://www.ft.com/content/6de86032-0a83-41ba-85a8-125ccce3b0be

15 Sujeet Indap, 'General Electric's Accounting Tactics Bared in SEC Settlement', *Financial Times*, 2 January 2021, https://www.ft.com/content/6de86032-0a83-41ba-85a8-125ccce3b0be

16 https://economictimes.indiatimes.com/news/et-explains/too-many-shadows-on-sun-whats-really-happening-at-indias-largest-pharma-firm/articleshow/66916260.cms?from=mdr

17 https://www.bloombergquint.com/business/sfio-says-top-executives-led-ilfs-to-its-ruin

18 https://indianexpress.com/article/business/banking-and-finance/ed-arrests-yes-bank-co-founder-rana-kapoor-in-a-money-laundering-case-7164110/

19 https://www.wsj.com/articles/wirecards-former-ceo-markus-braun-is-arrested-11592901759#:~:text=Wirecard%20AG's%20recently%20departed%20chief,about%20the%20once%2Dpromising%20company.

CHAPTER ONE: The (Un) Ethical Manager

1 Betwa Sharma, 'Business Today: Rajat Gupta Found Guilty of Insider Trading', 16 June 2012, https://www.businesstoday.in/current/world/rajat-gupta-insider-trading-sentence/story/185519.html

2 This example is author's own creation.

3 Mahzarin R. Banaji, Max H. Bazerman, and Dolly Chugh, 'How (Un)ethical Are You?' *Harvard Business Review*, December 2003, https://hbr.org/2003/12/how-unethical-are-you?autocomplete=true

4 https://www.cnbc.com/2020/08/19/lenders-deny-mortgages-for-blacks-at-a-rate-80percent-higher-than-whites.html

5 https://www.washingtonpost.com/news/wonk/wp/2018/03/28/redlining-was-banned-50-years-ago-its-still-hurting-minorities-today/

6 *Financial Times*, 'Citi Suspends Senior Bond Trader over Alleged Theft from Canteen', 3 February 2020, https://www.ft.com/content/b7c1952a-467b-11ea-aeb3-955839e06441

7 Nate Raymond, 'Ex-McKinsey Partner Arrested for Fraudulent Invoices, Expenses', Reuters, 5 January 2016, https://www.reuters.com/article/us-usa-crime-mckinsey-idUSKBN0UI1ZJ20160105

8 Gina Hall, 'Former McKinsey Partner Heads to Prison for Fraudulent Consulting Fees', *Chicago Business Journal*, 15 May 2018, https://www.bizjournals.com/chicago/news/2018/03/15/former-mckinsey-partner-heads-to-prison.html

9 http://www.nja.nic.in/P-948_Reading_Material/P-948_Audit_of_Fraud_in_economic_crimes/ACCOUNTING%20FRAUD.pdf

10 https://www.businesstoday.in/top-story/chanda-kochhars-fall-from-grace-here-is-how-she-was-caught-step-by-step/story/321344.html

11 CNN Money, 'Stewart Convicted on All Charges', 10 March 2004, https://money.cnn.com/2004/03/05/news/companies/martha_verdict/

12 https://www.cnbc.com/2019/01/13/ousted-nissans-chairman-ghosn-was-paid-8-million-last-year-by-a-dutch-entity--wsj.html

13 https://www.nytimes.com/2002/11/05/business/corporate-loans-used-personally-report-discloses.html

14 Merete Wedell-Wedellsborg, 'The Psychology behind Unethical Behavior', *Harvard Business Review*, 12 April 2019, https://hbr.org/2019/04/the-psychology-behind-unethical-behavior

15 https://www.businesstoday.in/current/corporate/fall-of-an-ace-banker-who-is-rana-kapoor-the-brain-behind-yes-bank/story/397838.html

16 https://www.theguardian.com/business/2016/mar/02/vw-ceo-martin-winterkorn-told-about-emissions-scandal

17 Reedy, 'Study Explores Why Employees Cheat'.

18 https://www.nytimes.com/2019/07/02/obituaries/lee-iacocca-dead.html

19 https://www.pwc.com/gx/en/services/forensics/economic-crime-survey.html

20 EY, *Is This the Moment of Truth for Corporate Integrity? Global Integrity Report 2020*, 2020, https://assets.ey.com/content/dam/ey-sites/ey-com/en_gl/topics/assurance/assurance-pdfs/ey-is-this-the-moment-of-truth-for-corporate-integrity.pdf

21 Dan Ariely, *The Honest Truth about Dishonesty: How We Lie to Everyone—Especially Ourselves* (Harper, 2013).

22 *The Economist*, 'Twilight of the Tax Haven', 5 June 2021, https://www.economist.com/finance-and-economics/2021/06/03/twilight-of-the-tax-haven

23 Donald R. Cressey, *Other people's money; a study in the social psychology of embezzlement* (Montclair, N.J., Patterson Smith, 1973).

24 https://edition.cnn.com/2013/07/02/us/enron-fast-facts/index.html

25 standard.com/about/who-is-vijay-mallya

CHAPTER TWO: Corporate Con Artists

1 https://www.cbsnews.com/news/bp-and-iran-the-forgotten-history/

2 https://www.nytimes.com/1972/03/22/archives/itt-said-to-seek-chile-coup-in-70-anderson-says-white-house-was.html

3 https://www.ft.com/content/778739c4-f869-11db-a940-000b5df10621

4 https://brandequity.economictimes.indiatimes.com/news/advertising/asci-processes-complaints-against-415-advertisements/68662681

5 https://economictimes.indiatimes.com/news/politics-and-nation/sfio-completed-investigations-against-361-companies-last-fiscal-government/articleshow/78126455.cms

6 https://www.nytimes.com/2018/05/09/business/china-sentences-anbang-founder-to-18-years-for-fraud.html

7 *The New York Times*, 'The Opioid Drugs Scandal Is Depressingly Familiar', 16 July 2019, https://www.ft.com/content/7cf7b242-a6e1-11e9-984c-fac8325aaa04

8   *The New York Times*, 'American Overdose by Chris McGreal—Prescription for Carnage', 7 December 2018, https://www.ft.com/content/19277234-ee63-11e8-8180-9cf212677a57

9   https://www.reuters.com/article/us-usa-court-pfizer-idUSBRE9B80K020131209

10 https://www.forbes.com/sites/larryhusten/2011/11/22/merck-pleads-guilty-and-pays-950-million-for-illegal-promotion-of-vioxx/?sh=1b8cf28220f4

11 Tiash Saha, 'Pharmaceutical Technology: The Biggest Ever Pharmaceutical Lawsuits', 25 June 2019, https://www.pharmaceutical-technology.com/features/biggest-pharmaceutical-lawsuits/

12 *Financial Times*, 'Lekoil Fake Loan Probe Puts Spotlight on Bahamas Broker', 21 January 2020, https://www.ft.com/content/cdd989fe-3955-11ea-a6d3-9a26f8c3cba4

13 https://www.bloombergquint.com/business/qatar-s-intervention-saved-lekoil-from-10-million-loss-in-scam

14 *The New York Times*, 'Berkshire Hathaway Says Blue Chip Law Firm Aided Fraud', 14 October 2020, https://www.nytimes.com/2020/10/14/business/Berkshire-Hathaway-Warren-Buffett-fraud.html?searchResultPosition=10

15 https://economictimes.indiatimes.com/industry/healthcare/biotech/pharmaceuticals/ranbaxy-to-pay-500-mn-to-us-govt-for-settlement-of-lawsuits-related-to-drug-safety/articleshow/20033918.cms?from=mdr

16 https://www.nasdaq.com/articles/what-ranbaxys-fraud-says-about-state-big-pharma-research-2013-11-08

17 https://www.business-standard.com/article/news-cm/cadila-healthcare-slumps-on-getting-warning-letter-from-usfda-115123100268_1.html

18 https://www.thehindubusinessline.com/companies/us-fda-warns-sri-krishna-pharma-for-cgmp-rule-violations/article8498399.ece

19 BBC News, 'Japan's Kobe Steel Indicted over Quality Scandal', 20 July 2018, https://www.bbc.com/news/business-44895564

20 https://www.usatoday.com/story/money/2017/06/25/takata-air-bag-scandal-timeline/103184598/

21 https://www.bbc.com/news/business-42096165

22 https://www.bloomberg.com/news/videos/2015-10-15/toyo-tire-admits-rubber-quality-data-manipulated

23 https://www.huffpost.com/archive/in/entry/tata-steel-uk-_n_9644644

24 https://www.pwc.com/gx/en/services/forensics/economic-crime-survey.html

CHAPTER THREE: Corruption and Corporations

1   Daniel Gallas, 'Brazil's Odebrecht Corruption Scandal Explained', BBC News, 17 April 2019, https://www.bbc.com/news/business-39194395

2   https://www.wsj.com/articles/peru-cancels-pipeline-contract-with-odebrecht-1485197176

3 *Financial Times*, 'Ericsson to Pay US More Than $1bn over Foreign Bribery', 7 December 2019, https://www.ft.com/content/d026b9c0-1876-11ea-8d73-6303645ac406

4 Liz Alderman, 'Airbus to Pay $4 Billion to Settle Corruption Inquiry', *The New York Times*, 31 January 2020, https://www.nytimes.com/2020/01/31/business/airbus-corruption-settlement.html?searchResultPosition=9

5 https://www.u4.no/publications/the-credibility-of-corruption-statistics

6 *Financial Times*, 'College Bribery: School for Scandal', Lex, 16 March 2019; Jennifer Medina, Katie Benner, and Kate Taylor, 'Actresses, Business Leaders and Other Wealthy Parents Charged in U.S. College Entry Fraud', *The New York Times*, 12 March 2019, https://www.nytimes.com/2019/03/12/us/college-admissions-cheating-scandal.html?module=inline

7 Transparency International, *Corruption Perceptions Index,* 2020, https://www.transparency.org/en/cpi/2020/index/nzl#

8 https://www.indiatoday.in/business/story/cbi-arrests-bhushan-steel-vice-chairman-in-bribery-case-203214-2014-08-07

9 https://www.forbes.com/sites/robertolsen/2021/01/18/samsung-billionaire-heir-jay-y-lee-sentenced-to-25-years-in-prison-for-bribery/?sh=f09c44c344b3

10 https://www.bbc.com/news/business-38644114

11 https://www.ft.com/content/31037500-7340-11e7-aca6-c6bd07df1a3c

12 Sandra Laville, 'Top Oil Firms Spending Millions Lobbying to Block Climate Change Policies, Says Report', *The Guardian*, 22 March 2019, https://www.theguardian.com/business/2019/mar/22/top-oil-firms-spending-millions-lobbying-to-block-climate-change-policies-says-report

13 *Financial Times*, 'Shell Faces Dutch Criminal Charges over Nigeria Oil Deal', 1 March 2019, https://www.ft.com/content/850c8212-3bf9-11e9-b72b-2c7f526ca5d0

14 https://www.usatoday.com/story/opinion/2018/02/04/google-investing-millions-political-process-cost-doing-business-david-boaz-column/1079715001/

15 https://www.livemint.com/companies/news/cognizant-used-l-t-to-bribe-govt-officials-in-india-1550426741937.html

16 https://www.sec.gov/news/press-release/2019-12

17 Jessie Yeung, 1 in 2 Indians Paid a Bribe at least Once in the Past Year, Survey Finds', CNN, 28 November 2019, https://edition.cnn.com/2019/11/27/asia/india-corruption-bribe-intl-hnk-scli/index.html

18 Transparency International, *Corruption Perceptions Index.*

19 https://www.comunicarseweb.com/sites/default/files/ey-corporate-misconduct-individual-consequences.pdf

20 Malyaban Ghosh, 'Govt and Industry Needs to Change the Way They Interact: R C Bhargava', Livemint, 7 May 2020, https://www.livemint.com/news/india/govt-and-industry-needs-to-change-the-way-they-interact-r-c-bhargava-11588858607910.html

21 *Financial Times*, 'UK's Poor Record on Corporate Crime Comes under Attack', 6 March 2019, https://www.ft.com/content/52101b3e-3f51-11e9-b896-fe36ec32aece

22 https://www.millerchevalier.com/publication/fcpa-spring-review-2019

23 https://www.hindustantimes.com/business/satyam-scam-all-you-need-to-know-about-india-s-biggest-accounting-fraud/story-YTfHTZy9K6NvsW8PxIEEYL.html

24 *Financial Times*, 'Deutsche Bank Pays Nearly $125m to Resolve US Bribery and Fraud Claims', 9 January 2021, https://www.ft.com/content/8bdf8fc9-0820-437c-b18c-fb6be6a517c0

25 https://www.ft.com/content/9810d9a6-0f90-11ea-a225-db2f231cfeae

26 *Financial Times*, 'Glencore Faces Swiss Criminal Probe over Alleged DRC Corruption', 20 June 2020, https://www.ft.com/content/4ecf86da-2cc1-4c7e-a5fd-7b2da1efe3f9

27 Ibid.

28 *The New York Times*, 'China Sentences Former Bank Chief to Death in Rare Move', 5 January 2021, https://www.nytimes.com/2021/01/05/business/china-huarong-death-penalty.html?searchResultPosition=1

29 https://www.weforum.org/agenda/2018/12/the-global-economy-loses-3-6-trillion-to-corruption-each-year-says-u-n

30 https://ficci.in/SEdocument/20254/FICCI-EY-Report-Bribery-corruption.pdf

CHAPTER FOUR: Technology Tall Tales

1 Robin Banerjee, *Who Blunders and How: The Dumb Side of the Corporate World* (New Delhi: SAGE Publications, 2019).

2 Experian, *The 2018 Global Fraud and Identity Report*.

3 https://www.nytimes.com/2019/11/11/business/google-ascension-health-data.html

4 https://www.bbc.com/news/technology-46590890

5 *Financial Times*, 'Why Google Thinks We Need to Regulate AI', February 2020, https://www.ft.com/content/3467659a-386d-11ea-ac3c-f68c10993b04

6 *Financial Times*, 'IBM and Microsoft Sign Vatican Pledge for Ethical AI', 20 February 2020, https://www.ft.com/content/5dc6edcc-5981-11ea-a528-dd0f971febbc

CHAPTER FIVE: Cybercrimes

1 *Financial Times*, 'Cybercrime Threat in a Cashless Economy', 14 August 2017, https://www.ft.com/video/3b94938b-4923-4dcc-a3ff-2ac33331b8d8

2 https://punemirror.indiatimes.com/news/india/delhi-cm-arvind-kejriwals-daughter-duped-of-rs-34000-in-e-commerce-fraud/articleshow/80758566.cms

3　Steven C. Tiell, 'The Case for Data Ethics', *Outlook*, 2015, https://www.accenture.com/_acnmedia/Accenture/Conversion-Assets/DotCom/Documents/Global/PDF/Dualpub_9/Accenture-Outlook-TechVision-Data Ethics-v3.pdf

4　https://www.bloomberg.com/news/articles/2018-11-20/the-email-scam-that-has-swiped-billions-from-executives

5　https://www.ukfinance.org.uk/system/files/Fraud%20the%20facts-%20 August%202018.pdf

6　BBC News, 'Mystery as Quadriga Crypto-cash Goes Missing', 5 March 2019, https://www.bbc.com/news/technology-47454528

7　https://www.reuters.com/business/finance/exclusive-crypto-crime-down-2021-through-april-defi-fraud-record-ciphertrace-2021-05-13/

8　https://www.cnbc.com/2019/03/22/majority-of-bitcoin-trading-is-a-hoax-new-study-finds.html

9　https://www.fca.org.uk/publication/annual-reports/annual-report-2019-20.pdf

10　https://www.ft.com/content/f4791553-7ec0-40fc-8056-f3b72c789d08

11　https://www.ft.com/content/66dbc3ba-848a-4206-8b97-27c0e384ff27

12　https://www.reuters.com/article/britain-marriott-dataprotection-idUSL8N2FK5HC

13　https://gadgets.ndtv.com/internet/news/dominos-india-data-breach-13tb-files-customer-details-credit-card-numbers-2416829

14　This example is author's own creation.

15　https://www.livemint.com/companies/news/indigo-cautions-against-fake-job-offers-11607578042043.html

16　https://ico.org.uk/about-the-ico/news-and-events/news-and-blogs/2020/10/ico-fines-british-airways-20m-for-data-breach-affecting-more-than-400-000-customers/

17　PwC, 'Digital Fraud'.

18　https://www.bbc.com/news/business-53055351

19　https://edition.cnn.com/2019/04/05/europe/ireland-airbnb-hidden-camera-scli-intl/index.html

20　https://www.thehindu.com/news/national/other-states/union-hrd-minister-smriti-irani-spots-cctv-camera-at-changing-room-fir-filed/article7065251.ece

21　*Financial Times*, 'Finland Police Hunt Blackmailer Who Hacked Psychotherapy Centre's Records', 26 October 2020, https://www.ft.com/content/569798b7-3b9e-4b9c-ba91-fd4cde1647f4

22　https://www.forbes.com/sites/chuckbrooks/2021/03/02/alarming-cybersecurity-stats-------what-you-need-to-know-for-2021/

CHAPTER SIX: Banking Deceits

1　https://www.business-standard.com/article/finance/frauds-reported-at-banks-financial-institutions-decreased-in-2020-21-rbi-121052700748_1.html

2 https://www.moneylife.in/article/rbi-extends-curbs-over-3-maharashtra-based-cooperative-banks-customers-pay-for-banks-fault/61157.html

3 https://www.newindianexpress.com/nation/2020/apr/21/vijay-mallyas-legal-setback-in-rs-9000-crore-money-laundering-case-gives-hope-to-cbi-ed-2133092.html

4 https://theprint.in/economy/indian-banks-could-add-rs-10-lakh-crore-in-npas-due-to-covid-ex-finance-secretary-garg/407504/

5 https://theconversation.com/how-wells-fargo-encouraged-employees-to-commit-fraud-66615

6 *The New York Times*, 'World-class Fraud: How B.C.C.I. Pulled It Off—A Special Report.; At the End of a Twisted Trail, Piggy Bank for a Favored Few', 12 August 1991, https://www.nytimes.com/1991/08/12/business/world-class-fraud-bcci-pulled-it-off-special-report-end-twisted-trail-piggy-bank.html

7 https://www.livemint.com/industry/banking/rbi-affidavit-details-how-it-was-fooled-by-scam-hit-pmc-bank-11574176023270.html

8 https://scroll.in/article/868825/explained-how-did-the-alleged-rs-11000-crore-nirav-modi-punjab-national-bank-scam-go-unnoticed

9 https://www.businesstoday.in/current/corporate/winsome-diamonds-case-cbi-files-chargesheet-against-3-former-canara-bank-officials/story/279706.html

10 https://www.thehindu.com/news/national/ed-arrests-zoom-developers-director-in-bank-loan-default-case/article18374129.ece

11 https://timesofindia.indiatimes.com/india/cbi-registers-case-against-2-directors-of-varun-industries-for-loan-default-of-rs-330-28cr/articleshow/51814994.cms

12 https://economictimes.indiatimes.com/industry/banking/finance/banking/reid-taylor-s-kumars-head-for-bankruptcy-after-loan-defaults-of-over-rs-5000-crore/articleshow/63226882.cms?from=mdr

13 https://www.thehindu.com/business/markets/sebi-bars-dsq-software-dalmia-from-capital-markets-for-7-yrs/article5201000.ece

14 Rajesh Naidu and Sachin Dave, 'Cox & Kings' Business Model Offers Clues to Bond Default', *The Economic Times*, 8 July 2019, https://economictimes.indiatimes.com/markets/bonds/cox-kings-business-model-offers-clues-to-bond-default/articleshow/70122678.cms?from=mdr

15 Munish Chandra Pandey, 'Cox & Kings Used Fake Customers to Launder Thousands of Crores: ED', *India Today*, 8 June 2020, https://www.indiatoday.in/india/story/cox-kings-used-fake-customers-to-launder-thousands-of-crores-ed-1686967-2020-06-08

16 https://www.business-standard.com/about/what-is-il-fs-crisis

17 https://www.businessstandard.com/article/finance/number-of-wilful-defaulters-rises-to-2-494-fm-informs-parliament-121072701036_1.html

18 https://www.moneycontrol.com/news/business/wilful-defaulters-owe-rs-1-5-lakh-crore-to-public-sector-banks-how-big-is-the-mess-5583011.html

19 https://www.moneylife.in/article/top-wilful-defaulters-here-is-the-list-of-2426-who-together-owe-rs147-lakh-crore-to-public-sector-banks/60959.html; https://economictimes.indiatimes.com/industry/banking/finance/banking/top-100-wilful-defaulters-owe-lenders-rs-84632-crore/articleshow/80753675.cms?from=mdr

20 https://www.consultancy.uk/news/23600/value-of-large-fraud-in-uk-booms-to-more-than-1-billion

21 BusinessToday.in, 'NCLT Slams Jaiprakash Associates for Fraudulently Using Jaypee Infratech's Land to Bag Further Loans', 18 May 2018, https://www.businesstoday.in/current/corporate/jaypee-nclt-jaiprakash-associates-jaypee-infratech-land-loans/story/277198.html

22 Munish Pandey, 'Trial in Bhushan Steel Case against 283 Accused Would Require a Stadium, Says Lawyer', *India Today*, 11 July 2019, https://www.indiatoday.in/india/story/trial-in-bhushan-steel-case-against-283-accused-would-require-a-stadium-says-lawyer-1566942-2019-07-11

23 *Financial Times*, 'Chinese Police Launch Dragnet for Peer-to-peer Lenders', 19 February 2019, https://www.ft.com/content/761f523a-337e-11e9-bd3a-8b2a211d90d5

24 https://www.businessinsider.com/chinese-p2p-investors-lost-115-billion-in-regulatory-crackdown-2020-8?IR=T

25 Shaikh Zoaib Saleem, 'Lessons for P2P Lending in India', Livemint, 12 September 2018, https://www.livemint.com/Money/tuI4wvfqdbVH9nQVYC1M5I/Lessons-for-P2P-lending-in-India.html

CHAPTER SEVEN: The Art of Hiding Shady Wealth

1 https://www.nytimes.com/2019/11/18/nyregion/bruce-bagley-money-laundering-venezuela.html

2 'This story is author's own creation inspired by 'Money Laundering in the EU', https://people.exeter.ac.uk/watupman/undergrad/ron/methods%20and%20stages.htm

3 https://www.theguardian.com/world/2017/mar/20/the-global-laundromat-how-did-it-work-and-who-benefited

4 https://www.ft.com/content/e231dbe0-6124-11e9-b285-3acd5d43599e

5 https://newsoncompliance.com/danske-bank-the-story-of-europes-biggest-money-laundering-scandal/

6 https://newsoncompliance.com/danske-bank-the-story-of-europes-biggest-money-laundering-scandal/

7 *Financial Times*, 'Westpac Accused of Australia's Biggest Money Laundering Breach', 20 November 2019, https://www.ft.com/content/3598cb7a-0b27-11ea-bb52-34c8d9dc6d84

8 https://www.thehindubusinessline.com/companies/ed-attaches-assets-worth-48104-crores-of-rei-agro-in-a-bank-fraud-case/article28781866.ece#

9   https://theprint.in/india/billionaire-laxmi-mittals-brother-pramod-jailed-for-fraud-led-opulent-life-despite-debts/269029/

10 https://economictimes.indiatimes.com/industry/banking/finance/banking/rbi-imposes-fine-of-rs-11-crore-on-seven-public-sector-banks/articleshow/70501404.cms?from=mdr

11 https://www.theguardian.com/business/2018/sep/21/is-money-laundering-scandal-at-danske-bank-the-largest-in-history

12 *The Times of India*, 'South Korean Tries Washing Money over Virus Fears, Suffers Loss', 2 August 2020, https://timesofindia.indiatimes.com/world/mad-mad-world/south-korean-tries-washing-money-over-virus-fears-suffers-loss/articleshow/77312921.cms

13 https://www.theguardian.com/business/2018/may/21/breaking-bad-to-the-paradise-papers-all-you-need-to-know-about-money-laundering

14 Oriana Zill and Lowell Bergman, 'The Black Peso Money Laundering System', *Frontline*, https://www.pbs.org/wgbh/pages/frontline/shows/drugs/special/blackpeso.html

15 Lucy Papachristou, 'Six Convicted in Black Market Peso Exchange Scheme', 14 February 2019, https://www.occrp.org/en/27-ccwatch/cc-watch-briefs/9238-us-six-convicted-in-black-market-peso-exchange-scheme

16 *The New York Times*, 'Stream of Foreign Wealth Flows to Elite New York Real Estate', 7 February 2015, https://www.nytimes.com/2015/02/08/nyregion/stream-of-foreign-wealth-flows-to-time-warner-condos.html

17 https://www.thehindubusinessline.com/opinion/columns/slate/all-you-wanted-to-know-aboutshell-companies/article9818149.ece#

18 Yatish Yadav, 'Strict Punishment in Offing for 3.38 Lakh Shell Company Owners', *Firstpost*, 3 October 2019, https://www.firstpost.com/india/strict-punishment-in-offing-for-3-38-lakh-shell-company-owners-centre-to-deploy-dri-fiu-cbdt-cbi-for-probe-ed-to-verify-how-funds-are-managed-laundered-7447881.html

19 *Financial Times*, 'Students' Bank Accounts Frozen amid Money Laundering Concerns', 28 February 2019, https://www.ft.com/content/96840328-3b6b-11e9-b856-5404d3811663

20 *Financial Times*, 'Lloyds Freezes 8,000 Offshore Jersey Accounts in Dirty Money Push', 24 June 2019, https://www.ft.com/content/85e377e8-8fa2-11e9-aea1-2b1d33ac3271

21 https://www.nytimes.com/2012/07/01/business/how-delaware-thrives-as-a-corporate-tax-haven.html

22 *The New York Times*, 'What Are the Panama Papers?' 4 April 2016, https://www.nytimes.com/2016/04/05/world/panama-papers-explainer.html?action=click&module=RelatedCoverage&pgtype=Article&region=Footer

23 Moneylife, 'Mix of Bollywood, Glamour, Sports in Latest "Panama Papers" Expose', 7 April 2016, https://www.moneylife.in/article/mix-of-bollywood-glamour-sports-in-latest-panama-papers-expose/46401.html

24 Moneylife, 'Niira Radia Now surfaces in "Panama Papers"', 6 April 2016, https://www.moneylife.in/article/niira-radia-now-surfaces-in-panama-papers/46368.html

25 Moneylife, 'Now, Bahamas Papers Expose on 475 India-linked Names with Offshore Accounts', 22 September 2016, https://www.moneylife.in/article/now-bahamas-papers-expose-on-475-india-linked-names-with-offshore-accounts/48248.html

26 https://www.huffpost.com/archive/in/entry/13-ways-in-which-indians-will-convert-their-black-money-into-whi_a_21605148

27 https://timesofindia.indiatimes.com/india/amid-rush-for-white-money-pune-business-converts-cash-into-black/articleshow/56163232.cms

CHAPTER EIGHT: Ponzi Schemes

1 *The New York Times*, '2 Charged in Ponzi Scheme Built around "Hamilton" Tickets', 27 January 2017, https://www.nytimes.com/2017/01/27/nyregion/hamilton-ponzi-scheme.html?searchResultPosition=4

2 *The New York Times*, 'In the Decade since Madoff, Ponzi Schemers Try New Tactics', 22 September 2019, https://www.nytimes.com/2019/09/22/business/ponzi-scheme-bernie-madoff.html?searchResultPosition=3

3 https://www.nytimes.com/2019/09/22/business/ponzi-scheme-bernie-madoff.html

4 https://www.indiatvnews.com/news/india-ima-ponzi-scam-main-accused-mohammed-mansoor-khan-arrested-from-delhi-536313

5 https://www.forbes.com/sites/jordanmaglich/2014/10/31/on-fifth-anniversary-of-rothsteins-1-2-billion-ponzi-scheme-questions-remain/?sh=5dc0e074b145

6 https://www.newsday.com/long-island/crime/panoramic-view-co-owner-sentenced-to-12-years-for-ponzi-scheme-1.14177430

7 *The New York Times*, 'Manhattan Restaurateur Admits Running $12 Million Ponzi Scheme', 11 May 2017, https://www.nytimes.com/2017/05/11/nyregion/hamlet-peralta-admits-ponzi-scheme.html?searchResultPosition=34

8 Adelphia Communications: https://www.sec.gov/news/press/2002-110.htm; Barings Bank: https://www.businessinsider.com/rogue-trader-barings-bank-anniversary-2015-2?IR=T#leeson-was-promoted-from-settlements-clerk-to-broker-at-barings-in-1992-2; LIBOR manipulations by Barclays: https://www.theguardian.com/business/2017/jan/18/libor-scandal-the-bankers-who-fixed-the-worlds-most-important-number

9 https://www.india.com/news/india/164-ponzi-companies-vanished-after-raising-public-money-finance-minister-arun-jaitley-1024099/

10 *Financial Times*, 'Allen Stanford's Ponzi Scheme Victims Have Been Shortchanged', 12 February 2019, https://www.ft.com/content/17324ff8-2a22-11e9-9222-7024d72222bc

11 Erik Larson and Christopher Cannon, 'Madoff's Victims Are Close to Getting Their $19 Billion Back', Bloomberg, 8 December 2018, https://www.bloomberg.com/graphics/2018-recovering-madoff-money/

12 https://theprint.in/india/rose-valley-has-returned-rs-10500-crore-of-investor-money-says-ed/517368/

13 *Financial Times*, 'China Warns Public over "Blockchain" Ponzi Schemes', 24 August 2018, https://www.ft.com/content/d6dee2ae-a76d-11e8-8ecf-a7ae1beff35b

14 https://www.reuters.com/world/china/china-central-bank-vows-crackdown-cryptocurrency-trading-2021-09-24/

15 https://www.reuters.com/legal/litigation/4-billion-onecoin-fraud-jurisdiction-dooms-claims-against-ex-big-law-partner-2021-09-22/

16 https://www.financialexpress.com/india-news/bitcoin-investment-scam-promoter-of-bitconnect-held/1284996/

17 https://www.businesstoday.in/latest/corporate/story/cryptocurrency-guru-arrested-for-bitcoin-ponzi-schemes-scam-could-run-into-rs-13000-crore-105449-2018-04-05

18 https://www.ftc.gov/news-events/press-releases/2019/10/multi-level-marketer-advocare-will-pay-150-million-settle-ftc

19 https://www.cnbctv18.com/business/goodwin-jewellers-fraud-all-you-need-to-know-4678031.htm

20 https://www.businesstoday.in/latest/corporate/story/ed-arrests-three-promoters-of-agri-gold-group-in-connection-to-rs-6380-ponzi-scam-282337-2020-12-23

21 https://www.ndtv.com/business/enough-is-enough-says-supreme-court-sahara-to-lose-aamby-valley-10-facts-1682497

22 Speak Asia: https://www.business-standard.com/article/current-affairs/mastermind-of-speak-asia-fraud-arrested-113112600680_1.html; Saradha: https://www.dnaindia.com/business/photo-gallery-saradha-scam-all-you-need-to-know-about-decade-old-chit-fund-fraud-2716284; Rose Valley: https://www.iasparliament.com/current-affairs/economy/rose-valley-scam-explained

CHAPTER NINE: Stock and Commodity Market Swindles

1 https://www.thehindu.com/business/markets/jignesh-shah-arrested-in-nsel-scam/article5986149.ece

2 https://economictimes.indiatimes.com/markets/stocks/news/heres-what-may-have-led-to-chitra-ramkrishnas-exit-from-nse/articleshow/56092505.cms?from=mdr

3 https://www.nytimes.com/2020/03/20/opinion/coronavirus-burr-loeffler-stocks.html?searchResultPosition=1

4 DOJ still investigating coronavirus stock sales by Sen. Burr, but drops probes of Loeffler: https://www.cnbc.com/2020/05/26/coronavirus-doj-investigates-burr-stock-sales-drops-loeffler-feinstein-probes.html

5 *Financial Times*, 'How Steven Cohen Survived an Insider Trading Scandal', 7 February 2017, https://www.ft.com/content/efda2ca2-ec69-11e6-930f-061b01e23655

6 https://www.nytimes.com/2017/02/01/books/review-black-edge-an-account-of-a-hedge-fund-magnate-and-insider-trading.html

7 https://www.thehindubusinessline.com/markets/stock-markets/price-rigging-down-insider-trading-up/article33836372.ece

8 https://economictimes.indiatimes.com/markets/stocks/news/sebi-imposes-rs-27-cr-fine-on-ndtv-promoters-prannoy-roy-and-radhika-roy-for-violating-regulatory-norms/articleshow/79944765.cms?from=mdr

9 https://www.livemint.com/market/stock-market-news/rakesh-jhunjhunwala-summoned-by-sebi-over-aptech-insider-trades-11580151574639.html

10 https://www.sebi.gov.in/enforcement/orders/nov-2018/settlement-order-in-respect-of-mr-rakesh-jhunjhunwala-in-the-matter-of-geometric-limited_41191.html

11 https://www.thehindu.com/business/markets/what-is-the-karvy-stock-scandal-all-about/article30233018.ece; https://economictimes.indiatimes.com/wealth/invest/karvy-stock-broking-scandal-how-retail-investors-can-safeguard-against-such-frauds/articleshow/72303278.cms?from=mdr

12 https://www.moneylife.in/article/over-rs1000-crore-at-risk-at-anugrah-stockbrokers-and-associates/61330.html

13 Pravin Palande, 'Economic Milestone: Stock Market Scam (1992)', *Forbes India*, 20 August 2014, https://www.forbesindia.com/article/independence-day-special/economic-milestone-stock-market-scam-(1992)/38457/1

14 https://www.thehindu.com/business/Industry/frauds-and-scams-throwback-to-k10-era/article23041874.ece

15 Jordan Belfort, *The Wolf of Wall Street* (Bantam Books: 2007, September 25).

16 https://www.ndtv.com/business/company-with-no-sales-gains-4-300-in-small-stocks-boom-as-retail-investors-frenzy-reaches-extreme-levels-2286007

17 https://www.nytimes.com/2021/03/18/business/penny-stocks-trading.html

18 *Financial Times*, 'Nikola Shares Fall after Short Seller Claims Business Us an "Intricate Fraud"', 8 September 2020, https://www.ft.com/content/653096d3-e338-4d24-bab9-4fcb89f5402e

19 https://www.ft.com/content/75a94988-2dc4-4bb1-b65d-e744636504cd

CHAPTER TEN: Insurance Imposture

1 https://www.hindustantimes.com/cities/man-fakes-his-death-to-claim-rs-1-5-cr-insurance-murders-friend/story-qX7J0Qsy5zEZskSRfQ1ZVO.html

2 https://timesofindia.indiatimes.com/india/man-murders-wife-2-days-after-buying-policy-gets-life-term/articleshow/73624703.cms

3 Stephen Cheetham, 'Back Pain Is a Massive Problem Which Is Badly Treated', *The Economist*, 18 January 2020, https://www.economist.com/briefing/2020/01/18/back-pain-is-a-massive-problem-which-is-badly-treated

4 *The Economist*, 'A Bondholder Finds a Sneaky Way to Trigger Insurance against Default', 3 May 2018, https://www.economist.com/finance-and-economics/2018/05/03/a-bondholder-finds-a-sneaky-way-to-trigger-insurance-against-default

5 https://www.nytimes.com/2018/09/04/world/asia/nepal-everest-rescue-fraud.html; https://www.nytimes.com/2019/01/25/world/asia/nepal-everest-insurers-fraud.html

6 https://www.seattletimes.com/nation-world/near-everests-slopes-a-helicopter-rescue-fraud-preys-on-trekkers/

7 https://economictimes.indiatimes.com/industry/banking/finance/insure/insurance-frauds-how-data-analytics-and-rigorous-checks-are-trying-to-eliminate-bogus-claims/articleshow/73509077.cms?from=mdr

8 *The Economist*, 'Puke for Payout, the Scam Making Holiday Firms Sick', 20 July 2017, https://www.economist.com/britain/2017/07/20/puke-for-payout-the-scam-making-holiday-firms-sick

9 *The New York Times*, 'Where the Frauds Are All Legal', 7 December 2019, https://www.nytimes.com/2019/12/07/opinion/sunday/medical-billing-fraud.html?searchResultPosition=2

10 https://www.formotiv.com/lemonade-loss-ratio/

11 https://www.economist.com/united-states/2018/07/05/why-detroit-is-the-most-expensive-city-in-america-to-buy-car-insurance

12 https://www.economist.com/finance-and-economics/2010/07/08/claim-and-misfortune

13 https://www.outlookindia.com/outlookmoney/insurance/frauds-in-insurance-sector-3706

14 https://www.fbi.gov/stats-services/publications/insurance-fraud

15 RGA, *RGA 2017: Global Claims Fraud Survey*, 2017, https://www.rgare.com/docs/default-source/knowledge-center-articles/rga-2017-global-claims-fraud-survey-white-paper---final.pdf?sfvrsn=601a588_0

CHAPTER ELEVEN: Accounting Artifice

1 *The New York Times*, 'Report Details How Lehman Hid Its Woes', 11 March 2010, https://www.nytimes.com/2010/03/12/business/12lehman.html; Wharton, 'Lehman's Demise and Repo 105: No Accounting for Deception', 31 March 2010, https://knowledge.wharton.upenn.edu/article/lehmans-demise-and-repo-105-no-accounting-for-deception/

2 https://en.wikipedia.org/wiki/Enron_scandal

3 https://en.wikipedia.org/wiki/WorldCom_scandal

4 https://en.wikipedia.org/wiki/Satyam_scandal

5 https://www.reuters.com/article/us-steinhoff-intln-accounts-idUSKCN1 QW2C2

6 https://www.firstpost.com/india/sc-judgment-in-amrapali-group-case-a-welcome-step-but-opacity-of-noidas-real-estate-market-remains-a-problem-7042201.html

7 Theo Francis and Ted Mann, 'GE Says It Has Received "Wells Notice" from SEC Relating to Accounting Investigation', *The Wall Street Journal*, 6 October 2020, https://www.wsj.com/articles/ge-says-it-has-received-wells-notice-from-sec-relating-to-accounting-investigation-11602008493?mod=searchres ults&page=1&pos=1

8 https://www.wsj.com/articles/sec-investigating-mattels-accounting-11582672709

9 Jing Yang, 'Behind the Fall of China's Luckin Coffee: A Network of Fake Buyers and a Fictitious Employee', *The Wall Street Journal*, 28 May 2020, https://www.wsj.com/articles/behind-the-fall-of-chinas-luckin-coffee-a-network-of-fake-buyers-and-a-fictitious-employee-11590682336?mod=sear chresults&page=10&pos=16

10 https://www.bloomberg.com/news/articles/2019-09-27/fiat-chrysler-fined-40-million-for-u-s-sales-reporting-fraud

11 https://www.nytimes.com/2019/12/23/business/bmw-sec.html

12 https://www.nytimes.com/2004/08/05/business/bristol-myers-agrees-to-settle-accounting-case.html

13 https://www.wsj.com/articles/SB117882466341398931

14 Michael Connor, 'Diebold to Pay $25 Million to Settle Accounting Fraud Charges', *Business Ethics*, 2 June 2010, https://business-ethics.com/2010/06/02/1519-diebold-to-pay-25-million-to-settle-accounting-fraud-charges/

15 https://www.washingtonpost.com/archive/business/2001/05/16/sunbeam-accused-of-fraud/4e03a2b8-c4da-4a00-bea8-f0cb55cb8d77/

16 https://www.nytimes.com/1992/12/12/business/comptronix-dismisses-chief-in-bogus-earnings-scandal.html

17 https://www.livemint.com/news/world/indian-american-pleads-guilty-in-17-million-bank-fraud-11600226964100.html

18 https://www.acfe.com/rttn2016/docs/2016-report-to-the-nations.pdf

19 https://www.nytimes.com/2001/05/16/business/sec-accuses-former-sunbeam-official-of-fraud.html

20 https://www.nytimes.com/2010/07/23/business/23dell.html

21 https://www.frc.org.uk/getattachment/88bd8c45-50ea-4841-95b0-d2f4f48069a2/2018-UK-Corporate-Governance-Code-FINAL.PDF

22 https://www.sebi.gov.in/sebi_data/attachdocs/1441284401427.pdf

23 NFRA: https://taxguru.in/company-law/form-nfra-1-applicability.html; KAM: https://news.cleartax.in/standard-on-auditing-sa-701-applicable-for-statutory-audits/1359/; CARO 2020: https://taxguru.in/company-law/mca-deffers-applicability-caro-2020-fy-2021-22.html

24 https://studycafe.in/not-auditors-job-to-be-a-bloodhound-icai-president-95860.html

CHAPTER TWELVE: Ominous Omens of Financial Frauds

1   Ridhima Saxena, 'SFIO Says Top Executives Led IL&FS to Its Ruin', Bloomberg Quint, 6 December 2018, https://www.bloombergquint.com/business/sfio-says-top-executives-led-ilfs-to-its-ruin

2   KPMG, *Global Banking Fraud Survey*, May 2019, https://assets.kpmg/content/dam/kpmg/cl/pdf/2019-05-kpmg-chile-advisory-banking-fraud.pdf

3   https://economictimes.indiatimes.com/industry/services/consultancy-/-audit/pwc-resigns-as-an-auditor-of-eveready-industries-citing-inter-group-transaction/articleshow/70010488.cms?from=mdr

4   https://www.livemint.com/industry/banking/bsr-associates-resigns-as-statutory-auditor-of-il-fs-investment-managers-1561122245782.html; https://www.livemint.com/companies/news/pwc-resigns-as-statutory-auditor-of-reliance-capital-and-reliance-home-finance-1560320418338.html

5   *Financial Times*, ;Deloitte Resigns from Indian Non-bank Lender', 6 August 2019, https://www.ft.com/content/8e2f7026-b858-11e9-8a88-aa6628ac896c

Epilogue

1   https://www.nytimes.com/2019/05/10/nyregion/anna-delvey-sorokin.html
2   https://globescan.com/2020-sustainability-leaders-report/
3   https://www.moneycontrol.com/india/stockpricequote/finance-housing/dewanhousingfinancecorporation/DHF
4   https://economictimes.indiatimes.com/yes-bank-ltd/stocks/companyid-16552.cms
5   https://www.ft.com/content/29d6c95c-8bff-39e6-9502-584f10366a2f

Scan QR code to access the
Penguin Random House India website